Mastering Lisp Programming
From Basics to Expert Proficiency

Contents

Introduction

Lisp, an acronym for List Processing, is one of the oldest high-level programming languages, first developed in the late 1950s by John McCarthy. Known for its rich expressive power and unique syntax, Lisp has influenced the development of many other programming languages and remains relevant for various applications today, ranging from artificial intelligence to web development.

The purpose of this book, "Mastering Lisp Programming: From Basics to Expert Proficiency," is to provide a comprehensive introduction and an in-depth exploration of the Lisp programming language. This book is designed to be accessible to beginners while also offering detailed insights and advanced knowledge for experienced programmers.

The first chapter lays the groundwork by answering the fundamental question: What is Lisp? Here, a historical perspective will be provided to understand how Lisp came into being and why it has stood the test of time. Furthermore, the practical advantages of learning Lisp will be discussed, illustrating its ongoing significance and various applications.

Installation instructions for setting up a Lisp programming environment will follow. Modern development environments and interactive computing have made it significantly easier to get started with Lisp. The procedures for installing a Lisp interpreter or compiler on different operating systems will be covered in detail to ensure a smooth start for the reader.

Next, a first look at the Lisp language will be provided. This involves an initial exploration of the basic syntax, including symbolic expressions (S-expressions), which form the core of Lisp's powerful syntax. A brief introduction to the Read-Eval-Print Loop (REPL), an interactive programming environment, will also be included. The REPL serves as an invaluable tool for learning and experimenting with Lisp.

Following the exploration of basic syntax, readers will be guided through the creation of simple Lisp programs. These initial exercises will help in solidifying the introductory concepts and offer hands-on experience in writing and running Lisp code.

Finally, an overview of the Lisp community and resources will be included. This will encompass a discussion of online forums, tutorials, documentation, and other such resources where readers can seek help, collaborate, and further their learning.

This introductory chapter forms the foundation upon which the subsequent, more complex topics will be built. The chapters that follow will delve into essential aspects such as Basic Lisp Syntax and Semantics, Lisp Data Structures, Functions and Functional Programming, Control Structures in Lisp, and many more. Each chapter aims to provide a complete understanding of the topic and is structured to facilitate gradual and comprehensive learning.

The journey through this book aims to equip readers with the skills necessary to master Lisp, allowing them to harness its full potential in solving complex problems efficiently and elegantly. By the end of this book, readers will have gained both theoretical knowledge and practical expertise, enabling them to program confidently and creatively in Lisp.

Chapter 1

Introduction to Lisp

Lisp, a pioneering high-level programming language, has had a significant impact on the development of modern computing. Originating in the late 1950s by John McCarthy, Lisp introduced revolutionary concepts in symbolic computation and functional programming. This chapter covers the history and significance of Lisp, provides installation guidelines for setting up a Lisp environment, offers an initial exploration of Lisp's syntax and the REPL, includes simple programming exercises, and provides an overview of community resources and support. This foundation prepares readers for more advanced topics in subsequent chapters.

1.1   What is Lisp?

Lisp, short for "LISt Processing," is a family of programming languages with a long history and distinctive, fully parenthesized prefix notation. Introduced in 1958 by John McCarthy, Lisp was constructed as a practical mathematical notation for computer programs, influenced heavily by the lambda calculus. This section delves deeply into the defining characteristics, underlying paradigms, and core features of Lisp, shedding light on why it remains relevant after more than six decades.

Lisp is primarily recognized for its powerful features in symbolic computation, a key area in artificial intelligence (AI) research. Its core philosophies include code as data (homoiconicity) and the extensive use of recursion. The language's syntax and semantics enforce these principles, resulting in concise and expressive programs.

Lisp syntax is minimalistic and relies heavily on s-expressions (symbolic expressions) for both code and data representation.   An s-expression is either an atom or a list of s-expressions. This uniform representation simplifies parsing and manipulation of code within the language itself. Here's an example of a simple Lisp expression:

```
(+ 1 2 3 4)
```

The above expression represents the summation of the numbers 1, 2, 3, and 4. The operator appears before its operands, characteristic of prefix notation, which eliminates the need for operator precedence rules found in infix notations.

Homoiconicity is manifested in Lisp through its treatment of code as data. This allows Lisp programs to manipulate and transform code with the full power of Lisp's computational capabilities. Code manipulation is often employed through macros, which are constructs that generate code at compile time, enabling powerful abstractions and domain-specific languages.

Lisp's macro system is one of the most advanced in programming languages. Macro definitions are similar to function definitions but instead of computations, they result in code that is then executed. Here is an example of a simple macro that repeats an expression n times:

```
(defmacro repeat (n &rest body)
  `(loop for i from 1 to ,n do
     ,@body))
```

When used, this macro expands into a loop construct:

```
(repeat 3 (print 'Hello))
```

The above call expands to:

```
(loop for i from 1 to 3 do
  (print 'Hello))
```

This allows developers to create high-level, readable abstractions without sacrificing performance or expressive power.

Lisp supports multiple programming paradigms, including functional, procedural, and object-oriented programming. Its functional programming features are particularly strong, with first-class functions and a rich set of higher-order functions. Functions in Lisp can be created using the lambda keyword:

```
(lambda (x) (+ x 1))
```

This expression returns an anonymous function that increments its argument by one. Functions are first-class citizens in Lisp, meaning they can be passed as arguments, returned as values, and stored in variables.

Lisp's procedural programming capabilities are evident in its imperative constructs, including conditionals, loops, and variable assignments. Here's an example of a simple conditional statement:

```
(if (> x 0)
    (print 'Positive)
    (print 'Non-Positive))
```

This conditional checks whether x is greater than zero and prints "Positive" if true, otherwise "Non-Positive."

Object-oriented programming in Lisp is supported through systems like the Common Lisp Object System (CLOS), which provides multiple inheritance, method combination, and dynamic dispatch. The following example defines a simple class and a method in CLOS:

```
(defclass person ()
  ((name :initarg :name :accessor person-name)
   (age :initarg :age :accessor person-age)))

(defmethod greet ((p person))
  (format t "Hello, my name is ~a and I am ~a years old." (person-name p) (person-age
    p)))
```

To create an instance of the person class and invoke the greet method:

```
(let ((p (make-instance 'person :name "Alice" :age 30)))
  (greet p))
```

The integration of these paradigms within Lisp provides developers with the flexibility to choose the most appropriate approach for a given problem, fostering an environment conducive to exploratory and innovative programming.

The enduring influence of Lisp on other programming languages is evident in many modern languages that borrow concepts originally introduced by Lisp, including garbage collection, first-class functions, and interpreters for interactive programming.

Lisp's rich history and distinctive features make it a valuable language for both academic inquiry and practical application. Learning Lisp exposes programmers to fundamental concepts in computer science and programming language theory, offering a deep understanding of topics that are highly applicable across a variety of other languages and systems.

1.2 History of Lisp

Lisp (LISt Processing) is among the oldest high-level programming languages, created in 1958 by John McCarthy at the Massachusetts Institute of Technology (MIT). Lisp's development was driven by McCarthy's interest in problem solving, artificial intelligence, and symbolic computation. As its name suggests, Lisp is particularly adept at processing lists and other symbolic structures, setting it apart in the early days of computer programming.

Lisp's innovation lies in its facilitation of manipulating programs as data. This stems from its representation of both code and data using the same data structure: the list. Such a representation provides immense flexibility, enabling self-modifying code, a distinctive feature that was ahead of its time.

The primary motivations for developing Lisp included:

- The need for an effective method to represent complex symbolic expressions.

- Funded research into artificial intelligence, which required a language capable of symbolic reasoning.

- Curiosity in exploring mathematical logic and the practical computations derived from it.

Milestones in the Evolution of Lisp:

- 1958-1959: Initial conceptualization and development of Lisp by John McCarthy, alongside Steve Russell, Timothy Hart, and Mike Levin. The language was based on the notation of Alonzo Church's Lambda Calculus. To illustrate the early Lisp implementation:

```
(defun factorial (n)
  (if (= n 0)
      1
      (* n (factorial (- n 1)))))
```

14

The above code snippet defines a recursive function to compute the factorial of a number.

- 1960: The publication of McCarthy's seminal paper, *Recursive Functions of Symbolic Expressions and Their Computation by Machine*, laid the theoretical foundation for Lisp.

- 1962: The pioneering work on the first Lisp interpreter by Steve Russell resulted in the appearance of Lisp 1.5, an evolutionary step incorporating several practical utilities.

- 1966: The introduction of Maclisp, which extended the language's capabilities by enhancing performance and managing symbol tables more efficiently.

- 1970s: Development of other dialects such as InterLisp and Scheme. Scheme simplified Lisp by introducing lexical scoping and first-class continuations. These two facets fundamentally impacted subsequent functional programming languages.

  Example of Scheme syntax:

  ```
  (define (square x) (* x x))
  ```

- 1984: The standardization of Common Lisp, a dialect developed to unify features across different versions. The *Common Lisp the Language* book by Guy L. Steele established the groundwork for this standardization.

- 1990: The publication of the ANSI Common Lisp standard, solidifying Common Lisp as a robust, industry-recognized language with a standardized library of functions and packages.

- 2000s: Advancements in open-source implementations like SBCL (Steel Bank Common Lisp) and Clozure CL, ensuring Lisp remains relevant in modern computer science and AI applications.

Lisp's constructs, such as car and cdr, which access the elements of lists, and the powerful cons operation to construct lists, have significant precedents.

Lisp's impact extends well beyond its syntactical innovations. It introduced several key paradigms:

- **Functional Programming Paradigm:** The emphasis on functions as first-class citizens laid the groundwork for functional programming languages.

- **Garbage Collection:** Early adoption of automated memory management influenced later high-level languages.

- **Metaprogramming:** Lisp's metaprogramming capabilities, allowing programs to manipulate themselves, inspired the development of macro systems in numerous modern languages.

Lisp has cultivated a unique community and culture, characterized by a deep commitment to exploring the theoretical and practical dimensions of computation. This culture persists today, reflected in the vibrant, ongoing development of current Lisp systems.

The historical development of Lisp is not a mere evolutionary process but a sequence of landmark innovations, each propelling computing technology into new realms. This history enables us to appreciate not just the technical facets but also the ingenuity underpinning modern computational paradigms.

1.3   Why Learn Lisp?

Lisp stands as a cornerstone in the evolution of programming languages, offering unique attributes that make it valuable for both historical understanding and practical application. Initially introduced by John McCarthy in 1958, Lisp has been influential in the development of subsequent languages and computing paradigms. Several factors underscore the importance of learning Lisp, which we will explore in detail.

Expressive Power and Flexibility: One of Lisp's most distinctive characteristics is its expressive power. Due to its simple and consistent syntax, Lisp enables the creation of highly readable and concise code. The use of s-expressions, which represent both code and data, allows seamless manipulation of program structures. This feature is particularly beneficial in domains such as symbolic computation, artificial intelligence, and rapid prototyping where dynamic and adaptable code is essential.

```
(defun factorial (n)
  (if (= n 0)
      1
      (* n (factorial (- n 1)))))

(factorial 5)
```

Output:
120

Macro System: Another compelling reason to learn Lisp is its powerful macro system. Unlike macros in many other languages, Lisp macros operate on the abstract syntax tree (AST), providing the capability to introduce new syntactic constructs and transform code during compilation. This metaprogramming capability offers advanced programmers unparalleled control and the ability to tailor the language to specific needs.

```
(defmacro when (condition &rest body)
  `(if ,condition
      (progn ,@body)))

(when (= 1 1)
  (print "Condition is true"))
```

Output:
"Condition is true"

Functional Programming: Lisp is inherently suited for functional programming, which emphasizes the application of functions and immutable data. This paradigm is becoming increasingly relevant due to its suitability in concurrent and parallel programming. Functions are first-class citizens in Lisp, meaning they can be passed as arguments, returned from other functions, and stored in data structures. This functional approach facilitates the development of modular and maintainable codebases.

```
(mapcar #'(lambda (x) (* x x)) '(1 2 3 4))
```

Output:
(1 4 9 16)

Influence on Modern Languages: Many features present in modern languages can trace their origins back to Lisp. For instance, higher-order functions, garbage collection, and REPL (Read-Eval-Print Loop) environments were pioneered by Lisp. Learning Lisp provides deeper insights into these concepts, enhancing one's ability to understand and utilize them in other programming contexts.

Educational Value: Lisp serves as an excellent educational tool, offering clarity in illustrating key programming concepts such as recursion, list manipulation, and the implementation of interpreters. Its minimalist

17

syntax reduces cognitive load, allowing learners to focus on algorithmic thinking rather than syntactic details.

```
(let ((list '(1 2 3 4)))
  (reverse list))
```

Output:
(4 3 2 1)

Community and Ecosystem: Over the decades, a robust and sup-portive community has grown around Lisp. Resources such as forums, mailing lists, and open-source projects provide valuable support for learners and practitioners. Furthermore, variants such as Common Lisp and Scheme offer different flavors of the language, catering to diverse needs and preferences.

Legacy and Longevity: Lisp's longevity is a testament to its robust-ness and adaptability. Despite the proliferation of newer languages, Lisp has remained relevant due to its foundational qualities and contin-ued evolution. This enduring presence makes it a worthwhile invest-ment for any programmer seeking to grasp the underlying principles of computing.

Learning Lisp equips individuals with a unique skill set, enhancing their problem-solving capabilities and broadening their understanding of pro-gramming paradigms. As such, mastering Lisp is not merely an aca-demic exercise but a strategic advantage in the ever-evolving land-scape of software development.

1.4   Installing a Lisp Environment

Installing a Lisp environment involves selecting a Lisp implementation, downloading the relevant software package, and setting it up on your operating system. There are multiple implementations of Lisp, each with its own features and support. The most commonly recommended implementations are SBCL (Steel Bank Common Lisp), CLISP, and CCL (Clozure Common Lisp). Here, the focus will be on installing SBCL, which is widely used for its performance and extensive library support.

- **SBCL**: A high-performance Common Lisp compiler known for its robust and fast execution.

- **CLISP**: An interpreter and compiler that is highly portable.

- **CCL**: Offers a balance between ease of use and performance.

System Requirements

Before proceeding with the installation, it is necessary to ensure that your system meets the minimum requirements for the selected Lisp implementation. For SBCL, make sure that you have:

- A compatible operating system (Windows, macOS, or a Unix-like system such as Linux)

- At least 50MB of free disk space

- An internet connection for downloading the software package

Installation on Unix-like Systems

Unix-like systems, including Linux and macOS, generally have package managers that simplify software installation.

To install SBCL on a Debian-based system such as Ubuntu, you can use the apt package manager:

```
sudo apt update
sudo apt install sbcl
```

On Red Hat-based systems, use the dnf or yum package manager:

```
sudo dnf install sbcl
```

For macOS users, Homebrew is the preferred package manager. First, ensure that Homebrew is installed, and then use the following commands:

```
brew update
brew install sbcl
```

Installation on Windows

Installing SBCL on Windows requires downloading the binary from SBCL's official website. Follow these steps:

- **Navigate to** http://www.sbcl.org/platform-table.html.

- Find the Windows binary corresponding to your machine's architecture (32-bit or 64-bit).

- Download and extract the zip file to a location of your choice.

- Add the path to the SBCL executable to your system's PATH environment variable to run sbcl from the command prompt.

Adding SBCL to PATH (Windows)

After extracting SBCL, locate the sbcl.exe file. Assuming it is extracted to C:/sbcl, follow these steps to add it to the PATH:

- Right-click on This PC, and choose Properties.

- Click on Advanced system settings.

- Under System Properties, navigate to the Advanced tab and click on Environment Variables.

- In the System variables section, find the Path variable, select it, and click Edit.

- Add the path to the directory containing sbcl.exe (e.g., C:/sbcl).

Verification

To ensure SBCL is installed correctly, open the terminal or command prompt and type:

```
sbcl
```

You should see output similar to the following:

```
This is SBCL 2.1.8 ...
*
```

If the SBCL prompt (*) appears, the installation has been successful.

Installing Emacs and SLIME

While SBCL can be used directly from the command line, integrating it with an editor like Emacs significantly enhances the development experience. SLIME (the Superior Lisp Interaction Mode for Emacs) is a popular Emacs mode for Common Lisp development.

Steps to install Emacs and SLIME:

- Install Emacs: Use your package manager or download from https://www.gnu.org/software/emacs/.

```
# On Debian-based systems
sudo apt install emacs

# On macOS using Homebrew
brew install emacs
```

- Download and install SLIME: To install SLIME, you can use MELPA (Milkypostman's Emacs Lisp Package Archive). Add the following to your .emacs or init.el file:

```
(require 'package)
(add-to-list 'package-archives
             '("melpa" . "https://melpa.org/packages/") t)
(package-initialize)

;; Install SLIME if not already installed
(unless (package-installed-p 'slime)
  (package-refresh-contents)
  (package-install 'slime))
```

- Configure SLIME to work with SBCL: In your .emacs or init.el file, add:

```
(setq inferior-lisp-program "sbcl")
(add-to-list 'load-path "/path/to/slime")
(require 'slime)
(slime-setup)
```

After these steps, opening Emacs and typing M-x slime should start SLIME and connect to the SBCL REPL.

Deploying a Lisp development environment involves selecting the appropriate implementation, installing it using system-specific package managers or binaries, and enhancing the setup with an editor and tools like Emacs and SLIME. This integrated approach provides a powerful and efficient environment for mastering Lisp.

1.5   A First Look at Lisp

Lisp, an acronym for *List Processing*, is uniquely characterized by its minimalist and highly expressive syntax. Understanding Lisp's fundamental syntax and semantics is crucial to leveraging its full power. This section delves into the core elements of Lisp syntax and provides practical examples to help you get started.

Atoms and Lists are the foundational building blocks of Lisp. An atom can be either a symbol or a number. Symbols are typically identifiers

21

for variables or functions, while numbers include integers, floating-point values, and complex numbers.

Lisp expressions, also known as forms, are either atomic or composite. Composite forms consist of lists, where the first element is often an operator or a function, followed by its arguments. For example:

```
(+ 2 3)
(setq x 10)
(/ (* 5 2) (- 8 2))
```

In the above examples:

- The first expression adds 2 and 3 using the + operator.

- The second expression uses the setq function to assign the value 10 to the variable x.

- The third example demonstrates nested function calls, where we first multiply 5 and 2, then divide the result by the difference of 8 and 2.

Lisp evaluates these expressions step-by-step. For arithmetic operations, the usual mathematical precedence rules apply within the context of nested expressions. Let's explore the evaluation process using a more complex expression:

```
(* (+ 1 2) (- 10 4))
```

During evaluation, Lisp processes this form as follows:

- Evaluate (+ 1 2) which results in 3.

- Evaluate (- 10 4) which results in 6.

- Multiply the two results: (* 3 6), yielding 18.

18

An essential feature of Lisp is its treatment of functions as first-class citizens. This means you can pass functions as arguments, return them from other functions, and assign them to variables. Consider the following example showcasing function definition and execution:

```
(defun square (x)
  "Calculate the square of x."
  (* x x))

(square 5)
```

Here, we define a function $square$ that returns the square of its argument x. The string following the function's argument declaration serves as a documentation string that describes the function's purpose. When invoked with x set to 5, the result is:

25

Lisp's REPL (Read-Eval-Print Loop) is an interactive programming environment that allows incremental code development and testing. The REPL reads an input expression, evaluates it, prints the result, and loops back for the next input. This interactive feedback loop is invaluable for learning and experimenting with Lisp.

Here is an example REPL session to illustrate basic variable operations and function calls:

```
CL-USER> (setq a 7)
7
CL-USER> (setq b 3)
3
CL-USER> (+ a b)
10
CL-USER> (square b)
9
```

In this session:

- $(setq\ a\ 7)$ assigns 7 to the variable a.
- $(setq\ b\ 3)$ assigns 3 to the variable b.
- $(+\ a\ b)$ evaluates to 10, the sum of a and b.
- $(square\ b)$ returns 9, the square of b.

Variables in Lisp persist beyond their initial creation within the REPL, and their values can be updated and interacted with in subsequent commands. This persistent state makes the REPL a powerful tool for incremental programming tasks.

Further distinguishing Lisp are its $macros$, which allow the creation of new syntactic constructs in a way that resembles rewriting Lisp code. Macros are pivotal in extending the language and introducing new control structures and constructs. However, they represent a more advanced aspect of Lisp that we will explore in subsequent chapters.

Handling lists is another cornerstone of Lisp programming. Lists can store heterogeneous elements, including numbers, symbols, and even other lists. Here is a basic example of list manipulation:

23

```
(setq my-list '(1 2 3 4))
(car my-list)
(cdr my-list)
(cons 0 my-list)
```

In these expressions:

- (setq my-list '(1 2 3 4)) assigns a list containing 1, 2, 3, 4 to my-list.

- (car my-list) returns 1, the first element of my-list.

- (cdr my-list) returns a list (2 3 4), which is my-list without its first element.

- (cons 0 my-list) creates a new list by adding 0 to the front, resulting in (0 1 2 3 4).

These operations illustrate the basic list-handling functions: car (which returns the first element), cdr (which returns the rest of the list minus the first element), and cons (which constructs a new list).

By mastering these foundational concepts, you will be well-prepared to explore more complex aspects of Lisp programming, ultimately leading to a deep understanding of its powerful features and idiomatic usage.

1.6   Basic REPL Usage

An essential feature of Lisp that greatly enhances its utility and interactive development capabilities is the Read-Eval-Print Loop (REPL). This environment allows developers to write and execute code incrementally, making it an invaluable tool for both learners and experienced programmers. Mastering the REPL involves understanding its components: the reader, the evaluator, and the printer.

The reader parses the Lisp code entered by the user. This parsing process involves converting the textual representation of code into Lisp data structures. The evaluator then processes these data structures, executing the code they represent. Finally, the printer outputs the result of the evaluation back to the user, completing the loop.

To start using the REPL, it is usually executed from the command line or through an integrated development environment (IDE) that supports

24

Lisp. For instance, if you have SBCL (Steel Bank Common Lisp) installed, you can start the REPL by typing sbcl in your terminal.

```
$ sbcl
This is SBCL 2.1.0, an implementation of ANSI Common Lisp.
More information about SBCL is available at <http://www.sbcl.org/>.

SBCL is free software, provided as is, with absolutely no warranty.
It is mostly in the public domain; some portions are provided under
BSD-style licenses. See the CREDITS file for more information.
[1]>
```

The REPL prompt, shown here as [1]>, is ready to accept and evaluate Lisp expressions. These expressions can be as simple as numbers, symbols, and lists, or more complex forms involving functions and macros.

Let's explore some basic REPL operations:

```
;; Addition of numbers
(+ 1 2)
```

Evaluating this line in the REPL:

```
3
```

The REPL evaluates the expression (+ 1 2), which adds the numbers 1 and 2, resulting in 3. Notice how the entire process from input to output is immediate, fostering a highly interactive coding experience.

More complex operations can also be executed. For instance, creating and applying a function:

```
;; Define a function to square a number
(defun square (x)
  (* x x))

;; Call the function
(square 4)
```

The REPL output would be:

```
16
```

The square function takes a single argument x and returns its square. The call to (square 4) evaluates to 16.

The REPL also supports defining and manipulating variables:

```
;; Define a variable
(setq a 10)

;; Retrieve the value of the variable
a
```

25

This results in:

10

The setq command is used to assign 10 to the variable a, and retrieving a displays its value.

Handling errors is also straightforward within the REPL. Consider an undefined function:

```
;; Call to an undefined function
(foo)
```

The REPL would return:

The function FOO is undefined.

The REPL's error messages are descriptive, assisting in debugging by pinpointing issues directly.

Finally, complex expressions involving conditionals and loops can be evaluated in the REPL:

```
;; Conditional expression
(if (> 5 3)
    'yes
    'no)
```

Evaluating this returns:

YES

Here, the if statement checks if 5 is greater than 3, and since the condition is true, it returns YES.

Using the REPL effectively builds a strong foundation in Lisp programming. It supports rapid iteration and experimental coding, facilitating a deeper comprehension of concepts through immediate feedback. As readers work through examples and exercises, the interactive REPL environment will prove indispensable, making the experience both productive and educational.

1.7   Simple Lisp Programs

In this section, we delve into crafting simple programs in Lisp, leveraging the knowledge gleaned from earlier chapters. Lisp's syntax and unique features play a pivotal role in simplifying seemingly complex problems. Understanding these aspects will solidify your foundation and prepare you for more advanced Lisp programming.

We will explore the following elementary programs:

- A program that computes factorial of a number.

- A program that checks if a number is prime.

- A program that performs basic list manipulations.

First, ensure your Lisp environment is correctly set up, as discussed in the "Installing a Lisp Environment" section. Launch the REPL to experiment with the following programs.

Factorial Calculation

The factorial of a non-negative integer n is the product of all positive integers less than or equal to n. It is denoted as $n!$. For $n = 0$, 0! is defined as 1. The factorial function can be defined recursively in Lisp:

```
(defun factorial (n)
  (if (<= n 1)
    1
    (* n (factorial (- n 1)))))
```

To execute this function and compute the factorial of 5, you can run the following command in the REPL:

```
(factorial 5)
```

The output is:

```
120
```

The recursive nature of the above function illustrates a typical Lisp approach for problem-solving. The base case for $n \leq 1$ is defined to return 1, and for other values, it recursively calls itself, reducing the problem size each time.

Prime Number Checker

A prime number is greater than 1 and has no positive divisors other than 1 and itself. Checking for prime numbers involves verifying that no integer less than the number itself divides it without a remainder.

We define a helper function first to check divisibility, and then use it to check for prime numbers.

```
(defun divisible (a b)
  (= (mod a b) 0))

(defun prime-p (n)
```

27

```
(if (< n 2)
    nil
    (loop for i from 2 to (sqrt n) never (divisible n i)))))
```

To check if 17 is a prime number, execute:

(prime-p 17)

The output confirms:

T

The divisible function uses the modulo operation to test if b divides a without a remainder. The prime-p function employs a loop to iterate from 2 up to the square root of n, checking divisibility. If no divisors are found, the number is prime.

Basic List Manipulations

Lisp's powerful list manipulation capabilities stem from its core design. We explore fundamental list operations such as constructing a list, accessing elements, and appending lists.

Constructing and accessing list elements:

```
(setq mylist (list 1 2 3 4 5))
(first mylist) ; Access the first element
(rest mylist) ; Access the rest of the list
(nth 2 mylist) ; Access the third element (0-based index)
```

Executing these lines in the REPL yields:

1
(2 3 4 5)
3

Appending two lists:

```
(setq list1 (list 'a 'b 'c))
(setq list2 (list 'd 'e 'f))
(append list1 list2)
```

The resulting output is:

(A B C D E F)

Here, setq is used to assign lists to the variables mylist, list1, and list2. The first and rest functions access the first element and the remaining elements of the list, respectively. The nth function retrieves elements based on a zero-indexed position. The append function concatenates list1 and list2.

Understanding and practicing these basic Lisp programs provide an essential groundwork for programming in Lisp. By mastering these simple examples, learners gain confidence and readiness to tackle more intricate problems in subsequent chapters.

1.8 Community and Resources

Engaging with the Lisp community and utilizing the myriad of resources available are pivotal steps for deepening your understanding and proficiency in Lisp programming. The vibrant and supportive Lisp community, along with a wealth of resources, play essential roles in the learning process.

Lisp has a rich history and a robust community that spans decades, providing ample opportunities for collaboration, learning, and skill enhancement.

Online Communities:

- comp.lang.lisp: One of the oldest and most active Usenet newsgroups dedicated to the discussion of Lisp topics.

- Stack Overflow: A popular Q&A platform where you can ask Lisp-related questions and receive answers from experienced programmers.

- Reddit: The r/lisp subreddit is a community of enthusiasts and professionals who share news, projects, and discussion on various Lisp topics.

- Discord and Slack Channels: Many communities have created chat channels on platforms like Discord and Slack where you can engage in real-time discussions with other Lisp programmers.

Mailing Lists:

- Common-Lisp.net Mailing Lists: A central hub for various mailing lists associated with different Lisp projects and general Lisp discussions.

- lisp-lang.org: Offers various resources including links to popular mailing lists in the Lisp community.

Conferences and Workshops:

29

- European Lisp Symposium (ELS): An annual event that brings together practitioners, researchers, and educators to discuss advancements in Lisp.

- International Lisp Conference (ILC): A major event in the Lisp community that features presentations, workshops, and networking opportunities.

- Lisp Meetups: Local meetups in various cities where Lisp enthusiasts can gather, share projects, and learn from each other.

Books and Publications:

- *Practical Common Lisp* by Peter Seibel: A comprehensive and practical guide to learning Common Lisp.

- *The Art of the Metaobject Protocol* by Gregor Kiczales, Jim Des Rivières, and Daniel G. Bobrow: An in-depth look at one of the most powerful features of Common Lisp.

- *On Lisp* by Paul Graham: A deep dive into advanced Lisp techniques and macros.

Online Tutorials and Documentation:

- Lisp Bootcamp: An interactive series of tutorials designed to teach Lisp from the ground up.

- Common Lisp HyperSpec: The definitive reference for the Common Lisp programming language.

- learn X in Y minutes: Concise reference guides for Lisp that provide quick overviews of syntax and key functions.

Source Repositories:

- GitHub: A plethora of Lisp projects, libraries, and educational resources are hosted on GitHub. Explore popular repositories, contribute to projects, and utilize code examples for learning.

- Quicklisp: The library manager for Common Lisp, making it easy to download, install, and manage Lisp libraries.

Development Tools:

- SLIME (Superior Lisp Interaction Mode for Emacs): An Emacs mode for Common Lisp development that provides a wide range of features for coding, debugging, and interaction.

- Sly: A fork of SLIME that offers additional features and an enhanced user experience.

- LispWorks: A comprehensive, commercial Lisp development environment with rich debugging and development tools.

Beginner-Friendly Guides:

- Lisp for the Web: A tutorial series focused on using Lisp for web development.

- The Land of Lisp: A whimsical and engaging guide intended to make learning Lisp fun and accessible through games and interactive projects.

Engaging with these community and resources not only enhances understanding and keeps one updated with the latest advancements in Lisp but also fosters a strong network with peers sharing similar interests. Such interactions often lead to collaborative projects, peer learning, and career opportunities.

Chapter 2

Basic Lisp Syntax and Semantics

This chapter covers the fundamental building blocks of Lisp programming, including expressions and atoms, basic data types, and symbolic expressions (S-expressions). It explores the structure and manipulation of lists, the use of quoting and evaluation, and the handling of atoms and variables. Additionally, it delves into defining and using variables, incorporating comments in code, performing basic arithmetic and Boolean operations, and making function calls. An understanding of special forms and proper indentation is also provided to ensure code readability and effectiveness.

2.1 Lisp Expressions and Atoms

Lisp expressions are the fundamental building blocks of Lisp programming. Lisp stands for "LISt Processing," which signifies its powerful capabilities in handling lists. In Lisp, everything is either an atom or a list. This section will delve into the details of these basic entities, helping you understand their structure and use.

An atom in Lisp is a single, indivisible unit of data, which can be a number, a string, or a symbol. Atoms are the simplest forms of expressions. When combined, atoms and lists constitute all Lisp code and data structures.

Atoms: Atoms include numbers, strings, and symbols.

- Numbers: Numerical atoms represent integers or floating-point numbers.

- Strings: Strings are sequences of characters enclosed in double quotes (e.g., "example").

- Symbols: These represent identifiers, variables, or functions in Lisp.

Lists: Lists are sequences of zero or more elements enclosed in parentheses. Elements can be atoms or other lists, enabling the construction of nested lists.

Basic expressions in Lisp either evaluate to a value or perform some computation. Atoms, when evaluated, typically return their value. Evaluating more complex expressions often entails function calling, which will be explored in subsequent sections.

```
42
3.14
"Hello, World!"
'atom
```

Here, 42 and 3.14 are numerical atoms, "Hello, World!" is a string atom, and 'atom is a symbol. Notice the use of the single quote before atom. This quote denotes that atom is a symbol and should not be evaluated.

Evaluation Rules for Atoms: 1. Numbers evaluate to themselves. 2. Strings evaluate to themselves. 3. Symbols evaluate to the value bound to them.

When writing Lisp code, it is crucial to understand the distinction between a symbol and its value. For instance, the symbol pi might be bound to the value 3.14. Evaluating pi would yield 3.14, while 'pi indicates the symbol itself, not its value.

```
(setq pi 3.14)
pi
=> 3.14
'pi
=> pi
```

In the above code, pi is bound to 3.14 using setq. Evaluating pi returns 3.14, whereas 'pi returns the symbol pi.

Lists and Their Evaluation

The syntax for lists includes parentheses containing zero or more elements separated by spaces.

```
()
(1 2 3 4)
("this" "is" "a" "list")
(+ 1 2 3)
```

()
(1 2 3 4)
("this" "is" "a" "list")
(+ 1 2 3)

The empty list () is also a valid list. Lists in Lisp are recursive structures, meaning elements within a list can be lists themselves. Evaluating an empty list returns itself; however, evaluating non-empty lists generally invokes a function call. The first element in a non-empty list is expected to be a function or operator, and the remaining elements are arguments to this function.

The example $(+ 1 2 3)$ represents a function call to the addition operation $+$, with the arguments 1, 2, and 3. The list evaluates to the sum of the numbers, which in this case is 6.

An essential aspect of Lisp is the uniformity of its syntax: both code and data are represented as lists. This means code can be manipulated as easily as data, providing powerful metaprogramming capabilities. Developing an understanding of how lists and atoms function is fundamental to leveraging Lisp effectively.

2.2   Basic Data Types

In Lisp, understanding the various data types is fundamental to writing efficient and effective programs. This section discusses the primary data types available in Lisp, including atoms, numbers, characters, strings, and lists. Each data type has unique properties and uses, which we will explore in detail.

Lisp programs manipulate different kinds of data, and recognizing how these data types interact and are used is critical for mastering Lisp programming.

Atoms are the simplest type of data in Lisp and consist of symbols and numbers. Symbols in Lisp are used as identifiers for variables, functions, and other entities. Symbols can include a wide range of characters, except those with specific syntactic meanings in Lisp (such as parentheses and spaces).

A number in Lisp can be an integer or a floating-point number. Integers are whole numbers and can be positive, negative, or zero. Lisp supports arbitrarily large integers, limited only by the machine's memory.

```
123
-4567
0
```

Floating-point numbers, on the other hand, represent real numbers and can include fractions.

```
3.14159
-2.71828
1.0
```

Characters in Lisp are represented using the #
notation, followed by the character. Each character has a corresponding numerical representation based on its position in the ASCII or Unicode table.

```
#\a
#\b
#\Space
#\Newline
```

Strings in Lisp are sequences of characters enclosed in double quotes. They can span multiple lines and include any valid character.

```
"This is a string"
"123"
"Multi-line
string"
```

Lists, a quintessential data type in Lisp, are sequences of elements enclosed in parentheses. Lists can contain a mixture of data types, including atoms, numbers, strings, characters, and even other lists.

```
(1 2 3)
("a" "b" "c")
(1 "two" 3.0)
```

There are several important operations for working with lists, such as car, cdr, and cons. The car operation retrieves the first element of a list, while cdr returns the remainder of the list after removing the first element. The cons operation constructs a new list by inserting an element at the beginning of an existing list.

```
(car '(1 2 3)) ; returns 1
(cdr '(1 2 3)) ; returns (2 3)
(cons 0 '(1 2 3)) ; returns (0 1 2 3)
```

Understanding these basic data types and operations allows for the construction of complex data structures and the implementation of sophisticated algorithms in Lisp programs.

Mastering data types and their manipulations form the cornerstone of Lisp programming proficiency.

2.3 Symbolic Expressions (S-expressions)

In Lisp, the fundamental structure for representing code and data is the symbolic expression, commonly referred to as an S-expression. An S-expression can be either an atom or a list. Atoms are indivisible entities like numbers, symbols, or characters, whereas lists are ordered collections of S-expressions enclosed in parentheses. Understanding S-expressions is crucial as they form the backbone of Lisp programming.

A single number, such as 42, is an example of an atomic S-expression:

42

Similarly, a symbol, say foo, is also an atomic S-expression:

foo

Lists, on the other hand, are represented by parentheses and can contain any combination of atoms and other lists. For instance, the following is a list containing the symbol bar and the number 3:

(bar 3)

Lists can be nested to any level of complexity, making Lisp highly expressive. An example of a nested list is:

((a 1) (b 2) (c 3))

In this example, the outer list contains three inner lists, each being

37

an S-expression with a symbol and a number. The uniform representation of code and data in Lisp as S-expressions allows for powerful metaprogramming capabilities, where programs can manipulate other programs as data.

Construction and Manipulation of S-expressions

To construct lists, Lisp provides the cons, list, and related functions. The cons function takes two arguments and constructs a pair, with the first argument being the head (or car) and the second argument being the tail (or cdr). Here is an example illustrating cons:

```
(cons 'a '(b c))
```

This expression outputs:

```
(a b c)
```

The list function is used to create a list from multiple arguments:

```
(list 'x 'y 'z)
```

The result is:

```
(x y z)
```

To access the elements of a list, one can use the car and cdr functions. car retrieves the first element, while cdr retrieves the rest of the list. For the list (foo bar baz), the car and cdr functions behave as follows:

```
(car '(foo bar baz))
(cdr '(foo bar baz))
```

The outputs are:

```
foo
(bar baz)
```

Syntactic and Semantic Aspects of S-expressions

The syntax of S-expressions is straightforward: atoms and lists. However, their semantics, or the meaning they represent, can vary significantly depending on context. Atoms can represent variables, constants, or function names. Lists can represent function calls, code blocks, or data structures.

Consider the list:

(+ 3 4)In this context, the list represents a function call to the addition function (+) with arguments 3 and 4. When evaluated, this list returns

7. The evaluation process is crucial for understanding Lisp programs: it interprets S-expressions as code to be executed.

Evaluation rules for S-expressions are managed by Lisp's reader and evaluator. The reader translates textual representations into internal S-expression data structures. The evaluator processes these structures to produce results. Understanding this dual role of S-expressions—both as code and data—is essential for Lisp programming.

Self-Referential Nature of S-expressions

An important property of S-expressions is their self-referential capability, allowing for sophisticated program manipulation techniques. Since Lisp programs are S-expressions, the language provides primitives to evaluate, construct, and decompose these structures.

This is evident in macros, which allow generating code programmatically. A simple macro might transform an S-expression template into another form before evaluation. For instance:

```
(defmacro square (x)
  '(* ,x ,x))
```

This macro defines a template for squaring a number, where x is an S-expression. The backquote (') and comma (,) syntaxes are used for template and value insertion respectively.

By mastering S-expressions, Lisp programmers can leverage the full power of the language's metaprogramming capabilities, creating code that is both concise and expressive.

Hence, a thorough grasp of symbolic expressions equips one with the tools necessary for effective and advanced Lisp programming. The uniformity in representing code and data through S-expressions underpins the language's powerful and elegant design.

2.4   Lists and Their Structure

In Lisp, lists are foundational data structures, integral to both code and data representation. Understanding their structure and manipulation is paramount to mastering Lisp programming. A list in Lisp is an ordered collection of elements, which can include atoms, other lists, or a mix of both.

An empty list, represented as '() or nil, is a base case in list processing. Lists can be created by enclosing elements in parentheses. For instance, the list containing the elements 1, 2, and 3 is represented as:

```
(list 1 2 3)
```

Here, list is a built-in function that constructs a list from the given elements.

A pivotal concept in list structure is the cons cell. A cons cell, or pair, is a fundamental building block of lists. It comprises two parts: the car (the first element) and the cdr (the rest of the list). For example, the list (1 2 3) is constructed using cons cells as follows:

```
(cons 1 (cons 2 (cons 3 nil)))
```

Each list is recursively defined as either an empty list or a cons cell whose cdr is a list. This recursive definition facilitates powerful recursive functions for list processing.

Consider the following recursive function to calculate the length of a list:

Algorithm 1: Length of a List

  Input: A list lst
  Result: The length of lst
1 **if** (null lst) **then**
2 | **return** 0;
3 **end**
4 **else**
5 | **return** 1 + (length (cdr lst));
6 **end**

In Lisp code, this would be defined as:

```
(defun length (lst)
  (if (null lst)
      0
      (+ 1 (length (cdr lst)))))
```

Evaluating (length '(1 2 3)) results in 3, demonstrating the recursive traversal of the list structure.

Lists can also be manipulated using functions such as car and cdr. The car function returns the first element, while the cdr function returns the rest of the list (excluding the first element). Here are examples:

```
(car '(1 2 3)) ; Returns 1
(cdr '(1 2 3)) ; Returns (2 3)
```

These primitive operations are critical for breaking down and recon-
structing lists.

Appending lists is another common operation, conducted using the append function. It concatenates multiple lists:

```
(append '(1 2) '(3 4)) ; Returns (1 2 3 4)
```

Similar to cons, but it combines entire lists rather than individual elements.

Lists are not restricted to a single type of element. They can be heterogeneous, containing diverse data types. For instance, consider:

```
(list 1 'two 3.0 "four") ; Returns (1 'two 3.0 "four")
```

This flexibility enhances the expressive power of Lisp in various domains, from symbolic computation to artificial intelligence.

Furthermore, nested lists are simply lists whose elements are themselves lists. This leads to complex data structures that can model hierarchical relationships naturally. For example, the nested list:

```
(list (list 1 2) (list 3 4))
```

represents a 2D matrix.

To recap, mastering lists involves understanding their construction via
cons cells, manipulating them with car and cdr, and leveraging Lisp's
functions for recursive operations. This knowledge forms the bedrock
of more advanced Lisp programming techniques and applications.

2.5   Quoting and Evaluation

In Lisp programming, quoting and evaluation are fundamental concepts
that dictate how expressions are interpreted by the Lisp interpreter. It is
essential to understand these concepts to effectively write and assess
Lisp code.

In Lisp, every expression is evaluated unless it is explicitly quoted. Evaluation involves interpreting an expression, computing, and returning its

41

value. There are instances where a programmer intends to refer to an expression itself rather than its evaluated value; this is where quoting becomes necessary.

Quoting Quoting an expression in Lisp prevents it from being evaluated. Instead, the expression is treated as a literal. The primary mechanism for quoting is the single quote character '.

Consider the following examples:

```
(+ 2 3) ; This will be evaluated to 5
'( + 2 3 ) ; This will not be evaluated, it is treated as the list (+ 2 3)
```

When expressions are quoted, they are simply returned as they are. The quote operator ' can be elaborated using the quote function:

```
(quote (+ 2 3)) ; This is equivalent to '+ 2 3
```

Quoting becomes particularly necessary when defining lists of symbols or other data structures which should not be directly evaluated.

Evaluation Evaluation is the process of computing the value of an expression. In Lisp, evaluation follows specific rules based on the type of the expression.

1. *Atoms*: If an expression is an atom, whether it's a number, string, or symbol, it evaluates to its value or binding.

```
42 ; This evaluates to 42
"hello" ; This evaluates to the string "hello"
```

2. *Lists*: If an expression is a list, Lisp treats the first element as an operator or function to apply and the rest as arguments.

```
(+ 2 3) ; This evaluates to 5
(cons 1 '(2 3)) ; This evaluates to the list (1 2 3)
```

Expressions involving function calls undergo evaluation by first evaluating each argument and then applying the function to the resulting values.

Quote Special Form The quote is a special form in Lisp. Unlike functions, special forms are not evaluated in the typical left-to-right manner. Instead, special forms have their own evaluation rules. The quote form returns its argument unevaluated.

Using quote:

```
(quote a) ; Returns the symbol a, not its value or binding
(quote (+ 2 3)) ; Returns the list (+ 2 3), unevaluated
```

The need to control evaluation with quote is pivotal in macro definitions and other advanced Lisp constructs where raw symbolic data needs to be manipulated before evaluation.

Quasi-Quoting A more flexible quoting mechanism is quasi-quoting, provided by the backtick` character. Quasi-quoting allows selective evaluation within quoted expressions using the comma , operator.

Example:

```
`(list ,(+ 2 3) 4) ; This evaluates to (list 5 4)
```

In quasi-quoting, the expression within the backtick is treated as quoted, but subexpressions preceded by a comma are evaluated.

This example demonstrates quasi-quoting combined with comma usage to inject evaluated expressions:

```
(setq a 10)
(setq b 20)
`(sum ,a ,b) ; This evaluates to (sum 10 20)
```

Finally, combining these quoting mechanisms enhances Lisp's ability to handle code as data and meta-programming, foundational elements of the language's flexibility and power.

2.6 Atoms and Variables

In Lisp, atoms are the fundamental building blocks of the language, representing the indivisible elements that cannot be subdivided. They include numbers, symbols, and strings. Understanding atoms and how they are used as variables forms a core aspect of Lisp programming.

Atoms can be categorized as either numeric or non-numeric. Numeric atoms include integers and floating-point numbers, while non-numeric atoms (symbols) are names that primarily serve as identifiers.

Numeric Atoms: Numeric atoms in Lisp are straightforward; they denote integer or floating-point values.

```
42 ; an integer atom
```

3.14 ; a floating-point atom

Non-Numeric Atoms: Non-numeric atoms are generally symbolic names. These symbols can be used as constants, variables, or function names.

x ; a symbolic atom
hello ; another symbolic atom

When using symbols as variables, they must be assigned values. Variable assignment in Lisp is typically done using the setq special operator. The setq operator takes two arguments: the name of the variable and the value to be assigned to it.

(setq x 10) ; Assigns the value 10 to the variable x
(setq message "Hello, World!") ; Assigns the string "Hello, World!" to
    the variable message

Once variables are defined, they can be used in expressions just like any other data type. For example:

(setq result (+ x 5)) ; Uses the variable x in an arithmetic expression,
    assigns the result to another variable

A key characteristic of Lisp variables is dynamic typing. Unlike statically-typed languages, Lisp variables do not have a fixed data type. A single variable can hold an integer, a floating-point number, a string, or any other type of data at different times in the program's execution.

(setq dynamicVar 42) ; Initially an integer
(setq dynamicVar "Forty-two") ; Later assigned to a string

Another important point is the use of symbols as constants. To define constants, Lisp uses the defconstant special operator.

(defconstant pi 3.14159) ; Defines pi as a constant with a value of
    3.14159

It's important to note that once defined, constants cannot be changed during the program's execution, preserving their integrity.

Variables are scoped either globally or locally. By default, variables defined with setq are global. That is, they are accessible throughout the

44

program after their definition. For local scope, Lisp provides constructs such as let and let*.

The let construct is used to create new variables with local scope within a block of code. Variables defined within a let block are not accessible outside it.

```
(let ((x 5)
      (y 10))
  (+ x y)) ; Returns 15
; x and y are not accessible here
```

The variables x and y exist only within the body of the let expression. The scope of these variables is local to the let block.

The let* construct is similar to let, but it allows sequential bindings. Each binding can reference the previously defined ones.

```
(let* ((x 5)
       (y (+ x 10)))
  (* x y)) ; Returns 75
```

In this example, the variable y is assigned a value that depends on the value of x. Such sequential bindings are useful when the value of a variable must be determined based on previous bindings.

Additionally, Lisp uses the concept of "special variables" or "dynamic variables", which are declared using the defvar or defparameter constructs. These variables are somewhat global but allow for dynamic scope.

```
(defvar *global-var* 100) ; Creates a dynamic variable with an initial
      value of 100
```

Note the convention of enclosing special variable names in asterisks (*). This helps signal to the programmer that the variables are special or dynamically scoped.

Through manipulation of atoms and variables, Lisp provides great flexibility and power. Understanding how to properly declare, use, and scope these elements is essential for effective Lisp programming. This knowledge builds a solid foundation for tackling more advanced topics in Lisp.

2.7 Defining and Using Variables

In Lisp, variables can hold references to data, making them essential for managing and manipulating information within programs. Defining and using variables in Lisp is facilitated by specific constructs and conventions. Understanding these constructs is essential for writing efficient and clear Lisp code.

Variables in Lisp are typically defined using the defvar and setq constructs. While defvar is used to declare and optionally initialize a global variable, setq is more versatile and is used for both global and local variables, for assigning values after variables are defined.

To declare a global variable, use the defvar construct. Below is an example of using defvar:

```
(defvar *global-variable* 100)
```

In this example, the variable *global-variable* is declared and initialized with the value 100. The naming convention, using asterisks around the variable name, is a common practice to indicate global scope in Lisp.

After declaring a variable, you can use setq to assign a new value to it:

```
(setq *global-variable* 200)
```

Here, *global-variable* is assigned a new value of 200. The setq construct can also declare and assign values to local variables within a function or block scope.

Consider the following example, which demonstrates the use of setq for local variables inside a function:

```
(defun compute-area (radius)
   (let ((pi 3.14159)
         (area))
     (setq area (* pi radius radius))
     area))
```

In this function, pi and area are local variables, defined within the scope of the let block. The setq construct assigns the value of the expression (* pi radius radius) to the variable area. The value of area is then returned as the function result.

Lisp also includes the defparameter construct, similar to defvar, but it always re-initializes the variable with the provided value:

```
(defparameter *global-parameter* 300)
```

Each time defparameter is evaluated, *global-parameter* will be re-initialized to 300.

It is crucial to understand scope in Lisp, which determines the visibility and lifetime of variables. Lisp primarily supports two kinds of scope: lexical (or static) scope and dynamic scope. Lexical scope is the most commonly used, defined by the structure of the code, whereas dynamic scope depends on the runtime call stack.

Lexical scope in Lisp is achieved using constructs like let and lambda. For example:

```
(let ((x 10)
      (y 20))
  (+ x y))
```

In this code, the variables x and y are locally scoped within the let block. They are not accessible outside this block, ensuring that the local bindings do not interfere with global variables of the same name, if any exist.

Dynamic scope, although less common, is implemented in Lisp using defvar for global variable declaration and setq for assignment within a dynamic context. An example illustrating dynamic scope involves the use of global variables within different function calls, where the value of a global variable can be altered dynamically by the functions.

Using appropriate variable naming conventions enhances code readability and maintainability. As a convention, variables for temporary or local use are named in lowercase letters with hyphens to separate words, while global variables often use asterisks to visually indicate their scope. This distinction helps developers quickly understand the context and scope of each variable.

Effective variable management is key to avoiding common issues such as name clashes or unintended variable shadowing. Lisp's disciplined approach to defining and using variables, with constructs like defvar, setq, let, and lambda, provides a robust framework for variable handling, ensuring both flexibility and clarity in code development.

2.8 Comments in Lisp Code

Comments in Lisp are crucial for making the code understandable to humans, providing context, and explaining intricate logic. They do not impact the execution of the program since the Lisp interpreter ignores them. Comments can significantly improve the maintainability and readability of the code, especially in collaborative environments or long-term projects.

In Lisp, single-line comments start with a semicolon ; and extend to the end of the line. There are also conventions for numbers of semicolons indicating the level or context of the commentary, which we will discuss in detail.

The basic syntax for a single-line comment is as follows:

```
; This is a single-line comment in Lisp
```

When a semicolon is placed before an expression, everything following it on the same line is ignored by the interpreter:

```
(+ 1 2) ; This adds 1 and 2
```

The output of the above code ignoring the comment is:

```
3
```

Levels of Comments

Lisp programmers often use different numbers of semicolons to denote the scope or importance of the comment: - A single semicolon ; is used for comments that are placed at the end of a line of code. - Double semicolons ;; align with the current indentation level and are used for comments on entire lines. - Triple semicolons ;;;, aligned with the code's start, often mark major sections or headings within the code. - Quadruple semicolons ;;;; serve as file headers or significant separators within a file.

Examples illustrating these conventions are:

```
;;; This is a major section comment
(defun add (x y)
  ;; This function adds two numbers
  (+ x y)) ; end of add function

(let ((a 5)
```

```
    (b 10))
;; Let binding for local variables
(+ a b)) ; end of let form
```

Multi-line Comments

In some Lisp dialects, like Common Lisp, multi-line comments are enclosed within #| and |#. This can be particularly useful for larger blocks of comments or for commenting out sections of code during debugging.

Example of a multi-line comment:

```
#|
This is a multi-line comment.
It can span multiple lines.
All text within this block is ignored by the interpreter.
|#
```

Another example where multi-line comments are used to disable sections of code:

```
(defun calculate (x y)
  (+ x y))

#|
;; Uncomment this code for debugging.
(defun debug-calculate (x y)
  (print (+ x y)))
|#

(calculate 5 10)
```

The output for the above code, ignoring the commented-out function debug-calculate, remains:

15

Best Practices

Effective commenting can distinguish between mere syntactical annotation and insightful commentary:

- Comments should be concise but informative, enhancing understanding without redundancy. - Always update comments when changing the code to prevent outdated or misleading information. - Use comments to explain the "why" behind complex logic or decisions, not the

49

"what", which is usually evident from the code itself. - Maintain good indentation and alignment for readability.

Here's a well-commented example to illustrate these practices:

```
;;; Main calculation section

(defun factorial (n)
    "Calculate the factorial of N recursively."
    (if (= n 0)
        1 ; Base case: 0! is 1
        (* n (factorial (- n 1)))))) ; Recursive call

(defun example-usage ()
    "Example usage of the factorial function."
    (let ((result (factorial 5))) ;; Calculate 5!
      (print result))) ; Expected output: 120

(example-usage)
```

Verbatim code output:

```
120
```

Well-placed and clear comments facilitate understanding and collaboration. Properly commented code not only elucidates the logic but also enhances readability and maintainability, making Lisp programming an efficient and enjoyable experience.

2.9 Basic Arithmetic and Boolean Operations

In Lisp, arithmetic and Boolean operations form the core of many computational tasks. This section elucidates the syntax and semantics of these operations, ensuring a comprehensive understanding of their usage.

Basic arithmetic operations in Lisp are performed using prefix notation, where the operator precedes the operands. The primary arithmetic operators are $+$, -, *, and /.

```
(+ 5 3) ; Addition: results in 8
(- 10 4) ; Subtraction: results in 6
```

```
(* 6 7) ; Multiplication: results in 42
(/ 20 4) ; Division: results in 5
```

The results from executing the above code are as follows:

```
8
6
42
5
```

In addition to simple arithmetic, Lisp can handle more complex expressions by nesting operations within each other. For example:

```
(+ (* 2 3) (/ 15 3)) ; Computes (2 * 3) + (15 / 3)
```

This expression yields:

```
9
```

Lisp also supports various numeric functions such as abs, sqrt, expt, and mod. These functions expand the arithmetic capabilities of the language.

```
(abs -10) ; Absolute value: results in 10
(sqrt 16) ; Square root: results in 4
(expt 2 3) ; Exponentiation: 2^3, results in 8
(mod 17 3) ; Modulus: 17 mod 3, results in 2
```

The Boolean domain in Lisp, represented primarily by the values T (true) and NIL (false), is essential for control structures and condition checking. Boolean operations are typically performed using functions such as and, or, and not.

```
(and t t) ; Logical AND: true
(and t nil) ; Logical AND: false
(or nil t) ; Logical OR: true
(not nil) ; Logical NOT: true
(not t) ; Logical NOT: false
```

The output of the above Boolean expressions are:

```
T
NIL
T
T
NIL
```

Lisp also provides relational operators to compare values. These operators include $<$, $>$, $<=$, $>=$, $=$, and $/=$. These operators return T for true and NIL for false when applied to numeric comparisons.

```
(< 4 5) ; Less than: true
(> 10 3) ; Greater than: true
(<= 7 7) ; Less than or equal: true
(>= 5 12) ; Greater than or equal: false
(= 10 10) ; Equal to: true
(/= 8 2) ; Not equal to: true
```

The execution results of these relational operators are:

```
T
T
T
NIL
T
T
```

Boolean expressions can be combined and nested to form complex logical statements. Consider the following example:

```
(and (> 10 2) (or (= 5 5) (not nil))) ; true AND (true OR true)
```

This yields:

```
T
```

Lisp's flexibility allows for user-defined arithmetic and Boolean functions using the defun keyword. For instance:

```
(defun is-even (n)
  "Check if a number is even."
  (= (mod n 2) 0))

(defun greater-than-five (x)
  "Check if a number is greater than five."
  (> x 5))
```

Executing the above functions:

```
(is-even 4) ; Check if 4 is even: true
(greater-than-five 10) ; Check if 10 is greater than five: true
```

Results in:

```
T
T
```

These operations and functions constitute the primary tools for performing arithmetic and logical computations in Lisp, laying a foundation for more complex programming structures.

2.10   Functions and Function Calls

In Lisp, functions are first-class citizens, meaning they can be treated like any other data type. They can be passed as arguments, returned from other functions, and assigned to variables. This flexibility provides a powerful tool for Lisp programmers in handling problem-solving tasks.

Functions in Lisp are defined using the defun keyword, which stands for "define function." The defun macro allows you to create a named function with a specified list of parameters and a body of code that represents the function's behavior. The general syntax for defun is as follows:

```
(defun function-name (parameter-list)
  "Optional documentation string."
  body)
```

Here, function-name is the name of the function, parameter-list is a list of parameters the function takes, and body contains one or more Lisp expressions that define what the function does. Let us look at an example:

```
(defun add-two-numbers (x y)
  "Adds two numbers x and y."
  (+ x y))
```

In this example, add-two-numbers is a function that takes two parameters, x and y, and returns their sum using the + operator. To call this function, you would use the following syntax:

```
(add-two-numbers 3 4)
```

This call returns 7.

Functions can return multiple values by using the values function. Here is an example to illustrate this:

```
(defun multiple-returns (a b)
  "Returns the sum and product of a and b."
  (values (+ a b) (* a b)))
```

53

Calling this function with arguments 3 and 4 would look like this:

```
(multiple-returns 3 4)
```

The above call would return two values: 7 and 12. To capture these values, you would use the multiple-value-bind construct:

```
(multiple-value-bind (sum product) (multiple-returns 3 4)
   (format t "Sum: ~a, Product: ~a~%" sum product))
```

This would output:

Sum: 7, Product: 12

Another important concept in Lisp functions is the use of lambda expressions. A lambda expression defines an anonymous function without a name. The general syntax is as follows:

```
(lambda (parameter-list)
   body)
```

For instance, you can define an anonymous function that adds two numbers:

```
(lambda (x y) (+ x y))
```

You can assign this lambda expression to a variable and use it like a regular function:

```
(setq add-func (lambda (x y) (+ x y)))
(funcall add-func 3 4)
```

This returns 7. The funcall function is used to call a function defined by a lambda expression or stored in a variable.

Lisp also supports higher-order functions, which are functions that take other functions as arguments or return them as results. One of the most common higher-order functions is mapcar, which applies a function to each element of a list:

```
(mapcar (lambda (x) (* x x)) '(1 2 3 4))
```

This call returns the list:

(1 4 9 16)

Recursive functions are a cornerstone of functional programming in

Lisp. A recursive function is one that calls itself until a base condition is met. For example, consider the factorial function:

```
(defun factorial (n)
  "Calculates the factorial of n."
  (if (= n 0)
      1
      (* n (factorial (- n 1)))))
```

When calling (factorial 5), the function computes the factorial of 5 by recursively calling itself until n equals 0.

Understanding these fundamental aspects of Lisp functions, including their definitions, calls, and advanced use cases, is essential for effective Lisp programming. This knowledge is foundational for developing more complex and powerful Lisp programs.

2.11 Special Forms and Their Uses

In Lisp, special forms are constructs with unique evaluation rules that differ from standard function calls. Unlike regular functions, special forms are integral to the language's syntax and are required to implement constructs fundamental to Lisp programming, such as conditionals, loops, and variable bindings.

Understanding how to use special forms effectively is crucial for mastering Lisp programming. Below, we will explore several essential special forms, including quote, if, cond, let, lambda, and defun.

quote

The quote special form is used to prevent the evaluation of expressions. By quoting an expression, you indicate to the Lisp interpreter that it should be treated as literal data rather than code to be executed. This is essential when working with symbolic data.

```
(quote (a b c)) ; returns (a b c)
```

An important syntactic sugar in Lisp is the use of the single-quote character as a shorthand for quote.

```
'(a b c) ; equivalent to (quote (a b c))
```

if

55

The if special form is the primary conditional construct in Lisp. It evaluates a test expression and, based on its truthiness, decides which of the subsequent expressions to evaluate and return.

```
(if test-expression
    consequent-expression
    alternative-expression)
```

For example:

```
(if (> 3 2)
    'yes
    'no) ; returns 'yes
```

cond

While if handles binary conditions, cond is preferable for multi-way branching. Similar to a series of nested if statements, cond evaluates conditions in sequence and executes the corresponding expression for the first true condition.

```
(cond
  ((< x 0) 'negative)
  ((= x 0) 'zero)
  ((> x 0) 'positive))
```

Each clause in the cond consists of a condition and a result expression. The first condition that evaluates to true will trigger its associated expression to execute.

let

The let special form facilitates local variable bindings. Variables defined within a let expression only exist within its body, ensuring modularity and preventing variable name clashes.

```
(let ((var1 val1)
      (var2 val2))
  body)
```

For instance:

```
(let ((x 2)
      (y 3))
  (+ x y)) ; returns 5
```

lambda

lambda allows for the creation of anonymous functions. These are functions not bound to a name and can be used where a named function
would typically be applied.

```
(lambda (param1 param2)
  body)
```

For example:

```
(lambda (x y)
  (+ x y))
```

This anonymous function can be used immediately or stored in a variable:

```
(let ((add (lambda (x y) (+ x y))))
  (add 3 4)) ; returns 7
```

defun

To define named functions, defun is used. This special form provides a
way to create reusable functions that are bound to symbols.

```
(defun function-name (param1 param2)
  body)
```

For example:

```
(defun add (x y)
  (+ x y))

(add 3 4) ; returns 7
```

These special forms are foundational elements of Lisp, enabling sophisticated control structures and functional abstraction. Understanding their mechanics and appropriate applications enhances the efficacy
and readability of Lisp code.

2.12   Proper Indentation and Readability Tips

Consistent indentation and readability significantly enhance the maintainability and clarity of Lisp code. Proper indentation ensures that
the structure of code is visually apparent, simplifying the tasks of reading and debugging. Maintaining readability involves following standard
conventions and practices that remove ambiguity and foster a professional coding environment.

Lisp code relies heavily on the use of parentheses to delineate expressions and function calls. To properly indent Lisp code, each sub-
expression should be indented in a manner that reflects its nested level
within the main expression. Indentation levels are typically managed by
aligning lines under the opening parenthesis of the line above.

Consider the following example, which displays improper indentation:

```
(defun factorial (n)
(if (<= n 1)
1
(* n (factorial (- n 1)))))
```

In the snippet above, the indentation does not accurately reflect the
structure of the code. Here is the same code snippet properly indented:

```
(defun factorial (n)
  (if (<= n 1)
      1
      (* n (factorial (- n 1)))))
```

In this properly indented version:

- The body of the defun is indented two spaces.

- The sub-forms of the if conditional are similarly indented under
  the keyword if.

- Each nested expression is indented to show its relationship to the
  parent expression.

Readability is further enhanced by adhering to consistent line breaks.
When expressions or function calls become too lengthy, breaking them
into multiple lines is advisable. For example:

```
(defun long-function-name (arg1 arg2 arg3 arg4)
```

```
(let ((result1 (some-calculation arg1 arg2))
      (result2 (another-calculation arg3 arg4)))
   (combine-results result1 result2)))
```

By breaking lines at coherent points, such as after a function name or at logical operators, the structure of code becomes clearer. Additionally, aligning related parts, such as arguments or variable declarations, vertically aligns the associated elements and makes dependencies more conspicuous.

Incorporating comments judiciously can also aid readability. Comments should be used to explain the purpose of code blocks, clarify non-obvious logic, and denote sections of code. However, they should not state the obvious or reiterate what the code is already conveying. Useful comments look like this:

```
(defun factorial (n)
  ;; Returns the factorial of n.
  ;; This is a classic recursive implementation.
  (if (<= n 1)
      1
      (* n (factorial (- n 1))))))
```

Avoid placing comments at the end of a line, as they can disrupt alignment and are often overlooked. It is better to place comments on their own line above the code they reference.

Naming conventions are another vital aspect of readability. Use descriptive names for variables and functions to communicate their roles and purposes. For instance, calculate-sum is preferred over cs, as it conveys clearer intent.

```
(let ((base-salary 50000)
      (bonus 5000))
  (+ base-salary bonus))
```

In this example, base-salary and bonus are descriptive, immediately informing the reader about their purpose within the code.

Whitespace usage also plays a pivotal role. Insert spaces around operators for better readability:

```
(+ a b)
(not= a b)
```

Instead of:

```
(+a+b)
(not=a=b)
```

Consistent use of whitespace enhances the visual separation between terms, reducing cognitive load.

Employing tools that automatically format and check Lisp code can help maintain these practices. Editors such as Emacs, with Lisp mode, automatically manage indentation and highlight syntax, aiding in adherence to conventions. Code linters or formatters further ensure that code remains clean and standardized.

Maintaining proper indentation and readability practices leads to cleaner, more understandable Lisp programs. This facilitates easier collaboration, debugging, and enhances overall code quality. Consequently, developing the discipline to follow these practices is an essential skill for proficient Lisp programmers.

Chapter 3

Lisp Data Structures

This chapter delves into the various data structures available in Lisp, beginning with lists and cons cells, and extending to vectors, arrays, strings, and characters. It explores the uses and implementations of hash tables, structures (structs), property lists, and association lists. Readers will learn techniques for creating and accessing complex data structures, as well as functions for manipulating these structures. Efficiency considerations for using different data structures are also discussed, ensuring that readers can make informed choices in their programs.

3.1   Introduction to Lisp Data Structures

Lisp is a highly flexible, dynamic language that excels in symbolic computation and accommodates a range of different data structures. Understanding the various data structures available in Lisp is critical to mastering the language, as they form the foundational elements for organizing and manipulating data within programs. Lisp provides several built-in data structures, including lists, cons cells, vectors, arrays, strings, characters, hash tables, structures (structs), property lists, and association lists. Each of these data structures has unique characteristics and use cases which we will explore throughout this chapter.

In Lisp, one of the most fundamental data structures is the list. A list in Lisp is a sequence of elements, which can be other lists, atoms, or a combination of both. Lists are defined by cons cells, where each cons cell is a pair of pointers typically referred to as the car (the first element) and the cdr (the rest of the list). For example, consider the following Lisp expression:

```
(cons 'a '())
```

This expression produces a list containing a single element a. The function cons constructs a new cons cell. The car points to a, and the cdr points to an empty list, denoted as '().

Another critical data structure in Lisp is the vector. A vector is a one-dimensional array that provides efficient access to elements using an index. Elements in a vector are stored contiguously in memory, allowing for faster access times compared to lists. Vectors can be created using the make-vector function:

```
(make-vector 5 0)
```

This creates a vector of length 5, with each element initialized to 0.

Lisp also supports multi-dimensional arrays. These arrays can be created using the make-array function, which allows specifying the dimensions of the array as well as the initial element:

```
(make-array '(2 3) :initial-element 0)
```

This example creates a 2x3 array where all elements are initialized to 0.

Strings in Lisp are sequences of characters. Strings are used for text manipulation and can be created using double quotes. For example:

```
"Hello, World!"
```

Strings are immutable, meaning that any operation that modifies a string actually creates a new string.

Characters, on the other hand, are individual symbols that constitute a string. Characters in Lisp are distinguished by a preceding backslash:

```
#\a
```

This represents the character a.

Lisp's hash tables allow for efficient key-value storage and retrieval. Hash tables are particularly useful when the relationship between keys and values is not inherently ordered. To create a hash table, use the make-hash-table function:

```
(make-hash-table :test 'equal)
```

This creates a hash table that uses the equal function for comparing keys.

Structures (structs) are another way to group related data together in Lisp. Structures are defined using the defstruct macro, which specifies the fields and their default values:

```
(defstruct person
  name
  age)
```

This defines a person structure with fields for name and age.

Property lists (plists) associate properties with values and are commonly used for passing optional arguments to functions. A plist is a list with an even number of elements, where odd-indexed elements are property names and even-indexed elements are corresponding values:

```
(setq my-plist '(name "John" age 30))
```

This sets my-plist to a property list associating name with "John" and age with 30.

Lastly, association lists (alists) are lists of pairs, where the car of each pair is the key and the cdr is the value. Alists can be manipulated using functions like assoc:

```
(setq my-alist '((name . "John") (age . 30)))
```

This sets my-alist to an association list with name mapped to "John" and age to 30.

Throughout the following sections, we will delve deeper into each of these data structures, examining their implementation, usage, and the functions provided by Lisp for their manipulation. This foundation will enable us to build and efficiently manage complex data structures within our Lisp programs.

3.2   Lists and Cons Cells

In Lisp, lists and cons cells are fundamental data structures that form the basis of most data manipulation operations. A cons cell, short for "construct," is a data structure with two components: the car (which stands for "contents of the address part of register") and the cdr (which stands for "contents of the decrement part of register"). Lists in Lisp are essentially chains of cons cells linked together.

A cons cell can be created using the cons function. The car and cdr of a cons cell can be accessed using the car and cdr functions, respectively.

```
(setq my-cons (cons 'a 'b)) ; Creates a cons cell (a . b)
(car my-cons) ; Returns 'a
(cdr my-cons) ; Returns 'b
```

The internal representation of a list is a chain of cons cells where the car contains an element of the list and the cdr contains either another cons cell or the special value nil, which denotes the end of the list.

```
(setq my-list (list 'a 'b 'c)) ; Creates a list (a b c)
(car my-list) ; Returns 'a
(cdr my-list) ; Returns (b c)
```

The list function is a convenient way to create lists of any length without the need to explicitly chain cons cells.

```
(list 'a 'b 'c) ; Returns (a b c)
(list 1 2 3 4 5) ; Returns (1 2 3 4 5)
```

Lists can also be built manually using nested cons cells, although this is less common in practice due to its complexity.

```
(cons 'a (cons 'b (cons 'c nil))) ; Returns (a b c)
```

The list structure can be visualized as follows:

```
(a . (b . (c . nil)))
```

Lists in Lisp are flexible and can grow dynamically. Various functions are available for manipulating lists, including append, reverse, and length.

```
(setq list1 '(1 2 3))
(setq list2 '(4 5 6))
```

```
(append list1 list2) ; Returns (1 2 3 4 5 6)
(reverse list1) ; Returns (3 2 1)
(length list1) ; Returns 3
```

Lists can contain any type of element, including other lists, enabling the creation of complex, nested structures.

```
(setq nested-list '(1 (2 3) (4 (5 6))))
(car nested-list) ; Returns 1
(cadr nested-list) ; Returns (2 3)
(caddr nested-list) ; Returns (4 (5 6))
```

The functions car, cdr, and their respective combinations such as caar, cadr, cdar, and cddr allow for deep extraction of nested list elements.

```
(caar '((a b) c d)) ; Returns 'a
(cadr '(x y z)) ; Returns 'y
(cdar '((p q) r s)) ; Returns '(q)
(cddr '(1 2 3 4)) ; Returns '(3 4)
```

To iterate over lists, Lisp provides several constructs, such as mapcar, dolist, and loop. Here is an example using dolist to sum a list of numbers:

```
(setq numbers '(1 2 3 4 5))
(setq sum 0)
(dolist (n numbers sum)
  (setq sum (+ sum n)))
; The sum will be 15 at the end
```

The mapcar function applies a given function to each element of a list, returning a list of results.

```
(mapcar #'1+ '(1 2 3 4 5)) ; Returns (2 3 4 5 6)
```

Each of these techniques leverages the inherent structure and properties of lists and cons cells in Lisp, allowing developers to create, process, and manipulate data efficiently. Understanding lists and cons cells is essential for mastering Lisp programming, as they are used pervasively in both simple and complex data handling tasks.

3.3   Vectors and Arrays

In Lisp, vectors and arrays are fundamental one-dimensional and multi-dimensional data structures, respectively. This section provides an in-depth exploration of their characteristics, usage, and manipulation using Lisp constructs. Understanding these structures is essential for efficiently managing complex data patterns in your programs.

Vectors in Lisp are fixed-length, one-dimensional arrays. They can store any type of data, including numbers, characters, symbols, and even other lists. The syntax for creating a vector, accessing its elements, and manipulating data within it is straightforward but powerful.

To create a vector, the vector function is employed:

```
(setq my-vector (vector 1 2 3 4 5))
```

In this example, my-vector is a five-element vector containing the integers from 1 to 5. We can access elements of this vector using the aref function. aref takes two arguments: the vector and the index of the element to be accessed. Note that Lisp uses zero-based indexing:

```
(aref my-vector 2) ; Returns 3
```

Modifying elements in a vector is achieved using the setf function in conjunction with aref:

```
(setf (aref my-vector 2) 10)
```

After executing the above code, the vector my-vector will be [1 2 10 4 5].

Arrays in Lisp extend the concept of vectors to more than one dimension. You can create arrays using the make-array function. In this case, it allows for specifying the dimensions and initializing them if necessary. The default is to create uninitialized arrays.

```
(setq my-array (make-array '(3 3))) ; Creates a 3x3 array
```

This command creates a 3x3 array without initializing the elements. Accessing elements in a multi-dimensional array requires specifying the indices for each dimension using aref:

```
(aref my-array 1 2) ; Accesses the element at row 1, column 2
```

66

Similarly, the setf function is used to modify elements in an array:

```
(setf (aref my-array 1 2) 42)
```

This sets the element at the second row and third column of my-array to 42. Additionally, initializing arrays with specific values during creation can simplify array setup. The :initial-element keyword argument does this:

```
(setq my-initialized-array (make-array '(2 2) :initial-element 0))
```

The above command creates a 2x2 array with all elements initialized to 0.

Lisp also supports displacement arrays, which allow parts of an array to share storage with another array. This can be useful for memory management and creating complex data structures.

```
(setq original-array (make-array 5 :initial-contents '(1 2 3 4 5)))
(setq displaced-array (make-array 3 :displaced-to original-array :
    displaced-index-offset 1))
```

Here, displaced-array shares its storage with original-array, starting at the second element. Changes in displaced-array will reflect in original-array and vice versa.

Dynamic arrays can be created using the adjust-array function. This allows resizing arrays as needed. When an array is adjusted, you can optionally choose to preserve the content of the original array by using the :initial-contents keyword.

```
(setq resizable-array (make-array 3 :initial-element 7))
(adjust-array resizable-array 5 :initial-contents '(7 7 7 7 7))
```

The example above adjusts resizable-array to a length of 5 and ensures all elements are initialized to 7.

Processing multiple elements in arrays is efficiently done using map functions. The mapcar function applies a specified function to each element of a list or array, returning a list of results.

```
(mapcar #'1+ my-vector)
```

This increments each element in my-vector by 1 and returns a new list. For arrays, map works similarly but keeps the structure of the array:

```
(map 'vector #'1+ my-vector)
```

The result is a new vector with each element incremented by 1.

Vectors and arrays enable efficient storage and manipulation of data in Lisp programs. Understanding their creation, access, and modification functions empowers you to build complex, high-performance data structures.

3.4   Strings and Characters

In Lisp, strings are sequences of characters. Each character within a string is an element of the type char, which is immutable and represents a single character. Strings themselves are mutable, allowing their elements to be read and modified. Characters in Lisp are represented using the Pound-Slash notation (#\), followed by the character itself.

A string literal in Lisp is enclosed in double quotes. For instance, "hello, world" is a string containing 12 characters (note that spaces and punctuation are counted as characters). To manipulate strings and characters effectively, you must understand the functions and operations available in Lisp.

Creating Strings and Characters

To create strings, you can either write a string literal or use the make-string function. Here are some examples:

```
; Creating a string literal
(setq my-string "hello, world")

; Making a string of length 5, initially filled with the character
(setq new-string (make-string 5 :initial-element #\space))
```

Characters can be created using the Pound-Slash notation as shown below:

```
; Creating characters
(setq char-a #\a)
(setq char-space #\space)
(setq char-newline #\Newline)
```

Accessing String Elements

To access individual elements of a string, the char function is used. The indexing is zero-based, which means the first character is at index 0.

```
; Accessing the first character of a string
(char "hello, world" 0) ; returns #\h

; Accessing the fifth character
(char "hello, world" 4) ; returns #\o
```

This function can also be used to check for a particular character at a given position:

```
; Checking if the first character is 'h'
(eq #\h (char "hello, world" 0)) ; returns T
```

Modifying Strings

Strings in Lisp can be modified using the setf macro in conjunction with the char function.

```
; Modifying a string
(setq my-string "goodbye")
(setf (char my-string 0) #\B) ; my-string now becomes "Boodbye"
```

It's important to note that directly modifying string literals may lead to undefined behavior in some Lisp implementations. Therefore, it's best to use string variables when modifications are necessary.

String Functions

Lisp provides a comprehensive set of functions for string manipulation. Some of the essential string functions include:

- string=: Compares two strings for equality.

  ```
  (string= "hello" "hello") ; returns T
  (string= "hello" "world") ; returns NIL
  ```

- string<: Checks if the first string is lexicographically smaller.

```
(string< "apple" "banana") ; returns T
```

- concatenate: Concatenates multiple strings into a single string.

```
(concatenate 'string "hello, " "world") ; returns "hello, world"
```

- substring: Extracts a substring from a given string.

```
(subseq "hello, world" 0 5) ; returns "hello"
```

- string-upcase and string-downcase: Converts a string to all upper-case or lowercase.

```
(string-upcase "hello") ; returns "HELLO"
(string-downcase "WORLD") ; returns "world"
```

- position: Finds the position of a character in a string.

```
(position #\w "hello, world") ; returns 7
```

These functions provide fundamental operations for working with strings, allowing for comparisons, concatenations, modifications, and various other manipulations.

Parsing and Formatting Strings

String parsing and formatting are essential tasks in many applications. Lisp offers functions for converting strings to other data types and vice versa. For instance, parse-integer converts a substring to an integer:

```
(parse-integer "12345") ; returns 12345
```

Similarly, to convert a number to a string, princ-to-string or format can be used:

```
; Using princ-to-string
(princ-to-string 12345) ; returns "12345"

; Using format
(format nil "~d" 12345) ; returns "12345"
```

70

The format function is particularly powerful and versatile. It produces formatted text based on a control string and a set of arguments. The control string contains directives for text formatting.

```
; Basic formatting
(format nil "The number is ~d." 12345) ; returns "The number is
    12345."

; Complex formatting with mixed types
(format nil "Hello, ~a! You have ~d new messages." "Alice" 3) ;
    returns "Hello, Alice! You have 3 new messages."
```

Efficiency Considerations

When dealing with large strings or performing extensive string manipulation, efficiency becomes a crucial aspect. While strings are flexible, their mutable nature can be both an advantage and a potential performance bottleneck. Frequent modifications to strings can lead to inefficiencies due to repeated allocations and copying.

To enhance performance:

- Prefer using adjustable arrays or vectors if your application involves extensive insertions or deletions.

- Use string buffers for accumulative string construction.

String buffers emulate a mutable sequence of characters with efficient concatenation capabilities.

```
(defparameter *buffer* (make-array 0 :element-type 'character :
    adjustable t :fill-pointer 0))

; Append characters to a buffer
(dotimes (i 3)
  (vector-push-extend #\X *buffer*))
*buffer* ; #(#\X #\X #\X)
```

Such practices help in managing memory usage efficiently, reducing the frequency of memory allocations and copying, and ultimately leading to faster string manipulations in performance-critical applications.

By understanding and applying these principles, you can handle strings and characters effectively in Lisp, ensuring both readability and efficiency in your code.

3.5   Hash Tables

Hash tables, also known as hash maps or dictionaries in other programming languages, provide an efficient method for storing and retrieving data using key-value pairs. In Lisp, hash tables are a versatile and powerful data structure, allowing constant-time complexity—on average—for insertion, deletion, and lookup operations.

To create a hash table in Lisp, the make-hash-table function is employed. This function allows customization through various keyword arguments such as :test for specifying the equality test and :size for providing an initial size hint.

```
(defparameter *phonebook* (make-hash-table :test 'equal))
```

The function make-hash-table initializes a hash table bound to the variable *phonebook*. The :test keyword argument is given the equality function equal, which will be used to determine whether two keys are the same.

To add entries to the hash table, the setf operator along with the gethash function is used. The syntax for inserting a key-value pair is shown below:

```
(setf (gethash "Alice" *phonebook*) "555-1234")
(setf (gethash "Bob" *phonebook*) "555-5678")
```

Here, "Alice" and "Bob" are keys associated with the values "555-1234" and "555-5678," respectively. The gethash function retrieves the value associated with a specified key if it exists, or inserts a new key-value pair if it does not.

Retrieving values from a hash table is straightforward. One can use gethash to fetch the value. If the key does not exist in the hash table, gethash returns nil by default.

```
(defparameter *alice-number* (gethash "Alice" *phonebook*))
```

In this example, *alice-number* would be set to "555-1234".

Sometimes, it is useful to know whether a key exists in the hash table.

This can be achieved by providing a second return value from gethash:

```
(multiple-value-bind (value present-p) (gethash "Alice" *phonebook*)
  (when present-p
    (format t "Alice's number is ~a~%" value)))
```

Here, value is bound to the fetched value, and present-p is T if the key was found, NIL otherwise.

Removing a key-value pair from the hash table is performed using remhash:

```
(remhash "Alice" *phonebook*)
```

This operation deletes the key "Alice" and its associated value from the hash table.

Hash tables can be iterated over using a variety of methods. A common approach is to use the maphash function, which applies a specified function to each key-value pair in the hash table:

```
(maphash (lambda (key value)
            (format t "~a: ~a~%" key value))
         *phonebook*)
```

Here, each key-value pair in *phonebook* is printed in the format "key: value".

To copy a hash table, the copy-hash-table function is used. This creates a shallow copy of the given hash table:

```
(defparameter *phonebook-copy* (copy-hash-table *phonebook*))
```

When selecting a hash table equality test, there are several options: eq, eql, equal, and equalp. Each has different use cases and performance implications. eq and eql are suitable when keys are symbols or numbers, respectively, offering the best performance. equal is necessary for comparing composed data structures like lists, and equalp provides the most lenient test, comparing data structures regardless of minor differences such as the case of characters.

Efficient hash table performance depends on factors like the size and distribution of the data. Lisp's hash tables handle resizing automatically, but specifying an initial size using the :size keyword can improve performance:

```
(defparameter *large-phonebook* (make-hash-table :size 1000 :test '
    equal))
```

This hash table is initialized with an estimated size of 1000 entries, optimizing initial memory allocation.

Implementing custom hash functions can further optimize hash table performance, although this is an advanced topic. Generally, built-in hash functions suffice for most applications.

Understanding hash tables and their functions is crucial for mastering Lisp, as they provide a foundational tool for managing associative data effectively.

3.6   Structures (Structs)

Structures, or structs, provide a way to group related data under a single composite entity. Structs in Lisp enable encapsulating heterogeneous information conveniently, facilitating organized and readable code. They are similar to structures in other programming languages such as C.

Structures in Common Lisp are defined using the defstruct macro. This macro effectively creates a new data type, providing accessor functions for each field or slot within the structure. Below is the syntax for defining a structure:

```
(defstruct structure-name
   slot1
   slot2
   ...
   slotN)
```

For illustrative purposes, consider an example where we define a structure to represent a point in a two-dimensional space:

```
(defstruct point
   x
   y)
```

In this definition, point is the structure name, and x and y are the slots representing the coordinates of the point. When it's necessary to create an instance of this structure, the make-structure-name function is used:

```
(setq p1 (make-point :x 3 :y 4))
```

This code creates a point p1 with x coordinate 3 and y coordinate 4. The make-point function automatically takes keyword arguments corresponding to the slot names.

To access the values of the slots in a struct, accessor functions automatically generated by defstruct are used. For instance:

```
(point-x p1) ; returns 3
(point-y p1) ; returns 4
```

Additionally, it is possible to set the values of slots in an existing structure using the setf macro:

```
(setf (point-x p1) 10)
(setf (point-y p1) 20)
```

With these changes, the point p1 is now located at coordinates (10, 20).

Common Lisp's defstruct also supports various options to customize the behavior and structure of structs. For instance, specifying default values for slots, including documentation strings, enabling type checking, and controlling accessor function names. Here is an example with several advanced features:

```
(defstruct (person
            (:constructor create-person (name age &key (gender '
               unknown) &aux (first-letter (char name 0))))
            (:type list)
            (:print-object custom-print))
   name
   age
   (gender 'unknown :type symbol)
   first-letter)
```

In this example:

- The person structure is defined with the slots name, age, gender, and first-letter.

- The :constructor option is used to define a custom constructor create-person with specific arguments.

- The :type option specifies that the internal representation of the structure should be as a list.

- The :print-object function (which needs to be defined separately) enables custom print behavior.

To create an instance of this structure, you would use:

```
(setq individual (create-person "Alice" 30 :gender 'female))
```

To access the slots:

```
(person-name individual) ; returns "Alice"
(person-age individual) ; returns 30
(person-gender individual) ; returns 'female
(person-first-letter individual) ; returns #\A
```

Proper utilization of these options can lead to more versatile and powerful data abstractions while maintaining readability and maintainability of the code.

Moreover, it is often necessary to compare structs for equality. Common Lisp provides equalp, which can compare struct instances by their contents:

```
(setq p2 (make-point :x 10 :y 20))
(equalp p1 p2) ; returns T because p1 and p2 have identical slot
    values
```

It is essential to understand the efficiency and overhead introduced by structures. While defstruct is versatile and straightforward, it should be used judiciously. Each structure introduces a small amount of computational overhead due to the accessor functions and slot management. However, the benefits of clear and structured code typically outweigh the minor performance costs in most applications.

Readers should now have a solid understanding of how structures work in Lisp, how to define and manipulate them, and how to leverage their functionality to build more organized and clear code.

3.7   Property Lists

In Lisp, property lists provide a flexible and efficient mechanism for associating metadata with symbols. Property lists, or "plists," are essentially lists of paired elements where the first element is the property name (a symbol) and the second element is the property value. Property lists are commonly used for symbol management, offering a way to attach additional information dynamically to symbols without needing to modify the symbol's core data structure.

Syntax and Basic Operations

The basic operations involving property lists are typically handled using the built-in functions get, putprop, remprop, and others.

Consider the following example:

```
(putprop 'example 'color 'red)
```

This command attaches the property color with the value red to the symbol example. To retrieve this property:

```
(get 'example 'color)
```

The output would be:

red

To remove a property from a symbol:

```
(remprop 'example 'color)
```

The property color is now removed from the symbol example.

Manipulating Property Lists

Property lists are versatile and can be manipulated using a variety of built-in functions. For instance, to add multiple properties to a symbol:

```
(putprop 'example 'size 'large)
(putprop 'example 'shape 'circle)
```

Now, the symbol example has properties color, size, and shape with corresponding values. To list all properties of a symbol:

```
(symbol-plist 'example)
```

The output for this would be:

(size large shape circle)

This shows the list of property-value pairs associated with example.

Efficiency Considerations

CHAPTER 3.   LISP DATA STRUCTURES

Property lists are more flexible but generally less efficient for frequent access and updates compared to other data structures like hash tables. Each retrieval or update operation on a property list involves traversing the list, which results in linear time complexity $\mathcal{O}(n)$, where n is the length of the list.

```
(defun get-value (prop plist)
  (if plist
      (if (eq prop (car plist))
          (cadr plist)
          (get-value prop (cddr plist)))))
```

This function get-value illustrates a simple recursive approach to finding a property in a property list.

Use Cases

A prevalent use case for property lists is in attaching metadata to symbols within interpreters or compilers. They can be used to store attributes, such as type information, scope details, or even documentation strings.

Consider a symbol var representing a variable in an interpreted language:

```
(putprop 'var 'type 'integer)
(putprop 'var 'scope 'local)
(putprop 'var 'initial-value 10)
```

This attaches three properties to the symbol var. To retrieve the variable's type:

```
(get 'var 'type)
```

The output would be:

```
integer
```

This example shows how property lists can be used to manage contextual information about symbols dynamically.

Property lists, while elegant and flexible, should be chosen judiciously in performance-sensitive applications. For metadata that requires frequent access or modification, alternatives like hash tables might be more appropriate despite the reduced flexibility.

In Lisp, property lists have their roots in the earliest versions of the language, highlighting their long-standing utility and ease of use. They offer a dynamic way to augment symbols with additional context, fitting seamlessly into Lisp's paradigm of dynamic typing and flexible data manipulation.

3.8 Association Lists

In Lisp, association lists (or a-lists) are a common way to implement simple key-value pair data structures. An association list is essentially a list where each element is a cons cell, with the car holding the key and the cdr holding the corresponding value. This format allows for straightforward association and retrieval of values corresponding to specific keys.

Creating and Using Association Lists

Creating an association list typically involves forming a list of cons cells. Each cons cell comprises a key and its associated value. For example, consider the following association list that maps symbols to numbers:

```
(setq my-alist '((a . 1) (b . 2) (c . 3)))
```

Here, my-alist is an association list where the key a is associated with the value 1, b with 2, and c with 3.

To retrieve the value associated with a key, we can use the built-in assoc function. This function searches the association list for the first cons cell whose car matches the specified key and returns that cons cell.

```
(assoc 'b my-alist)
```

The above code will return:

```
(b . 2)
```

We can access the value part of the cons cell using the cdr function:

```
(cdr (assoc 'b my-alist))
```

This will return:

```
2
```

Modifying Association Lists

Modifying association lists, such as adding new key-value pairs or updating existing ones, is straightforward. To add a new pair, we can use the cons function to add a new cons cell to the front of the list:

```
(setq my-alist (cons '(d . 4) my-alist))
```

Now, my-alist becomes:

```
((d . 4) (a . 1) (b . 2) (c . 3))
```

Updating an existing key-value pair requires searching the list for the key and modifying the associated value. Here's an example function that updates a value associated with a key:

```
(defun update-alist (key new-value alist)
  (let ((pair (assoc key alist)))
    (if pair
        (setcdr pair new-value)
        (setq alist (cons (cons key new-value) alist))))
  alist)
```

Using this function, we can update the value associated with key b to 42:

```
(setq my-alist (update-alist 'b 42 my-alist))
```

Now, my-alist becomes:

```
((d . 4) (a . 1) (b . 42) (c . 3))
```

Removing Elements from Association Lists

To remove a key-value pair from an association list, a common approach is to use the remove function to filter out the cons cell with the specified key:

```
(setq my-alist (remove-if (lambda (pair) (eq (car pair) 'b)) my-alist))
```

After executing this code, my-alist is updated to:

```
((d . 4) (a . 1) (c . 3))
```

Efficiency Considerations

While association lists are simple and convenient, their performance characteristics must be considered, especially for large datasets. The assoc function performs a linear search, which means that the average-case time complexity for lookups, insertions, and deletions is $O(n)$, where n is the number of elements in the association list.

For scenarios requiring frequent or fast lookups, hash tables are generally a more efficient alternative due to their average-case constant time complexity $O(1)$ for these operations. However, association lists can be more suitable for situations where the dataset is small, the overhead of hash table maintenance is undesirable, or the order of pairs needs to be preserved.

3.9 Creating and Accessing Complex Data Structures

In Lisp, creating and accessing complex data structures necessitates a comprehensive understanding of the foundational data types and a proficiency in combining these elements into more sophisticated forms. Building on our exploration of simpler data structures, we now delve into the conception and manipulation of more intricate, composite data structures such as nested structures, multi-dimensional arrays, and hybrid combinations of lists and hash tables.

Nested Structures

Nested structures in Lisp allow us to encapsulate several layers of information, enabling more sophisticated organization and retrieval methodologies. Given the flexibility of Lisp's defstruct, nested structures are straightforward to implement.

```
(defstruct person
  (name "")
  (age 0)
  (address (make-address)))

(defstruct address
  (street "")
  (city "")
  (zip 0))

(let ((john-doe (make-person :name "John Doe"
                  :age 30
                  :address (make-address :street "123 Lisp
                    Lane"
                              :city "Codeville"
                              :zip 12345)))))
  (print (person-name john-doe))
```

```
  (print (address-city (person-address john-doe)))))
```

In the above example, we define two structures: person and address.
The address structure is nested within person. By using defstruct for
both, interacting with the nested data becomes straightforward.

Multi-Dimensional Arrays

Lisp supports the creation of multi-dimensional arrays, which are crucial
for representing complex data in a tabular form or for modeling multi-
dimensional spaces.

```
(setq md-array (make-array '(3 3) :initial-element 0))

(setf (aref md-array 0 0) 1)
(setf (aref md-array 1 1) 2)
(setf (aref md-array 2 2) 3)

(dotimes (i 3)
  (dotimes (j 3)
    (format t "~A " (aref md-array i j)))
  (format t "~%"))
```

Here, make-array constructs a 3x3 array initialized to zeros. aref accesses elements within the array, allowing for setting and retrieving
values at specific indices.

Hybrid Data Structures: Lists and Hash Tables

Hybrid data structures, such as combinations of lists and hash tables,
enable advanced data organization. For instance, consider a scenario
where each entry in a list is a hash table representing a person's detailed information.

```
(setq people (list (make-hash-table :test 'equal)
                   (make-hash-table :test 'equal)))

(setf (gethash "name" (first people)) "Alice")
(setf (gethash "age" (first people)) 28)
(setf (gethash "city" (first people)) "Wonderland")

(setf (gethash "name" (second people)) "Bob")
(setf (gethash "age" (second people)) 34)
(setf (gethash "city" (second people)) "Builderland")
```

```
(dolist (person people)
  (format t "Name: ~A, Age: ~A, City: ~A~%"
          (gethash "name" person)
          (gethash "age" person)
          (gethash "city" person)))
```

In this example, we create a list called people where each element is a hash table. Each hash table stores details about a person. Accessing and updating individual person information is efficient due to the hash table's properties.

Accessing Complex Data Structures

Accessing elements within these complex structures requires a thorough understanding of the functions and their appropriate application. Utilize get, gethash, aref, and other accessor functions to retrieve data. Crucially, ensure the correct sequencing of access steps, especially in nested or hybrid structures.

```
(format t "John Doe's Zip: ~A~%"
        (address-zip (person-address john-doe)))

(format t "Value at [2,2] in md-array: ~A~%"
        (aref md-array 2 2))

(let ((alice (first people)))
  (format t "Alice's City: ~A~%"
          (gethash "city" alice)))
```

The examples illustrate accesses to: - The zip code in a nested structure - A specific index in a multi-dimensional array - A value from a hash table embedded in a list

Using these access techniques, Lisp programmers can efficiently manage and utilize complex data structures, optimizing their applications' performance and organization.

The creation and access principles outlined here are fundamental for developing larger, more sophisticated applications in Lisp, emphasizing the importance of structuring data efficiently and accessing it methodically.

3.10   Data Structure Manipulation Functions

In Lisp, manipulating data structures is a fundamental practice that empowers developers to create efficient and dynamic programs. This section focuses on the various functions available for manipulating different data structures within Lisp, ensuring you can handle and transform data as required by your applications.

For lists, the most ubiquitous data structure in Lisp, several key functions facilitate manipulation:

- car and cdr: These functions return the first element and the rest of the list, respectively. For example:

```
(car '(1 2 3 4)) ; outputs 1
(cdr '(1 2 3 4)) ; outputs (2 3 4)
```

- cons: This function constructs a new list by prepending an element to the front of an existing list. For instance:

```
(cons 0 '(1 2 3 4)) ; outputs (0 1 2 3 4)
```

- list: Creates a list from its arguments:

```
(list 1 2 3 4) ; outputs (1 2 3 4)
```

- append: Concatenates two or more lists. Example:

```
(append '(1 2) '(3 4)) ; outputs (1 2 3 4)
```

- length: Returns the number of elements in a list:

```
(length '(1 2 3 4)) ; outputs 4
```

- reverse: Reverses the elements of a list:

```
(reverse '(1 2 3 4)) ; outputs (4 3 2 1)
```

Vectors, on the other hand, are handled using different functions due to their fixed length and indexable nature. Below are key functions for vector manipulation:

- vector: Constructs a vector from given elements:

```
(vector 1 2 3 4) ; outputs #(1 2 3 4)
```

- aref: Accesses an element at a specific index:

```
(aref #(1 2 3 4) 2) ; outputs 3
```

- aset: Sets an element at a specific index. Note that aset mutates the original vector:

```
(let ((v #(1 2 3 4)))
  (aset v 2 99)
  v) ; outputs #(1 2 99 4)
```

- length: Returns the number of elements in a vector:

```
(length #(1 2 3 4)) ; outputs 4
```

- subseq: Extracts a subsequence from a vector:

```
(subseq #(1 2 3 4) 1 3) ; outputs #(2 3)
```

When dealing with hash tables, manipulation functions focus on key-value pairs:

- make-hash-table: Creates a new empty hash table:

```
(make-hash-table) ; creates an empty hash table
```

- gethash: Retrieves the value associated with a given key:

```
(let ((table (make-hash-table)))
  (setf (gethash 'a table) 1)
  (gethash 'a table)) ; outputs 1
```

- setf with gethash: Sets the value for a specified key:

```
(let ((table (make-hash-table)))
  (setf (gethash 'b table) 2)
  (gethash 'b table)) ; outputs 2
```

- remhash: Removes the key-value pair for a given key:

```
(let ((table (make-hash-table)))
  (setf (gethash 'c table) 3)
  (remhash 'c table)
  (gethash 'c table)) ; outputs NIL
```

- clrhash: **Clears all key-value pairs from the hash table:**

```
(let ((table (make-hash-table)))
  (setf (gethash 'd table) 4)
  (clrhash table)
  (gethash 'd table)) ; outputs NIL
```

For structures (structs), which are used to define complex data types, the following functions are pertinent:

- defstruct: **Defines a new structure type:**

```
(defstruct person
  name
  age) ; defines a struct type 'person'
```

- make-structure-name: **Creates an instance of the defined structure:**

```
(make-person :name "Alice" :age 30) ; outputs #S(
  PERSON :NAME "Alice" :AGE 30)
```

- structure-name-slot: **Accesses a slot value from a structure instance:**

```
(defparameter *p1* (make-person :name "Bob" :age 25)
  )
(person-name *p1*) ; outputs "Bob"
(person-age *p1*) ; outputs 25
```

- (setf structure-name-slot): **Sets a slot value in a structure instance:**

```
(setf (person-age *p1*) 26)
(person-age *p1*) ; outputs 26
```

86

Property lists (plists) also come with their specific manipulation functions:

- getf: Retrieves the value associated with a property:

```
(getf '(:a 1 :b 2) :a) ; outputs 1
```

- setf with getf: Sets the value for a specified property:

```
(let ((plist '(:a 1 :b 2)))
  (setf (getf plist :a) 10)
  plist) ; outputs (:a 10 :b 2)
```

- remf: Removes a property and its value from the list:

```
(let ((plist '(:a 1 :b 2)))
  (remf plist :a)
  plist) ; outputs (:b 2)
```

Association lists (alists) are managed using somewhat analogous functions:

- assoc: Finds the pair whose car is equal to the specified key:

```
(assoc 'key '((key . 1) (other . 2))) ; outputs (key . 1)
```

- acons: Constructs a new alist by adding a key-value pair:

```
(acons 'new-key 99 '((key . 1) (other . 2))) ; outputs ((
  new-key . 99) (key . 1) (other . 2))
```

- rassoc: Finds the pair whose cdr is equal to the specified value:

```
(rassoc 2 '((key . 1) (other . 2))) ; outputs (other . 2)
```

- pairlis: Constructs a new alist from two lists of keys and values:

```
(pairlis '(a b c) '(1 2 3)) ; outputs ((a . 1) (b . 2) (c . 3))
```

Through these functions, Lisp offers a robust suite for manipulating its wide array of data structures, providing developers with the power to efficiently handle and transform data in various forms. Proficiency in using these functions is crucial for crafting precise and optimized Lisp programs.

3.11   Efficiency Considerations for Data Structures

When selecting a data structure for a specific application in Lisp, efficiency considerations play a crucial role. The efficiency of a data structure can be evaluated in terms of time complexity, space complexity, and ease of use in algorithmic implementations. In this section, we analyze various data structures introduced in previous sections with respect to these efficiency metrics.

Time Complexity:

The time complexity of operations on data structures determines how the performance scales with the number of elements in the data structure. Consider the following common operations: access, insertion, deletion, and search.

- Lists and Cons Cells:
    - Access: Accessing elements in a list is, in the worst case, $O(n)$, as it requires traversing from the head of the list.
    - Insertion: Inserting an element at the beginning of a list using cons is $O(1)$. However, inserting at a position other than the head requires traversal $O(n)$.
    - Deletion: Deleting an element involves searching for it $O(n)$ and then adjusting pointers $O(1)$ once found.
    - Search: Searching for an element in a list is $O(n)$ as each element must be examined.

- Vectors and Arrays:
    - Access: Indexing an element is $O(1)$, thanks to the direct access nature of arrays.
    - Insertion: Inserting requires shifting subsequent elements $O(n)$ in the worst case.
    - Deletion: Similar to insertion, deletion involves shifting elements $O(n)$.
    - Search: A linear search is $O(n)$, though sorted arrays may use binary search to reduce complexity to $O(\log n)$.

- Hash Tables:

88

- Access: Accessing an element typically averages $O(1)$ due to hashing, though in the worst case, it can degrade to $O(n)$ if collisions are not handled.
- Insertion: Insertions average $O(1)$.
- Deletion: Deletions also average $O(1)$.
- Search: Search operations are $O(1)$ on average.

- Property Lists:

  - Access: Access time is $O(n)$, as it requires linear search through the list.
  - Insertion: Inserting is $O(1)$ assuming insertion at the head.
  - Deletion: Deleting is $O(n)$ for the search plus $O(1)$ for removing.
  - Search: Searches are $O(n)$.

- Association Lists:

  - Access: Accessing an element is $O(n)$.
  - Insertion: Insertion time is $O(1)$ if adding to the front.
  - Deletion: Deletion involves searching $O(n)$ then removing $O(1)$.
  - Search: Search time is $O(n)$.

Space Complexity:

Space complexity evaluates the amount of memory required by a data structure, important for applications handling large datasets or operating within memory constraints.

- Lists and Cons Cells: Lists inherently have a space overhead due to the storage of both the element and the pointer to the next cons cell. Therefore, space complexity is $O(n)$ plus the overhead for pointers.

- Vectors and Arrays: Vectors and arrays have $O(n)$ space complexity, requiring contiguous memory allocation. Fixed-size arrays are inefficient if their full capacity is not used.

- Hash Tables: Hash tables can be highly efficient, averaging $O(n)$ space. However, poor hash functions or excessive collisions can lead to wasteful memory use.

- Property Lists: Property lists combine elements with their property values, leading to $O(n)$ space complexity but with additional overhead for properties.

- Association Lists: These lists similarly have $O(n)$ space complexity, with the added space for each key-value pairing.

Algorithmic Considerations:

Algorithmic efficiency is crucial in optimizing program performance. Specific operations may favor one data structure over another based on their complexity profiles.

```
;; Example: Finding an element in different data structures

;; List search (O(n))
(defun find-in-list (elem lst)
  (find elem lst))

;; Vector search (O(n) linear, O(log n) binary if sorted)
(defun find-in-vector (elem vec)
  (loop for i from 0 below (length vec)
        when (equal elem (elt vec i))
        return i))

;; Hash table search (O(1))
(defun find-in-hashtable (key table)
  (gethash key table))
```

```
;; Example Output:
(find-in-list 'a '(b c a d)) ; => A
(find-in-vector 'a #(b c a d)) ; => 2
(setf ht (make-hash-table))
(setf (gethash 'a ht) 10)
(find-in-hashtable 'a ht) ; => 10
```

Understanding these efficiency considerations enables selecting the most appropriate data structure for a given task, balancing between speed and memory consumption. This knowledge is vital for optimizing Lisp programs and ensuring robust and scalable implementations.

90

Chapter 4

Functions and Functional Programming

This chapter provides an in-depth exploration of functions and functional programming in Lisp. It begins with defining functions and understanding lambdas and anonymous functions. The chapter then moves on to higher-order functions, scope, and closures. Key concepts of recursion, function composition, mapping, and reducing functions are explained. The principles of immutability and pure functions are introduced, along with an overview of functional programming paradigms and advanced techniques. These foundations equip readers with the skills to write robust, efficient, and elegant functional code in Lisp.

4.1   Introduction to Functions in Lisp

Functions are fundamental building blocks in Lisp programming. Understanding functions is essential for mastering Lisp, as they form the core of both procedural and functional paradigms. A function in Lisp is a first-class citizen, meaning it can be passed around as a value, returned from other functions, and assigned to variables.

Basic Anatomy of a Function   A function in Lisp typically consists of a name, a list of parameters, and a body that specifies the actions to be performed. The general syntax for defining a function using the defun keyword is as follows:

```
(defun function-name (parameter-list)
  body...)
```

For instance, to define a simple function that adds two numbers, you would write:

```
(defun add-numbers (a b)
  (+ a b))
```

To call this function, use:

```
(add-numbers 3 5)
```

The output of the above function call would be:

8

Anonymous Functions and Lambdas Lisp allows the creation of anonymous functions, also known as lambda functions. These are functions that do not have a name and are typically used for short operations or passed as arguments to higher-order functions. The lambda keyword is used to define anonymous functions.

Example of an anonymous function that squares a number:

```
(lambda (x) (* x x))
```

To apply this anonymous function to a number, you can use the funcall function:

```
(funcall (lambda (x) (* x x)) 4)
```

The output would be:

16

Higher-Order Functions Higher-order functions are functions that take other functions as arguments or return them as results. These functions are a powerful feature of Lisp, enabling the creation of more abstract and modular code. Examples of higher-order functions in Lisp include mapcar, reduce, and filter.

For example, mapcar applies a given function to each item in a list and returns a list of results:

```
(mapcar (lambda (x) (* x 2)) '(1 2 3 4))
```

The output of the above code is:

(2 4 6 8)

Function Composition   Function composition is the process of combining two or more functions to produce a new function. In Lisp, this can be achieved using labels for local functions or flet for temporary functions. Additionally, functions like compose can be used from various Lisp libraries.

Example of compose to create a new function combining two functions, f1 and f2:

```
(defun f1 (x) (+ x 5))
(defun f2 (x) (* x 2))
(defvar new-function (compose 'f2 'f1))
(funcall new-function 3)
```

The result would be:

16

Understanding Immutability and Pure Functions   In Lisp, functions may exhibit characteristics like immutability and purity. An immutable function does not modify its input arguments or any state outside the function's scope. A pure function is deterministic, meaning it always produces the same output given the same input and has no side effects. These attributes are crucial in functional programming as they facilitate reasoning about code behavior and enhance reliability.

Example of a pure function:

```
(defun pure-function (x)
  (+ x 10))
```

This function is pure because it does not alter any external state and consistently returns the same result for a given x.

Variable Scope and Closures   Lisp supports lexical scoping, where a variable's scope is determined by its position within the source code. Functions can capture and retain bindings from their defining scope, giving rise to closures.

Example of a closure:

```
(defun make-adder (x)
  (lambda (y) (+ x y)))

(defvar add5 (make-adder 5))
(funcall add5 10)
```

The output is:

15

Here, add5 is a closure that retains the binding of x from its environment.

Integrating these fundamentals provides a comprehensive understanding of functions in Lisp, enabling advanced functional programming techniques and robust code development. An emphasis on these principles solidifies the foundation necessary to delve deeper into complex Lisp programming paradigms.

4.2   Defining Functions

A function in Lisp is a first-class object, allowing it to be passed around as an argument, returned from other functions, and stored in variables. Defining a function establishes a new function object and binds it to a name in the current environment.

To define a function in Lisp, the defun macro is used. The syntax for defun is as follows:

```
(defun function-name (parameter-list)
  "Optional documentation string."
  body)
```

Here, function-name is the name of the function, parameter-list is a list of parameters the function takes, and body contains expressions that constitute the function's behavior. The function body is evaluated each time the function is called.

Consider the following example that defines a function to compute the square of a number:

```
(defun square (x)
  "Compute the square of x."
  (* x x))
```

In this case, the function square takes one parameter x and returns the product of x with itself. To invoke this function, you would use:

```
(square 5)
```

The output of the above call is:

25

Arguments passed to functions can have default values, which are specified within the parameter list in the following manner:

```
(defun greet (&optional name)
  "Greet the person with the given name or a default greeting."
  (if name
      (format t "Hello, ~a!" name)
      (format t "Hello, World!")))
```

Here, name is an optional argument. The function greet checks if name is provided; if not, it defaults to "World". For instance:

```
(greet "Alice")
```

The output is:

Hello, Alice!While calling greet without any argument:

```
(greet)
```

produces:

Hello, World!

Lisp also supports keyword arguments, which provide a more explicit way to pass arguments, enhancing code readability:

```
(defun make-rectangle (&key (width 1) (height 1))
  "Create a rectangle with specified width and height."
  (list :width width :height height))
```

This function make-rectangle creates a rectangle structure, and default values are specified for both width and height. Calling the function with keyword arguments looks like this:

```
(make-rectangle :width 5 :height 3)
```

Which results in:

```
(:WIDTH 5 :HEIGHT 3)
```

Scope of variables in functions plays a crucial role in their behavior. Lisp uses lexical scoping, meaning that the bindings of variables are determined by the textual context of the code. For example:

```
(defun outer (x)
  (let ((y 5))
    (defun inner ()
      (+ x y))))
```

Here, inner function is defined within outer. The variable y is local to outer and is accessible within inner due to lexical scoping. Therefore, the call (outer 3) followed by (inner) would have access to x and y.

Proper understanding of function definitions and scope helps in leveraging the power of Lisp's functional paradigm. The ability to create, manipulate, and utilize functions effectively forms the core strength of Lisp programming.

4.3   Lambdas and Anonymous Functions

In Lisp, functions are first-class citizens, meaning they can be passed as arguments to other functions, returned as values from other functions, and assigned to variables. One of the powerful features of Lisp is its support for *lambda* expressions, also known as anonymous functions. These are functions that are defined without being bound to an identifier.

To define a lambda expression in Lisp, the lambda keyword is used, followed by a parameter list and the function body. Consider the following example where a simple lambda expression is created to add two numbers:

```
(lambda (x y) (+ x y))
```

This lambda expression takes two parameters, x and y, and returns their sum.

Lambda expressions are particularly useful in scenarios where a short-lived function is required without the need to explicitly name it. They can be passed directly as arguments to higher-order functions, such as mapcar, reduce, or any user-defined function. Here is an example where a lambda expression is used with mapcar to square each number in a list:

```
(mapcar (lambda (x) (* x x)) '(1 2 3 4 5))
```

The output of the above code would be:

```
(1 4 9 16 25)
```

In addition to concise syntax, lambda expressions enhance code readability and maintainability by localizing the scope of functions to where they are needed. Let's explore another example in the context of filtering a list for even numbers using remove-if-not:

```
(remove-if-not (lambda (x) (evenp x)) '(1 2 3 4 5 6))
```

The output is:

```
(2 4 6)
```

It is important to understand that lambda expressions can capture variables from their surrounding lexical environment, forming what is known as a closure. This allows the lambda expression to access and manipulate those variables even if it is executed in a different scope. Here is an example that demonstrates this concept:

```
(let ((factor 10))
   (mapcar (lambda (x) (* x factor)) '(1 2 3 4 5)))
```

This code snippet uses let to bind factor to 10 and then defines a lambda expression that multiplies each element of the list by factor. The output will be:

```
(10 20 30 40 50)
```

The lambda expression forms a closure over the variable factor, allowing it to reference factor even outside the scope of the let form. This capability of closures is fundamental in functional programming for creating higher-order functions and enhancing code modularity.

Lambda expressions are also useful in defining functions that can take

97

variable numbers of arguments. These are known as variadic functions. Here is an example:

```
((lambda (&rest numbers) (apply '+ numbers)) 1 2 3 4 5)
```

The lambda expression uses &rest to collect all arguments into the parameter numbers, and then apply is used to sum them. The output is:

15

Lambda expressions can also be nested within other lambda expressions, creating complex functional constructs. Below is an example of nested lambda expressions to compute the derivative of a simple quadratic function at a given point:

```
((lambda (f)
   ((lambda (h)
      (lambda (x)
         (/ (- (funcall f (+ x h)) (funcall f x)) h)))
    0.0001))
 (lambda (x) (+ (* 3 x x) (* 2 x) 1))) 2
```

The outermost lambda takes a function f, and the inner lambda approximates the derivative of f using a small step size h. It then applies this to the function $(+ (* 3 x x) (* 2 x) 1)$ at the point $x = 2$. The approximate derivative at $x = 2$ is:

14.000300000012032

Lambda expressions provide a versatile and expressive way to create anonymous functions in Lisp. They enable the functional programming paradigms by allowing functions to be passed around as arguments, returned from other functions, and used in a very flexible manner to construct complex behaviors concisely.

4.4   Higher-Order Functions

Higher-order functions are a cornerstone of functional programming in Lisp. A higher-order function is defined as any function that takes one or more functions as arguments, or returns a function as a result. These functions are instrumental in creating more abstract and reusable pieces of code. Lisp provides a rich set of higher-order functions that facilitate operations on lists, among other data structures.

To illustrate the concept, consider the function mapcar, which applies a given function to each element of a list and returns a list of the results. The mapcar function is defined as:

```
(mapcar #'function_name list)
```

Here, function_name is a function that will be applied to each element of list. The use of #' is crucial as it denotes the function's reference.

```
(defun square (x)
  (* x x))

(mapcar #'square '(1 2 3 4 5))
```

The above code applies the square function to each element of the list '(1 2 3 4 5). The result of this operation will be:

```
(1 4 9 16 25)
```

Another example of a higher-order function in Lisp is apply. The apply function takes a function and a list of arguments and applies the function to those arguments.

```
(apply #' + '(1 2 3 4 5))
```

This results in:

```
15
```

Here, the apply function takes the function + and applies it to each element of the list '(1 2 3 4 5).

Another significant higher-order function is reduce (also known as fold). The reduce function recursively applies a function to elements of a list, effectively reducing the list to a single value.

```
(reduce #'+ '(1 2 3 4 5))
```

The result is:

```
15
```

Here, reduce starts by applying the + function to the first two elements of the list, then takes the result and applies the + function to the next element, continuing this process to the end of the list.

```
(reduce #'max '(1 4 3 2 5))
```

The resulting value is:

5

Demonstrates how reduce can also find the maximum element in a list.

A core utility in working with higher-order functions is the lambda expression, or anonymous function. Lambda expressions allow you to define functions without giving them a name. This flexibility can be particularly useful when you need simple, one-off functions.

```
(mapcar (lambda (x) (* x x x)) '(1 2 3 4 5))
```

This maps an anonymous function that cubes each number over the list '(1 2 3 4 5). The result will be:

(1 8 27 64 125)

Combining higher-order functions with lambda expressions enhances the expressive power of Lisp. Consider sorting a list of numbers in descending order:

```
(sort '(1 5 3 2 4) #'>
```

The result is:

(5 4 3 2 1)

Here, the sort function uses the > function to compare elements, thus sorting in descending order.

Another utility is the function composition, where two or more functions combine to form a new one. Although Lisp does not have a built-in operator for function composition, it can be implemented manually using higher-order function capabilities.

```
(defun compose (f g)
   (lambda (x) (funcall f (funcall g x)))))
```

Applying compose:

```
(defun increment (x) (+ x 1))
(defun double (x) (* x 2))

(funcall (compose #'double #'increment) 5)
```

This will result in:

12

The compose function creates a new function that first increments a number and then doubles it. The use of higher-order functions promotes cleaner, more readable, and adaptable code.

Functions like mapcar, apply, reduce, and the concept of lambda expressions bring considerable power and flexibility to Lisp programming, enabling a high level of abstraction and deft manipulation of functions and data.

4.5   Scope and Closures

Understanding scope in Lisp is fundamental to mastering functional programming. Scope determines the visibility and lifetime of variables within a program. In Lisp, there are two primary types of scope: lexical scope and dynamic scope. Lexical scope, also known as static scope, is the default in most modern Lisp dialects like Common Lisp and Scheme.

Lexical scope means that a variable's scope is determined by its physical location in the source code. When the compiler processes the code, it absorbs the structure defined by the nesting of the syntactic constructs. Variable bindings are associated with blocks of code during compile-time. Consider the following example to illustrate lexical scope in Common Lisp:

```
(let ((x 10)
      (y 20))
  (+ x y)) ; Outputs 30
```

In the above let construct, the variables x and y are bound to 10 and 20, respectively. These bindings are available within the let block but are not available outside it. Any attempt to use x or y outside the block would result in an error.

Dynamic scope, on the other hand, determines variable bindings based on the call stack at runtime. Historically, Lisp implementations used dynamic scope, but it has largely fallen out of favor due to its complexity and unpredictability. In dynamic scope, the search for a variable's value occurs in the call chain of the functions, as demonstrated in the following example:

```
(defvar *x* 5)
```

```
(defun foo ()
  (print *x*))

(defun bar ()
  (let ((*x* 10))
    (foo)))

(bar) ; Outputs 10
(foo) ; Outputs 5
```

In this example, the *x* variable within bar temporarily binds the value 10 to *x* for the duration of the call to foo. Once bar completes execution, the value of *x* is reverted to its global binding of 5. This behavior is the hallmark of dynamic scope.

Closures are closely related to lexical scope. A closure in Lisp is a first-class function with two parts: the function code and the referenced environment. A closure can access and manipulate variables that were in scope when the closure was created, even if those variables are not currently in scope when the closure is invoked. This encapsulated environment allows for powerful and flexible function definitions.

The following example showcases the creation and use of closures in Common Lisp:

```
(defun make-adder (x)
  (lambda (y)
    (+ x y)))

(setq add5 (make-adder 5))
(funcall add5 10) ; Outputs 15
```

The function make-adder returns a lambda function that adds its argument y to x. The returned lambda function is a closure that captures the environment where x was defined. Even though make-adder has finished execution, the closure retains access to x.

The concept of closure is particularly useful in scenarios requiring encapsulation and stateful behavior. For instance, closures can be employed to generate functions as return values or to maintain state across function invocations.

Applying closures within higher-order functions enhances their utility. Consider an example where closures are used with the mapcar function:

```
(defun make-multiplier (factor)
  (lambda (x)
    (* factor x)))

(setq double (make-multiplier 2))

(mapcar double '(1 2 3 4)) ; Outputs (2 4 6 8)
```

Here, the make-multiplier function generates a closure that multiplies its input by factor. The double closure is applied to each element in the list using mapcar, demonstrating how closures can carry and apply specific behaviors defined by captured environments.

In functional programming with Lisp, scope and closures are core concepts that lead to robust and maintainable code. Understanding the intricacies of lexical scope and the power of closures equips developers with a deeper ability to manipulate functions and variables effectively. The precision of lexical scoping, combined with the flexibility of closures, provides a powerful toolkit for functional programming paradigms.

4.6 Recursion in Lisp

In Lisp, recursion is an indispensable concept that is frequently utilized for solving problems that can be broken down into smaller, more manageable subproblems. Recursion is a fundamental programming paradigm where a function calls itself to solve a problem. This technique is especially powerful in Lisp due to its inherent support for functional programming and immutability.

Consider a simplistic example of calculating the factorial of a number using recursion. The factorial of a number n, denoted as $n!$, is defined as the product of all positive integers less than or equal to n. This can be expressed recursively:

$$n! = \begin{cases} 1 & \text{if } n = 0 \\ n \times (n-1)! & \text{if } n > 0 \end{cases}$$

In Lisp, this recursive definition of the factorial can be directly translated into code as follows:

```
(defun factorial (n)
  (if (<= n 0)
    1
    (* n (factorial (- n 1)))))
```

When the factorial function is invoked with a positive integer, it checks if the integer is less than or equal to zero. If so, it returns 1 (the base case). Otherwise, it multiplies the integer n by the factorial of $n-1$ (the recursive case).

To understand and debug recursive functions properly, it is crucial to grasp the concept of the call stack and how function calls are managed in memory. Each recursive call adds a new frame to the call stack, storing the state of the current function execution. Mismanagement of base cases or excessive depth in recursion can lead to a stack overflow error.

To illustrate this further, let's consider another classic recursive problem: the Fibonacci sequence. Each term in the Fibonacci sequence is the sum of the two preceding ones, typically starting with 0 and 1. The recursive definition of the Fibonacci sequence is:

$$Fib(n) = \begin{cases} 0 & \text{if } n = 0 \\ 1 & \text{if } n = 1 \\ Fib(n-1) + Fib(n-2) & \text{if } n > 1 \end{cases}$$

This definition can be implemented recursively in Lisp as follows:

```
(defun fibonacci (n)
  (cond
    ((= n 0) 0)
    ((= n 1) 1)
    (t (+ (fibonacci (- n 1)) (fibonacci (- n 2))))))
```

While straightforward, this implementation has significant performance drawbacks due to repeated calculations of the same Fibonacci numbers, leading to an exponential time complexity. To optimize this, we can use techniques like memoization, which store and reuse previously computed values. Here is a version using memoization:

```
(defvar *fibonacci-memo* (make-hash-table :test 'equal))

(defun fibonacci-memo (n)
```

```
(or (gethash n *fibonacci-memo*)
    (setf (gethash n *fibonacci-memo*)
       (cond
          ((= n 0) 0)
          ((= n 1) 1)
          (t (+ (fibonacci-memo (- n 1)) (fibonacci-memo (- n 2))
             ))))))
```

In this optimized version, a hash table *fibonacci-memo* is used to store computed Fibonacci numbers. The fibonacci-memo function first checks if the value of n is already in the hash table, returning it if so. Otherwise, it computes the value recursively and stores it in the hash table before returning the result.

It is also important to note tail recursion, a special form of recursion where the recursive call is the last operation performed within the function. Tail-recursive functions can be optimized by the compiler into iterative loops, reducing the call stack usage and preventing stack overflow. Consider the tail-recursive version of the factorial function:

```
(defun factorial-tail-rec (n &optional (acc 1))
  (if (<= n 0)
      acc
      (factorial-tail-rec (- n 1) (* n acc))))
```

In the factorial-tail-rec function, the recursive call is the last action performed, and an accumulator acc is used to carry the result of the multiplication. This allows Lisp compilers that support tail call optimization (TCO) to convert the recursion into a loop, maintaining constant stack space.

Understanding recursion in Lisp equips programmers with the ability to solve complex problems elegantly. By mastering both direct and tail recursion, and knowing when to leverage optimization techniques such as memoization, one can write efficient and maintainable Lisp code.

4.7 Function Composition

Function composition is a core concept in functional programming, including Lisp, which allows programmers to build complex operations by combining simpler functions. This technique involves creating a new function by chaining multiple existing functions together. The result of one function becomes the input for the next, enabling a modular and expressive coding style. When composing functions, the order of operations is crucial. The output of the last-called function in the composition is returned as the final result.

In Lisp, function composition can be achieved using several methods, including lambda functions and composition functions such as compose. Understanding how to effectively compose functions is essential for constructing readable and maintainable code.

We start by examining simple applications of function composition with examples of common Lisp operations. Let us consider two basic functions, square and increment:

```
(defun square (x)
  (* x x))

(defun increment (x)
  (+ x 1))
```

The square function takes a number and returns its square, while the increment function increases a number by one. To compose these functions, we create a new function that applies increment to an argument and then applies square to the result.

```
(defun square-of-increment (x)
  (square (increment x)))
```

In the example above, the function square-of-increment takes an input x, increments it by one using increment, and then squares the result using square. We can test this by calling:

```
(square-of-increment 3)
```

16

Here, the input 3 is incremented to 4 and then squared to yield 16.

For scenarios involving multiple functions, Lisp provides the compose function, which can be used to create a composition of any number of functions. The compose function returns a new function that is the composition of the provided functions. For example, suppose we also have a function that doubles a number:

```
(defun double (x)
  (* x 2))
```

106

We can compose increment, square, and double as follows:

```
(defun increment-square-double (x)
  ((compose 'double 'square 'increment) x))
```

Now, calling increment-square-double with an argument should apply increment first, then square, and finally double the result.

```
(increment-square-double 3)
```

32

Here, 3 is incremented to 4, squared to 16, and then doubled to 32.

Additionally, anonymous functions or lambda expressions can be composed similarly. For composition of lambda functions, consider an example where we want to add 1, then double, and then subtract 3:

```
(defun add1-double-sub3 (x)
  ((compose (lambda (n) (- n 3))
            (lambda (n) (* n 2))
            (lambda (n) (+ n 1))) x))
```

Running this function with input 4:

```
(add1-double-sub3 4)
```

9

The input 4 is first incremented by 1 to get 5, then doubled to 10, and finally 3 is subtracted resulting in 7.

For complex operations, combining more extensive and specialized functions could significantly simplify code compared to writing large monolithic functions. This modularity fosters code reuse and enhances readability such that each modular function is responsible for a single, well-defined task.

```
(defmacro compose-lambdas (&rest funs)
  (reduce (lambda (f g)
            `(lambda (x) (,f (,g x))))
          funs))
```

Using the compose-lambdas macro, we can create composed functions dynamically:

```
(setq composed-fn (compose-lambdas (lambda (n) (* n 3))
```

```
                              (lambda (n) (+ n 2))
                              (lambda (n) (sqrt n))))

(funcall composed-fn 16)
```

10.0

In this example, we first apply the square root function, then add 2 to
the result, and finally multiply by 3. The function composition method
provided by compose-lambdas makes it easier and clearer to construct
composite operations on the fly.

4.8 Mapping and Reducing Functions

Mapping and reducing functions are powerful abstractions in Lisp that
allow for efficient processing of sequences and collections. Both concepts lie at the heart of functional programming and facilitate concise
and expressive code.

Mapping Functions:

Mapping involves applying a function to each element of a list, producing a new list containing the results. The most common mapping function in Lisp is mapcar, which applies a given function to each element of
a list. Consider the following example, where we use mapcar to square
each number in a list:

```
(mapcar #'(lambda (x) (* x x)) '(1 2 3 4 5))
```

This code evaluates to (1 4 9 16 25). The lambda function takes an
element x and returns its square. Below is another example where we
convert a list of numbers to their corresponding strings:

```
(mapcar #'(lambda (n) (format nil "~a" n)) '(10 20 30))
```

This code evaluates to ("10" "20" "30"). Here, format function is used
to create the string representation of each number.

The mapping function generalizes well to multiple lists, as long as they
are of the same length. Consider the example:

```
(mapcar #'+ '(1 2 3) '(4 5 6))
```

This code returns (5 7 9). The function + is applied to corresponding

108

elements of the provided lists, summing each pair.

Reducing Functions:

Reducing functions take a list and combine its elements into a single result, using a given function. The most prominent reducing function in Lisp is reduce. It processes a list by applying the function cumulatively to pairs of elements until a single result is obtained. Consider the example:

```
(reduce #'+ '(1 2 3 4 5))
```

This code evaluates to 15. The + function is applied cumulatively: (+ (+ (+ (+ 1 2) 3) 4) 5).

Reduce also accepts keyword arguments to control its behavior. For instance, :from-end starts the reduction from the end of the list, and :initial-value can provide an initial accumulator value:

```
(reduce #'+ '(1 2 3 4 5) :initial-value 10)
```

This code increments the result by the initial-value, yielding 25 (10 + 15).

mapping and reducing functions combined:

Combining mapcar and reduce allows for sophisticated data transformations. For example, summing the squares of a list of numbers:

```
(reduce #'+ (mapcar #'(lambda (x) (* x x)) '(1 2 3 4 5)))
```

First, mapcar creates a list of squares: (1 4 9 16 25). Then, reduce sums these values to produce 55.

Handling complex data structures:

In real-world applications, data often involves nested lists or more complex structures. Mapping and reducing functions handle these scenarios well. Consider a list of lists:

```
(mapcar #'(lambda (lst) (reduce #'+ lst)) '((1 2 3) (4 5 6) (7 8 9)))
```

This code produces (6 15 24). Each sublist is summed individually using reduce.

Lisp's extensibility:

Leveraging Lisp's extensibility, we can define our mapping and reducing functions, working seamlessly with Lisp's built-in features. Consider implementing a custom map function:

```
(defun custom-map (func lst)
  (if (null lst)
      nil
      (cons (funcall func (car lst))
            (custom-map func (cdr lst)))))
```

This function custom-map recursively applies func to each element of lst, creating a new list. Testing it with a square function:

```
(custom-map #'(lambda (x) (* x x)) '(1 2 3 4 5))
```

The result is (1 4 9 16 25).

Similarly, a custom reduce function can be defined:

```
(defun custom-reduce (func lst &optional (accumulator (car lst)))
  (if (null (cdr lst))
      accumulator
      (custom-reduce func (cdr lst)
                     (funcall func accumulator (cadr lst)))))
```

This function custom-reduce iteratively applies func to the accumulator and the next element in lst. Testing with a sum function:

```
(custom-reduce #'+ '(1 2 3 4 5))
```

The result is 15.

Understanding and utilizing mapping and reducing functions empower Lisp programmers to handle complex data transformations effectively. These functional paradigms simplify and enhance the expressiveness of code, integral to mastering Lisp programming.

4.9   Immutability and Pure Functions

Immutability and pure functions are key tenets of functional programming that contribute to the creation of predictable, testable, and maintainable code. Understanding these principles is paramount for mastering Lisp programming, and functional programming paradigms more broadly.

Immutability refers to the concept that once a data structure is created,

110

it cannot be altered. Any modifications result in the creation of a new data structure, leaving the original one unaltered. In Lisp, lists are the primary data structures, and immutability can be enforced using constructs that prevent in-place modifications.

A pure function, on the other hand, is a function that, given the same input, will always produce the same output and does not cause any side effects (like modifying external state or variables). Pure functions are central to functional programming as they ensure that functions behave predictably and can be reasoned through mathematical logic.

Creating Immutable Data Structures

The immutability in Lisp is typically managed by constructing new lists from existing ones rather than modifying the original list. For example, the cons function can be used to create new lists without changing the existing ones. Here is an illustration of constructing an immutable list using cons:

```
(setq original-list '(1 2 3))
(setq new-list (cons 0 original-list))
```

In this example, original-list remains (1 2 3) while new-list becomes (0 1 2 3). The original list is left unmodified, adhering to the principle of immutability.

Immutability with set Functions

Lisp also provides functions like setcar and setcdr to modify lists directly, which contravenes the immutability principle. However, to adhere to functional programming principles, direct usage of these functions should be avoided. Instead, one should favor creation of new lists:

```
(setq original-list '(1 2 3))
(setq modified-list (append '(0) (cdr original-list)))
```

In this case, modified-list becomes (0 2 3), and original-list remains unchanged.

Pure Functions in Lisp

Pure functions are deterministic and side-effect-free. They are central to functional programming because they allow for easier reasoning about code behavior and facilitate parallel processing and memoization. Here is an example of a pure function in Lisp:

```
(defun add (x y)
  (+ x y))
```

The add function adheres to the definition of a pure function. For any given inputs x and y, it will always return the same result without modifying any external state or causing side effects.

Conversely, here is an impure function:

```
(setq global-counter 0)

(defun increment-counter (value)
  (setq global-counter (+ global-counter value))
  global-counter)
```

The function increment-counter modifies the external state, specifically global-counter, making it impure as its output depends on the global state and also changes it.

Enforcing Pure Functions

To enforce pure functional programming, ensure that all functions are pure by not relying on or modifying any outside state. Functions should only utilize their input parameters and return results based solely on those inputs.

A common pattern in Lisp to achieve pure functions is by using higher-order functions and recursion rather than relying on iterative constructs that modify shared state. Here is an example of a higher-order pure function that applies a given function to each element of a list, resulting in a new list:

```
(defun map-pure (fn lst)
  (if (null lst)
      nil
      (cons (funcall fn (car lst)) (map-pure fn (cdr lst)))))
```

In this example, map-pure takes a function fn and a list lst, applying fn to each element recursively, constructing a new list without altering the original list.

The properties of immutability and pure functions together yield several advantages:

- **Predictability**: Functions' behavior is consistent and reproducible.

112

- **Testability**: It is easier to test functions as they do not have dependencies on or alter external states.

- **Concurrency**: Pure functions with immutable data are inherently thread-safe, facilitating parallel computation.

- **Debugging**: Debugging is more straightforward as functions are self-contained and do not alter external states.

4.10   Functional Programming Paradigms

Functional programming is a paradigm that treats computation as the evaluation of mathematical functions. It avoids changing state and mutable data, emphasizing the application of functions. This paradigm contrasts with imperative programming, where the computation is primarily based on changing states and sequences of commands.

In Lisp, functional programming paradigms are leveraged to create clear, concise, and correct code. Key components of these paradigms include higher-order functions, immutability, pure functions, and first-class functions.

Higher-order Functions are functions that can take other functions as arguments or return functions as results. This concept is foundational in functional programming and allows for creating highly abstract and reusable code.

```
(defun apply-twice (f x)
  (funcall f (funcall f x)))

(defun square (x)
  (* x x))

(apply-twice #'square 2)
```

Output: 16

In this example, apply-twice accepts a function f and a value x. It applies the function f twice to x. The function square squares its argument, so applying it twice to 2 yields 16.

Immutability refers to the idea that data objects are unchangeable once created. Instead of altering an object, new objects are created with the desired changes. This principle is critical in functional program-

113

ming as it eliminates side effects, making functions easier to reason about, test, and parallelize.

```
(setq fruits '("apple" "banana" "cherry"))
(setq new-fruits (cons "date" fruits))
```

Output:
fruits: ("apple" "banana" "cherry")
new-fruits: ("date" "apple" "banana" "cherry")

Here, adding an element to the list fruits does not alter the original list but instead creates a new list new-fruits. This immutability ensures that data remains consistent and predictable.

Pure Functions are functions where the output solely depends on the input values and does not cause any side effects. This predictability makes pure functions integral to functional programming.

```
(defun add (x y)
  (+ x y))
```

(add 2 3)
Output: 5

The add function is pure because its output is solely determined by its inputs, and it does not modify any state or interact with the outside world.

First-class Functions mean that functions in Lisp are first-class citizens. They can be passed as arguments to other functions, returned as values from other functions, and assigned to variables.

```
(defun higher-order-example (f x)
  (funcall f x))

(setq increment (lambda (x) (+ x 1)))

(higher-order-example increment 5)
```

Output: 6

In this example, increment is a first-class function assigned to a variable and passed as an argument to higher-order-example, demonstrating its flexibility and power.

These principles are the building blocks of functional programming in Lisp. By combining them, programmers can construct robust and elegant code.

The power of functional programming in Lisp is further illustrated through *map* and *reduce* operations. The *map* function applies a given function to each element of a list, returning a list of results.

```
(defun double (x)
  (* 2 x))

(mapcar #'double '(1 2 3 4))
```

Output: (2 4 6 8)

The mapcar function applies double to each element of the list (1 2 3 4), producing a new list (2 4 6 8).

The reduce function, or fold in some languages, applies a function of two arguments cumulatively to the items of a sequence, from left to right, so as to reduce the sequence to a single value.

```
(reduce #'+ '(1 2 3 4))
```

Output: 10

Here, reduce sums the elements of the list (1 2 3 4), yielding 10. Such operations showcase the expressive power and succinctness of functional paradigms in Lisp.

By adhering to these principles, functional programming in Lisp yields code that is both powerful and elegant, allowing for the construction of complex programs with clarity and precision.

4.11 Advanced Functional Programming Techniques

Advanced functional programming techniques in Lisp offer powerful ways to create concise, flexible, and efficient code. These techniques build on the foundational principles of functional programming introduced in earlier sections, leveraging the expressive power of Lisp to handle complex operations with elegance and precision. This section delves into advanced topics such as memoization, lazy evaluation, combinators, and the use of macros for meta-programming, each adding a layer of sophistication to your functional programming repertoire.

Memoization: Memoization is a technique used to optimize functions by storing the results of expensive function calls and reusing the cached results for the same inputs. This is particularly useful for recursive functions where the same computations are repeatedly performed.

The following example demonstrates a memoized version of the Fibonacci function:

```
(defparameter *fib-cache* (make-hash-table :test 'equal))

(defun memoized-fib (n)
  (or (gethash n *fib-cache*)
      (setf (gethash n *fib-cache*)
            (if (<= n 1)
                n
                (+ (memoized-fib (- n 1))
                   (memoized-fib (- n 2)))))))
```

In this implementation, the *fib-cache* hash table is used to store previously calculated Fibonacci values. The memoized-fib function first checks if the result for n is already in the cache using gethash. If it is, the cached value is returned, otherwise the function computes the result, stores it in the cache using setf and gethash, and then returns the result.

Lazy Evaluation: Lazy evaluation delays the evaluation of expressions until their values are needed, which can lead to significant performance improvements by avoiding unnecessary computations.

In Lisp, lazy evaluation can be implemented using closures and the delay and force functions. Here's a basic example:

```
(defun delay (expression)
  (let ((evaluated nil)
        (result nil))
    (lambda ()
      (unless evaluated
        (setf result (eval expression))
        (setf evaluated t))
      result)))

(defun force (delayed-object)
  (funcall delayed-object))

(let ((lazy (delay (* 3 4))))
```

```
(format t "Value: ~a~%" (force lazy))) ; Outputs "Value: 12"
```

In this example, delay creates a closure that encapsulates the expression, postponing its evaluation. The force function triggers the evaluation when the result is required.

Combinators: Combinators are higher-order functions that use only function application and earlier defined combinators to define results from their arguments. Two notable combinators in functional programming are the Y combinator and the K combinator.

The Y combinator is used to enable recursion in a language that does not support named functions. Here is the Y combinator expressed in Lisp:

```
(defun Y (f)
  ((lambda (x) (funcall x x))
   (lambda (x) (funcall f (lambda (&rest args) (apply (funcall x x)
       args)))))))

(Y (lambda (rec)
     (lambda (n)
       (if (<= n 1)
         1
         (* n (funcall rec (- n 1)))))))
```

This implementation allows for the definition of recursive functions without explicit names. The inner lambda function ensures that recursion occurs by repeatedly applying f.

Macros for Meta-Programming: Macros in Lisp enable powerful meta-programming capabilities, allowing programmers to transform and generate code dynamically. Macros can be used to create domain-specific languages, implement control structures, or simplify repetitive code patterns.

Consider the following macro that creates a simple unless control structure:

```
(defmacro unless (condition &body body)
  '(if (not ,condition)
       (progn ,@body)))

(unless t
  (format t "This will not be printed."))
```

```
(unless nil
  (format t "This will be printed.~%"))
```

The unless macro uses quasi-quotation (backticks) and unquoting (commas) to construct the conditional expression. The progn form ensures that all body expressions are evaluated in sequence when the condition is nil.

By leveraging memoization, lazy evaluation, combinators, and macros, Lisp programmers can write highly efficient and expressive code, pushing the boundaries of functional programming techniques. These advanced techniques enhance the readability, maintainability, and performance of Lisp programs, embodying the true essence of functional programming.

Chapter 5

Control Structures in Lisp

This chapter focuses on the various control structures available in Lisp. It covers conditional expressions such as 'if' and 'cond', logical operators, and different types of loops including 'do', 'dolist', and 'dotimes'. Advanced topics include 'block' and 'return', 'case' and 'typecase' statements, and constructs like 'progn' and 'progv'. The chapter also addresses exception handling using 'catch' and 'throw', advanced loop constructs, and recursive control structures. Best practices for control flow are provided to help readers write clear, efficient, and maintainable Lisp code.

5.1   Introduction to Control Structures

Control structures in Lisp enable the execution of code conditional on certain conditions, the repetition of code blocks, and the termination of processes when specific criteria are met. These constructs are essential for building complex and efficient programs. This section introduces the fundamental control structures in Lisp, laying the groundwork for more advanced topics covered later in the chapter.

Control structures guide the flow of execution in a program. They are divided into several categories:

- Conditional Expressions

- Loops and Iterations

- Blocks and Returns

- Case and Typecase Statements

- Progn and Progv

- Exception Handling

- Recursive Control Structures

Lisp provides a rich set of control structures, more flexible and powerful compared to many other programming languages. They allow you to handle various logical operations and looping mechanisms with minimal syntax while ensuring high readability.

Here, we start with basic constructs and gradually extend to more sophisticated ones.

Consider the following basic conditional expression using if:

```
(if (> x 10)
    (print "x is greater than 10")
    (print "x is not greater than 10"))
```

This if expression evaluates the condition (> x 10). If the condition is true, it executes the first print statement; otherwise, it executes the second print statement.

In addition to the if statement, Lisp offers multiple ways to perform conditional evaluations, such as the cond expression, which allows a series of conditions and associated actions.

```
(cond
 ((> x 10) (print "x is greater than 10"))
 ((= x 10) (print "x is exactly 10"))
 (t (print "x is less than 10")))
```

The cond expression sequentially evaluates each condition until one evaluates to true, executing the corresponding action. The t symbol serves as a default case if no other conditions are true.

Loops are another integral part of control structures. They allow for repetitive execution of code blocks until certain conditions are met. For example, the dolist loop iterates over each element in a list:

```
(dolist (item '(1 2 3 4 5))
  (print item))
```

In this loop, dolist iterates over each item in the list '(1 2 3 4 5) and prints it.

Another common loop construct is dotimes which iterates a specified number of times:

```
(dotimes (i 5)
  (print i))
```

Here, dotimes repeats the loop body five times, printing the values of i from 0 to 4.

Advanced looping constructs are provided through the loop macro that supports a wide range of iteration patterns:

```
(loop for i from 1 to 10
     do (print i))
```

The loop macro simplifies writing loops with sophisticated iteration patterns such as stepping, collecting results, and conditional execution.

To control the flow and exit of blocks, Lisp employs block and return, allowing you to label a code block and exit early if needed:

```
(block example
   (dotimes (i 10)
     (when (> i 5)
       (return i))))
```

The above code creates a block labeled example, and the return exits this block and returns i the first time i exceeds 5.

Lisp also provides case and typecase statements for selective execution based on the value or type of a variable, respectively:

```
(case x
   (1 (print "one"))
   (2 (print "two"))
   (otherwise (print "other")))
```

The progn construct allows for grouping multiple expressions together so that they are evaluated in sequence as a single unit:

```
(progn
   (print "This prints first.")
   (print "This prints second."))
```

Exception handling in Lisp is managed through catch and throw, providing mechanisms for handling errors and unexpected conditions:

```
(catch 'example-tag
  (dotimes (i 10)
    (when (> i 5)
      (throw 'example-tag i)))))
```

Recursive control structures are essential in Lisp, allowing a function to call itself to solve a problem iteratively. Consider the factorial function:

```
(defun factorial (n)
  (if (<= n 1)
      1
      (* n (factorial (- n 1))))))
```

This factorial function recursively calls itself, reducing the problem size at each step.

The intricacies of these constructs will be explored in subsequent sections, facilitating a more in-depth understanding of how to apply them effectively for creating robust Lisp programs.

5.2 Conditional Expressions (if, cond)

In Lisp, conditional expressions determine the flow of execution based on boolean evaluations. They allow efficient decision-making pathways and are fundamental for writing logical and dynamic programs. This section focuses on the primary conditional expressions: if and cond.

if is the simplest form of conditional expression in Lisp. It follows the pattern (if test then-part else-part). The test expression is evaluated first. If the test yields a non-nil value (true), the then-part is executed; otherwise, the else-part is executed.

```
(if (> 3 2)
    (print "3 is greater than 2")
    (print "2 is greater than or equal to 3"))
```

When executed, the output is:

```
"3 is greater than 2"
```

In this example, the test expression (> 3 2) is true, so the then-part, which is (print "3 is greater than 2"), is executed. else-part is ignored.

The else-part is optional. If omitted and the test evaluates to false, nil is returned.

```
(if nil
    (print "This won't print"))
```

There is no output in this case since the test evaluates to nil, and there is no else-part.

The if expression is suitable for simple, binary decisions. For multiple conditions, the cond expression, which stands for "conditional," is more appropriate. cond can be seen as a sequence of if statements. It follows the pattern (cond (test1 result1) (test2 result2) ... (testN resultN)). Each pair (testN resultN) is evaluated in order. The first true testN triggers its corresponding resultN, and the execution exits the cond statement.

```
(cond ((> 3 2) (print "3 is greater than 2"))
      ((< 3 2) (print "3 is less than 2"))
      (t (print "3 is equal to 2")))
```

The output is:

"3 is greater than 2"

In this cond expression, the first test (> 3 2) is true, so (print "3 is greater than 2") is executed. Subsequent conditions are ignored.

The clause (t (print ...)), where t stands for true, serves as a default case when all previous tests evaluate to nil. This ensures that one of the resultN forms is always executed, provided the cond expression has a case with t.

```
(cond ((< 3 2) (print "3 is less than 2"))
      (t (print "This is the default case")))
```

The output is:

"This is the default case"

Nested if and cond expressions are also common. It's typical to find an if within a then-part or else-part, or another cond within a branch of a cond.

```
(if (< 3 5)
    (if (> 3 2)
```

```
        (print "3 is between 2 and 5")
        (print "3 is less than or equal to 2"))
  (print "3 is greater than or equal to 5"))
```

The output is:

"3 is between 2 and 5"

In the above nested if statement, the outer if checks whether $3 < 5$. Since it is true, the inner if is evaluated. The inner if then checks $3 > 2$, which is true. Thus, (print "3 is between 2 and 5") is executed.

cond can also be nested to handle more complex situations:

```
(cond ((> 3 4) (print "3 is greater than 4"))
      ((= 3 4) (print "3 is equal to 4"))
      (t
        (cond ((> 3 2) (print "3 is greater than 2"))
              ((= 3 2) (print "3 is equal to 2")))))
```

The output is:

"3 is greater than 2"

In this nested cond, the outer cond handles the checks for whether $3 > 4$ or $3 == 4$. Since both tests are false, the default case (t ...) executes another cond, which checks whether $3 > 2$ or $3 == 2$. Here, $(> 3\ 2)$ returns true, so (print "3 is greater than 2") is executed.

Practically, cond is often favored over nested if statements for its readability and its capability to handle multiple branching paths efficiently. Understanding and utilizing these conditional expressions effectively is essential in Lisp, as they form the foundation for various control flow constructs in the language.

5.3   Logical Operators

Logical operators are essential in any programming language for making decisions based on boolean logic. In Lisp, logical operators are used to construct more complex conditions and control structures. The primary logical operators in Lisp are and, or, not, and null. Each of these operators has specific behaviors that are crucial in the manipulation and evaluation of boolean expressions.

The and operator takes multiple arguments and returns t (true) if all

124

arguments evaluate to non-nil (true). If any argument evaluates to nil (false), the and operator immediately returns nil without evaluating the remaining arguments. This short-circuiting behavior ensures that and is efficient in terms of execution time.

```
(setq a 5)
(setq b 10)
(and (> a 2) (< b 20)) ; Evaluates to t, as both conditions are true
(and (> a 10) (< b 20)) ; Evaluates to nil, as the first condition is
    false
```

The or operator also takes multiple arguments but returns t if at least one argument evaluates to non-nil. If no arguments are non-nil, the or operator returns nil. Similar to and, the or operator employs short-circuit evaluation. It stops evaluating arguments as soon as it encounters a non-nil value.

```
(setq x 0)
(setq y 1)
(or (> x 5) (= y 1)) ; Evaluates to t, as the second condition is true
(or (> x 5) (< y 1)) ; Evaluates to nil, as both conditions are false
```

The not operator is unary and inverts the boolean value of its argument. If the argument is non-nil, not returns nil; if the argument is nil, not returns t.

```
(not nil) ; Evaluates to t
(not t) ; Evaluates to nil
```

The null operator checks if its argument is nil. It is synonymous with the not operator when the argument is a list or an atom. If the argument is nil, null returns t; otherwise, it returns nil.

```
(null nil) ; Evaluates to t
(null '()) ; Evaluates to t, as '() is equivalent to nil
(null 0) ; Evaluates to nil, as 0 is not nil
```

The combination of these logical operators allows the construction of complex logical expressions. These expressions are integral to the control flow mechanisms discussed in other parts of this chapter. For instance, logical operators are often embedded within conditional expressions such as if and cond to handle intricate decision-making processes.

125

Consider a more complex example where multiple conditions must be met for a given set of actions:

```
(defun check-conditions (a b c)
  (if (and (> a 0) (or (= b 1) (= c 2)))
      (format t "Conditions met.~%")
      (format t "Conditions not met.~%")))

(check-conditions 1 1 3) ; Evaluates to "Conditions met."
(check-conditions 1 0 2) ; Evaluates to "Conditions met."
(check-conditions -1 1 2) ; Evaluates to "Conditions not met."
```

In the above example, and ensures that a is greater than 0, and or allows either b to be 1 or c to be 2 for the overall condition to be true. Such logical operations are foundational to creating dynamic and responsive programs.

Additionally, advanced usage of logical operators can be found in recursive functions, exception handling, and iterative processing. Mastery of these operators vastly improves the ability to write concise and efficient Lisp code. Users are encouraged to practice these operators in diverse scenarios to internalize their behaviors and implications.

5.4 Loops and Iterations (do, dolist, dotimes)

In Lisp, loops and iterations provide powerful mechanisms to execute a set of instructions repeatedly. This section will delve into three primary constructs for iteration: do, dolist, and dotimes. Understanding these constructs is essential for manipulating collections and performing repetitive tasks efficiently.

The do construct offers extensive flexibility for creating complex loops. The syntax of do is as follows:

```
(do ((<var1> <init1> <step1>)
     (<var2> <init2> <step2>)
     ...)
    (<end-test> <result>)
  <body>)
```

Here, var1, var2, etc. are loop variables initialized to init1, init2, etc.

Within each iteration, step1, step2, etc. modify the loop variables. The loop terminates when end-test evaluates to true, and result is the value returned. The loop body, <body>, contains the operations executed during each iteration.

Consider an example where we sum integers from 1 to 10 using do:

```
(do ((i 1 (+ i 1))
     (sum 0 (+ sum i)))
    ((> i 10) sum)
   (format t "i=~d, sum=~d~%" i sum))
```

The output of the above loop will be:

```
i=1, sum=1
i=2, sum=3
i=3, sum=6
...
i=10, sum=55
```

This example illustrates the initialization of i and sum, the modification of these variables in each iteration, and the termination when i exceeds 10.

The dolist construct iterates over elements in a list. Its syntax is:

```
(dolist (<var> <list> [<result>])
   <body>)
```

Here, var represents the current element of list during each iteration. The loop evaluates <body> for each element. After traversing the entire list, result is returned (defaulting to nil if not specified).

To illustrate, let's iterate through a list of numbers and print them:

```
(dolist (x '(1 2 3 4 5))
   (format t "Element: ~d~%" x))
```

The output is:

```
Element: 1
Element: 2
Element: 3
Element: 4
Element: 5
```

Finally, the dotimes construct iterates a fixed number of times. Its syntax is:

```
(dotimes (<var> <count> [<result>])
   <body>)
```

127

The loop variable var takes on values from 0 to count - 1 during each iteration. The loop terminates after completing count iterations, returning result (defaulting to nil).

As an example, let's print the first 5 natural numbers using dotimes:

```
(dotimes (i 5)
  (format t "i=~d~%" i))
```

The output is:

```
i=0
i=1
i=2
i=3
i=4
```

The constructs do, dolist, and dotimes offer different approaches to iteration, catering to various use-cases. Selecting the appropriate construct based on the task ensures efficient and readable Lisp code. Whether iterating over lists, performing a set number of iterations, or running complex loops with multiple variables, these constructs are fundamental for procedural programming in Lisp.

5.5   Block and Return

In Lisp, 'block' and 'return' serve as advanced control structures that allow for delineating local exits within a function or a sequence of expressions. These structures provide mechanisms to explicitly define the boundaries for control flow and offer controlled exits from those regions.

The 'block' construct establishes a named block of code, enabling the grouped execution of expressions. The syntax for a 'block' is straightforward:

```
(block block-name
  expression-1
  expression-2
  ...
  expression-n)
```

Here, block-name can be any symbol, and it identifies the constructed block. The expressions encapsulated inside this block are evaluated in sequence. The value of the last expression is returned as the value of the block unless a 'return' statement is encountered.

The 'return' construct is used to exit a block prematurely and return a specified value. The syntax is:

```
(return from block-name value)
```

The return statement specifies the block from which to exit (using block-name) and the value to return when exiting.

Consider an example where a block is utilized for conditional evaluation and controlled exit:

```
(defun example-block-return (x)
  (block check-values
    (format t "Evaluating the value of x...~%")
    (if (< x 0)
        (return-from check-values "Negative value")
        (format t "x is non-negative.~%"))
    x))
```

In this example, the function example-block-return takes an argument x. An informational message is printed using format. If x is less than zero, return-from is used to exit the check-values block immediately and return the string "Negative value". Otherwise, "x is non-negative." is displayed, and the value of x is returned at the end of the block.

To demonstrate the execution of example-block-return, consider the following test cases:

```
(example-block-return -5)
```

```
Evaluating the value of x...
"Negative value"
```

```
(example-block-return 10)
```

```
Evaluating the value of x...
x is non-negative.
10
```

In the first test case, example-block-return evaluates x (-5) and exits the block, returning "Negative value". In the second case, x (10) is non-negative, so it prints the message and returns 10.

The use of block and return-from enhances readability and maintainability by explicitly denoting possible exit points from a sequence of expressions. Additionally, blocks can be nested, and return-from can specify which block to exit.

```
(defun nested-block-example (x y)
  (block outer
    (format t "Entering outer block...~%")
    (block inner
      (format t "Entering inner block...~%")
      (if (= x y)
          (return-from inner 'inner-exit))
      (format t "Exiting inner block...~%"))
    (return-from outer 'outer-exit)))
```

In this nested block example, the function nested-block-example evaluates whether x equals y. If so, it exits the 'inner' block while printing "inner-exit". If they are not equal, it proceeds to exit the 'outer' block and returns "outer-exit".

Test the nested block implementation as follows:

```
(nested-block-example 5 5)
```

```
Entering outer block...
Entering inner block...
inner-exit
```

```
(nested-block-example 3 4)
```

```
Entering outer block...
Entering inner block...
Exiting inner block...
outer-exit
```

This demonstrates the control flow where different exit points are executed based on specified conditions, leveraging the 'block' and 'return-from' constructs efficiently.

5.6   Case and Typecase Statements

The case and typecase statements in Lisp are essential tools for controlling program flow based on the value of expressions or the type of objects, respectively. These constructs enhance the readability and efficiency of code by providing a structured way to handle multiple conditions that would otherwise require a series of nested if or cond expressions.

130

Case Statement

The case statement evaluates an expression and chooses among many possible actions based on the value of that expression. It is similar to the switch statement in other programming languages. The general form of the case statement is as follows:

```
(case <keyform>
  (<key1> <result1>)
  (<key2> <result2>)
  ...
  (t <default-result>))
```

The <keyform> is evaluated first, and its value is compared against the keys (<key1>, <key2>, etc.). If a match is found, the corresponding result expression is evaluated and its value is returned. If no match is found, the expression associated with the t key (which acts as a default case) is evaluated and returned. The case statement is implemented using a property list, making key lookups efficient.

Example:

```
(case 3
  (1 'one)
  (2 'two)
  (3 'three)
  (t 'unknown))
```

In this example, the expression (case 3 ...) will evaluate to 'three because the value 3 matches the third key.

It is important to note that each key in the case statement can be a single value or a list of values. Here is an example using multiple values for keys:

```
(case 'b
  ((a e i o u) 'vowel)
  ((b c d f g) 'consonant)
  (t 'unknown))
```

In this case, 'b matches the second group, so the result is 'consonant.

Typecase Statement

The typecase statement is a type-based discriminator that chooses among many possible actions based on the type of an object. It is similar to the case statement but operates on types instead of values. The general form of the typecase statement is as follows:

```
(typecase <expression>
  (<type1> <result1>)
  (<type2> <result2>)
  ...
  (t <default-result>))
```

The <expression> is evaluated first, and the type of its result is compared against the specified types (<type1>, <type2>, etc.). If a match is found, the corresponding result expression is evaluated and its value is returned. If no match is found, the expression associated with the t type (which acts as a default case) is evaluated and returned.

Example:

```
(typecase 3.14
  (integer 'an-integer)
  (float 'a-float)
  (string 'a-string)
  (t 'unknown-type))
```

In this example, since 3.14 is a floating-point number, the above typecase form will evaluate to 'a-float.

Similar to the case statement, the typecase statement can handle multiple types for each case. Here is an example illustrating this:

```
(typecase "hello"
  ((integer float) 'number)
  (string 'text)
  (t 'unknown-type))
```

In this example, since "hello" is a string, the form evaluates to 'text.

Best Practices

When using case and typecase statements, the following best practices ensure efficient and maintainable code:

- Group related key values or types under a single branch to avoid redundancy.

- Always include a default case using t to handle unexpected values or types.

132

- Use descriptive symbols and expressions for readability.

- Avoid deeply nested case or typecase statements by breaking them into smaller, modular functions when necessary.

- Ensure that keys in case statements and types in typecase statements are mutually exclusive when possible to prevent ambiguous matches.

5.7 Progn and Progv

The progn and progv constructs are essential for mastering advanced control flow in Lisp. Both constructs enable the sequential evaluation of multiple expressions but serve different purposes and contexts within program execution.

progn is used to group multiple expressions, ensuring they are evaluated in sequence. This construct is particularly useful when a series of operations need to be executed, and only the value of the last expression is returned. It is often utilized within conditional statements or loops where multiple steps must be performed as part of a single logical unit. Here is a basic example of progn usage:

```
(progn
  (print "Step 1")
  (print "Step 2")
  (print "Step 3"))
```

The above code will print each of the strings "Step 1", "Step 2", and "Step 3" in sequence. The result of the entire progn expression will be the result of the print function called with "Step 3", which is the last expression.

In practice, progn is often used within other control structures to encapsulate a block of code that needs to be executed conditionally. For example:

```
(if (> x 5)
    (progn
      (print "x is greater than 5")
      (setq y (+ x 10)))
    (print "x is 5 or less"))
```

In this scenario, if x is greater than 5, both the print and setq expressions within the progn block will be executed. If x is not greater than 5, only the second print statement will be executed.

progv, on the other hand, dynamically binds a list of variables to corresponding values within its scope. This advanced construct is useful when the set of variables to be bound and their values are determined at runtime. The syntax for progv is:

```
(progv var-list val-list body...)
```

Here, var-list is a list of symbols that will be bound to the values in val-list, and body represents the expressions to be executed with these bindings. Consider the following example:

```
(let ((vars '(a b c))
      (vals '(1 2 3)))
  (progv vars vals
    (print a) ; prints 1
    (print b) ; prints 2
    (print c))) ; prints 3
```

In this example, the variables a, b, and c are dynamically bound to 1, 2, and 3 respectively within the scope of the progv expression. This kind of dynamic variable binding is particularly powerful in meta-programming and scenarios where the program needs to interact with varying sets of variables.

Both progn and progv showcase Lisp's flexibility and power in managing control flow and dynamic bindings. Proper utilization of these constructs can lead to more readable and maintainable code, enabling efficient execution of complex programmable logic.

5.8 Exception Handling with Catch and Throw

Exception handling is a crucial aspect of programming, providing a mechanism to manage runtime errors and other exceptional conditions that may arise during the execution of a program. In Lisp, the catch and throw constructs offer powerful tools for implementing such control flow structures.

134

The catch construct defines a context or a "catcher" that can catch a thrown value or expression. The throw construct, on the other hand, enables a program to exit from the dynamic extent of the catch and pass a value back to it. Here's a basic example:

```
(catch 'my-tag
  (if (= 1 1)
      (throw 'my-tag 'condition-met)))
```

In this example, the catch form specifies a tag, 'my-tag, which is used by the throw form to transfer control back to the catch, along with a return value 'condition-met. This mechanism can be visualized as defining an exit path from deeply nested computations back to a known point.

To understand how catch and throw can be used in more complex scenarios, consider the following practical example:

```
(defun search-element (list element)
  "Search for ELEMENT in LIST, returning its position or NIL if not
      found."
  (catch 'found
    (dotimes (i (length list))
      (when (equal (nth i list) element)
        (throw 'found i)))
    nil))
```

In this function, search-element, a loop iterates over a list to find the desired element. If the element is found, throw transfers control to the catch form, effectively returning the index of element. If the loop completes without finding the element, the function returns nil.

The use of catch and throw can also facilitate cleaner error handling. Consider the scenario where we wish to ensure certain preconditions before proceeding with computations:

```
(defun divide-safe (numerator denominator)
  "Performs safe division, handling division-by-zero errors."
  (catch 'error
    (if (= denominator 0)
        (throw 'error 'division-by-zero))
    (/ numerator denominator)))
```

In this divide-safe function, we check if the denominator is zero. If it is, we throw an error tagged with 'division-by-zero. Otherwise, we proceed with the division. During the invocation:

```
CL-USER> (divide-safe 10 5)
2

CL-USER> (divide-safe 10 0)
division-by-zero
```

The first call performs normally, while the second call catches the error and returns the error tag, ensuring the program doesn't encounter an operational error.

catch and throw can also be nested, allowing for sophisticated control flows. Consider the following example:

```
(defun nested-catch-throw ()
  "Demonstrates nested catch and throw usage."
  (catch 'outer
    (format t "Entering outer catch~%")
    (catch 'inner
      (format t "Entering inner catch~%")
      (throw 'outer 'thrown-from-inner))
    (format t "This won't print since throw unwinds to outer catch~%
      ")))
```

Here, a throw from within an inner catch unwinds the control flow to an outer catch, effectively skipping intervening code. When executed:

```
CL-USER> (nested-catch-throw)
Entering outer catch
Entering inner catch
thrown-from-inner
```

The output demonstrates that control is transferred directly from the inner throw to the outer catch, bypassing the intermediate statements.

Understanding and employing catch and throw in Lisp enables robust error handling and structured control flows, leading to more reliable and maintainable code. This ability to manage exceptional conditions gracefully is a testament to the flexibility and power intrinsic to Lisp's design.

5.9   Advanced Loop Constructs

In addition to the basic looping constructs covered in earlier sections, Lisp provides a variety of advanced loop constructs that allow for more sophisticated and flexible iteration patterns. These constructs enable a higher level of expressiveness and control, making it easier to write concise and efficient code for complex tasks.

loop is one of the most versatile and powerful iteration constructs available in Common Lisp. Unlike do, dolist, and dotimes, which have specific iteration patterns, the loop macro supports a wide range of iteration patterns through a rich set of keywords and options.

```
(loop for i from 1 to 10
    do (print i))
```

In the above example, loop iterates over the values from 1 to 10, printing each value. The for keyword introduces a variable i, which takes on successive values in the specified range. The do keyword introduces the body of the loop, which in this case consists of a single print statement.

loop can also handle more complex iteration patterns, such as nested loops and multiple variables.

```
(loop for i from 1 to 10
    for j from 10 downto 1
    do (format t "~d ~d~%" i j))
```

Here, i iterates from 1 to 10, while j iterates from 10 down to 1. The format function is used to print both variables on each iteration. The loop construct makes it straightforward to manage multiple iteration variables and nested loops without requiring explicit nesting.

Another powerful feature of loop is its ability to collect results. This can be particularly useful for generating lists or other collections based on the results of iterations.

```
(loop for i from 1 to 10
    collect i)
```

The collect keyword indicates that the values of i should be collected into a list. The resulting list, in this case, would be (1 2 3 4 5 6 7 8 9 10). This feature of loop simplifies the process of generating lists through iteration, which would otherwise require explicit list construction and manipulation.

loop also supports summing values, counting items, and other common aggregation operations through its built-in keywords.

```
(loop for i from 1 to 10
```

```
      sum i)
```

The sum keyword causes the values of i to be summed, resulting in the value 55 for this example. Similarly, the count keyword can be used to count the number of items satisfying a certain condition.

```
(loop for i from 1 to 10
      count (evenp i))
```

Here, count tallies the number of even values of i, using the evenp predicate. The count would be 5, as there are five even numbers between 1 and 10.

Another feature is the loop construct's ability to concatenate lists or string together values within the loop.

```
(loop for i from 1 to 5
      concat (format nil "~d " i))
```

The concat keyword indicates that the results of each iteration, formatted as strings in this case, should be concatenated together. The resulting string would be "1 2 3 4 5 ".

Lisp's loop construct includes advanced control capabilities such as conditional execution within the loop.

```
(loop for i from 1 to 10
      if (evenp i)
         collect i into evens
      else
         collect i into odds
      finally (return (list evens odds)))
```

In this example, the loop conditionally collects even and odd numbers into separate lists, using the if keyword. The finally keyword introduces end-of-loop processing, where the loop explicitly returns a list of the two collections.

With loop, it is possible to iterate over multiple sequences simultaneously.

```
(loop for a in '(1 2 3)
      for b in '(4 5 6)
      collect (list a b))
```

This example collects pairs of elements from two sequences into a list of lists: $((1\ 4)\ (2\ 5)\ (3\ 6))$. The for keyword is used with the in option to iterate over lists.

Algorithm 2: Looping through a list and computing squares

Input: A list of numbers numbers
Output: A list of their squares

1 squares ← empty-list;
2 **for** i ← *1* **to** length of numbers **do**
3   ⌊ squares ← append(squares, (nth i numbers)^2);
4 **return** squares

The loop construct's expressiveness extends beyond simple iteration into realms of conditionality, sequence management, aggregation, and end-of-loop processing, providing a comprehensive solution for complex iteration patterns.

This detailed examination of loop in Lisp emphasizes its flexibility and power, enabling more elegant and efficient iteration patterns that go beyond typical looping constructs.

5.10 Recursive Control Structures

In Lisp, recursion is a fundamental concept leveraged for a wide range of computational tasks. Unlike iterative constructs which rely on explicit looping mechanisms, recursion allows a function to call itself in order to solve smaller instances of a problem until a base case is reached. This method often results in more intuitive and elegant solutions for problems that are inherently recursive, such as those involving data structures like trees and lists.

Consider a simple example of calculating the factorial of a number n using recursion. The factorial of n (denoted as $n!$) is defined as the product of all positive integers less than or equal to n. This can be recursively defined as:

$$n! = \begin{cases} 1 & \text{if } n = 0 \\ n \times (n-1)! & \text{if } n > 0 \end{cases}$$

In Lisp, the corresponding recursive function can be implemented as follows:

```
(defun factorial (n)
  (if (<= n 0)
    1
    (* n (factorial (- n 1)))))
```

When the above function is called with an argument n, it checks if n is less than or equal to 0. If true, it returns 1; otherwise, it recursively calls itself with $n - 1$ and multiplies the result by n.

Recursive control structures in Lisp are not limited to numeric computations. They are also extensively used for operations on lists. For instance, a function to sum all elements of a list can be written as follows:

```
(defun sum-list (lst)
  (if (null lst)
    0
    (+ (car lst) (sum-list (cdr lst)))))
```

Here, the base case checks if the list is empty using null. If the list is empty, the function returns 0. Otherwise, it adds the first element of the list (retrieved using car) to the result of a recursive call to sum-list on the rest of the list (retrieved using cdr).

Recursion is also a powerful tool for tree traversal. Consider a binary tree where each node can have a left and a right child. A recursive function to compute the height of such a binary tree would look like this:

```
(defun tree-height (tree)
  (if (null tree)
    0
    (1+ (max (tree-height (left-child tree))
             (tree-height (right-child tree))))))
```

In this implementation, tree is assumed to be a structure with accessor functions left-child and right-child. The base case returns 0 if tree is null, representing an empty tree. Otherwise, it recursively computes the height of the left and right subtrees and returns the maximum of these heights plus one.

It is important to ensure that recursive functions in Lisp must have a well-defined base case to avoid infinite recursion. Each recursive call should make progress towards this base case.

Recursion is particularly suited for problems expressible in terms of subproblems of the same kind. However, recursion comes with its own set of limitations, primarily the potential for excessive memory usage due to maintaining multiple stack frames. To mitigate this, Lisp implementations often employ a technique known as tail-call optimization. A tail-recursive function is one where the final action of the function is a call to itself, allowing for optimization where the stack frame is reused.

Consider the following example of a tail-recursive factorial function:

```
(defun factorial-tail-rec (n &optional (acc 1))
  (if (<= n 0)
      acc
      (factorial-tail-rec (- n 1) (* n acc))))
```

Here, acc (accumulator) is used to store the intermediate results. The system can optimize this tail-recursive function to maintain constant stack space.

Understanding and effectively utilizing recursive control structures allow Lisp programmers to solve complex problems with clear, maintainable code.

5.11 Best Practices for Control Flow in Lisp

When developing software in Lisp, a thorough understanding of control flow and its effective management is key. Below are some best practices aimed at enhancing both the readability and efficiency of your Lisp programs by properly leveraging control structures.

- **Use Appropriate Conditional Constructs:** Select the most suitable conditional construct based on the complexity and requirements of the condition being evaluated. For simple binary conditions, if is ideal. When dealing with multiple branches, cond becomes more readable and manageable. Avoid nesting multiple if statements unnecessarily, which can lead to code that is difficult to read and debug.

```
;; Example of using 'if' for a simple condition
(if (> x 0)
    (print "Positive")
    (print "Non-positive"))
```

```
;; Example of using 'cond' for multiple branches
(cond
   ((> x 0) (print "Positive"))
   ((< x 0) (print "Negative"))
   (t (print "Zero")))
```

- **Prefer 'case' and 'typecase' for Multiple Values:** For cases where a value is compared against a set of constants or types, case and typecase are more efficient than multiple if or cond statements. These constructs not only improve readability but can also optimize execution.

```
;; Using 'case'
(case x
   (1 (print "One"))
   (2 (print "Two"))
   (otherwise (print "Other")))

;; Using 'typecase'
(typecase y
   (string (print "It's a string"))
   (integer (print "It's an integer"))
   (t (print "Other type")))
```

- **Minimize Global State by Using 'let' and 'let*':** The use of global state can lead to code that is difficult to understand and maintain. Instead, use let and let* to create local variables that limit the scope of data to the smallest possible context.

```
;; Example of using 'let' for local variables
(let ((a 10)
      (b 20))
   (print (+ a b)))
```

- **Utilize Proper Loop Constructs:** Make use of the appropriate looping construct for your specific use case. For fixed repetitions, dotimes is suitable, while dolist is intended for iterating over list elements. The do construct is versatile for more complex loops where both initialization and condition checking are required.

```
;; Example of using 'dotimes' for fixed repetitions
(dotimes (i 5)
  (print i))

;; Example of using 'dolist' for iterating over a list
(dolist (item '(1 2 3 4 5))
  (print item))
```

- **Avoid Deep Nesting:** Deeply nested structures are difficult to follow and understand. Where possible, refactor deeply nested code into separate functions or use constructs like progn to manage multiple step evaluations within a simpler structure.

```
;; Example of avoiding deep nesting using 'progn'
(when (condition1)
  (progn
    (do-first-task)
    (do-second-task)
    (do-third-task)))
```

- **Handle Exceptions Gracefully:** Use catch and throw to manage exceptions and control the flow of the program during error conditions. This approach ensures your program can handle unexpected situations more robustly.

```
;; Example of using 'catch' and 'throw' for exception handling
(catch 'error
  (if (not (valid-input-p input))
      (throw 'error "Invalid input"))
  ;; Normal processing
  (process-input input))
```

- **Ensure Proper Exit from Blocks:** When using block and return-from, ensure the logical exit points of your blocks are clear and clean. This clarity helps in understanding the control flow more efficiently, especially in complex operations.

```
;; Example of using 'block' and 'return-from'
(block my-block
  (do-something)
  (if (condition)
      (return-from my-block "Exit early"))
  (do-more-things))
```

- **Optimize Recursion with Proper Base Cases:** Ensure recursive functions have well-defined base cases to prevent infinite loops and stack overflow errors. Tail-recursive constructs should be employed to optimize performance when possible.

```
;; Example of a recursive function with a base case
(defun factorial (n)
  (if (<= n 1)
      1
      (* n (factorial (- n 1))))))
```

Employing these practices enhances the robustness, readability, and maintainability of Lisp programs, allowing developers to create more efficient and effective code.

Chapter 6

Macros and Meta-programming

This chapter explores the powerful features of macros and meta-programming in Lisp. It starts with defining simple macros and understanding macro expansion and evaluation. Advanced macro techniques, hygiene considerations, and the distinctions between macros and functions are discussed. Practical applications of macros, including code generation and debugging, are covered in detail. The chapter also introduces meta-programming concepts and offers best practices for writing effective and maintainable macros, providing readers with the tools to extend and customize the Lisp language efficiently.

6.1   Introduction to Macros

Macros in Lisp can be thought of as powerful tools that allow programmers to abstract and transform code before it gets evaluated. Unlike functions, which operate on values and expressions during runtime, macros operate on the code itself at compile-time, enabling the creation of new syntactic constructs and domain-specific languages. Understanding macros is fundamental for gaining proficiency in Lisp programming due to their ability to extend and customize the language efficiently.

Macros differ from functions primarily in the timing of their execution. While functions are executed at runtime on already evaluated arguments, macros are expanded at compile-time, which means they receive unevaluated code as their arguments and generate new code that is subsequently compiled and executed. This additional layer of code manipulation elevates the expressive power of Lisp and facilitates complex programming paradigms, such as metaprogramming.

The basic form of a macro definition in Common Lisp is given by the defmacro construct. Here's a simple example:

```
(defmacro when (condition &body body)
  '(if ,condition
       (progn ,@body)))
```

In this example, the when macro simplifies conditional execution. When the when macro is called, it transforms the code into an if statement with a progn block. To understand this better, consider the following usage of the when macro:

```
(when (> x 0)
  (print "x is positive")
  (setf y x))
```

The macro expands into:

```
(if (> x 0)
    (progn
      (print "x is positive")
      (setf y x)))
```

This code illustrates the power of macros: they simplify repetitive code structures and introduce new syntactic abstractions that make programs more readable and maintainable.

Macro expansion and evaluation are crucial processes to grasp. When the Lisp compiler encounters a macro call, it temporarily suspends the compilation, expands the macro, and then proceeds with the compilation of the expanded code. This allows the programmer to define new constructs in a way that seamlessly integrates with the core language syntax. You can explicitly see how a macro expands by using the macroexpand function:

```
(macroexpand '(when (> x 0)
                (print "x is positive")
```

146

```
                    (setf y x)))
```

The output will show the expanded form of the macro:

```
(if (> x 0)
    (progn
      (print "x is positive")
      (setf y x)))
```

Macro expansion fundamentally illustrates that macros are about code transformation. This transformation capability is what empowers macros to perform tasks that traditional functions cannot.

Coding conventions and hygiene are paramount when writing macros to avoid unintended side-effects and variable capture. Macros should be written to ensure that they do not inadvertently interfere with the surrounding code, a concept known as hygiene. Consider the following faulty macro:

```
(defmacro faulty-macro (x)
  '(let ((y ,x))
     (+ y 10)))
```

If the macro is used in a context where y has already been defined, it will cause unexpected behavior or errors. For instance:

```
(let ((y 5))
  (faulty-macro 3))
```

This conflict can be avoided by using gensym to generate unique variable names within the macro:

```
(defmacro safe-macro (x)
  (let ((temp (gensym)))
    '(let ((,temp ,x))
       (+ ,temp 10))))
```

When safe-macro is used, it will not interfere with any pre-existing variables named y:

```
(let ((y 5))
  (safe-macro 3))
```

This section lays the foundation for understanding macros, emphasizing their pre-evaluation, transformation capabilities, and the need for careful handling to maintain code hygiene. As we proceed, we will

147

delve deeper into advanced macro techniques and their practical applications in building more powerful and efficient Lisp programs.

6.2 Defining Simple Macros

In Lisp, macros are a powerful tool that allows the programmer to add new syntactic constructs to the language itself. Unlike functions, which operate on evaluated arguments, macros can manipulate their unevaluated arguments and generate code that will be evaluated later. This capability enables the construction of complex programs with concise and expressive code. Here, we will delve into the fundamental steps and concepts for defining simple macros in Lisp.

A macro is defined using the defmacro construct. The basic syntax for defmacro is as follows:

```
(defmacro macro-name (parameters)
  "optional-documentation-string"
  body-forms)
```

The macro-name is an identifier for the macro, parameters specifies the macro arguments, and body-forms are the forms that assemble the macro expansion. Once defined, a macro can be invoked like a function, but with the critical difference that Lisp first expands the macro before evaluating the result.

Consider a simple example where we define a macro named simple-macro that takes two arguments and returns their sum:

```
(defmacro simple-macro (a b)
  '(+ ,a ,b))
```

This macro uses the backquote (') to create a template for the resulting code, with the comma (,) before the variables a and b indicating that these are to be evaluated in the macro's environment before being inserted into the template.

To understand how this macro functions, let's expand it manually. Given the expression:

```
(simple-macro 3 4)
```

The macro expansion would result in:

(+ 3 4)

Thus, evaluating (simple-macro 3 4) results in 7.

A more complex example can illustrate handling multiple forms and integrating conditional logic within the macro body. Consider a macro that increments a variable if it is positive:

```
(defmacro inc-if-positive (var)
  '(if (> ,var 0)
       (incf ,var)
       ,var))
```

This macro uses the if conditional construct, the > function to check if the variable is positive, and the incf function to increment the variable. If the variable is not positive, it simply returns the variable unchanged.

With the expression:

```
(inc-if-positive x)
```

If x is 5, the macro expands to:

```
(if (> x 0)
   (incf x)
   x)
```

And if x is already 5, evaluating this results in x becoming 6.

Macros can also contain nested forms and leverage other macros within their definition. Here is a macro that demonstrates nesting:

```
(defmacro nested-macro (x y)
  '(let ((a ,x)
         (b ,y))
     (when (> a b)
       (list a b))))
```

This macro nests a let form to bind a and b to the values of x and y, respectively. It includes a when form, which checks if a is greater than b, and if so, it creates a list of a and b.

Given the expression:

```
(nested-macro 10 5)
```

The macro expands to:

```
(let ((a 10)
      (b 5))
  (when (> a b)
    (list a b)))
```

Evaluating this expression results in the list $(10\ 5)$ because 10 is indeed greater than 5.

As shown, defining simple macros involves creating syntactic templates that manipulate unevaluated code and generate meaningful expressions. The use of backquote, comma, and nested forms allows for flexible and powerful code generation capabilities.

6.3   Macro Expansion and Evaluation

Understanding macro expansion and evaluation is crucial in mastering the use of macros in Lisp. Macros allow us to introduce new syntactic constructs in a flexible and dynamic manner. Unlike functions, macros manipulate the code itself during compilation or interpretation, resulting in more powerful and efficient programs.

When a macro is called, it undergoes a process known as macro expansion. This process involves recursively transforming the macro calls into their expanded forms until no more macros are left to expand. Let's delve deeper into this process with an illustrative example.

Consider a simple macro incf that increments a variable:

```
(defmacro incf (var)
  `(setq ,var (+ ,var 1)))
```

In the above macro definition, backquote ("`") is used to create a template for the output, and comma (",") is used to evaluate the expressions within the template. When incf is called, it replaces itself with the corresponding setq form.

For instance, the macro call (incf x) expands to:

```
(setq x (+ x 1))
```

To further explore this, let us manually expand a nested macro form. Consider a macro with-temp-var that creates a temporary variable initialized to a given value:

```
(defmacro with-temp-var ((var init) &body body)
  `(let ((,var ,init))
     ,@body))
```

Combining this with our incf macro, we can write:

```
(with-temp-var (x 10)
  (incf x)
  (print x))
```

Manually expanding this step-by-step:

1. Expand with-temp-var:

```
(let ((x 10))
  (incf x)
  (print x))
```

2. Next, expand incf within the body of let:

```
(let ((x 10))
  (setq x (+ x 1))
  (print x))
```

At this point, the code is fully expanded, and the Lisp interpreter or compiler can evaluate it.

Another important concept is *macro evaluation*. Unlike functions, macros do not evaluate their arguments immediately. Instead, they take their arguments as raw unevaluated code and transform them. This allows macros to operate on the structure of the code itself. For instance:

```
(incf (* 2 3))
```

The above would result in an error because (* 2 3) is not a valid variable. Now, consider another macro when defined as follows:

```
(defmacro when (condition &body body)
  '(if ,condition
       (progn ,@body)))
```

Here, when takes a condition and a body of code. It expands into an if expression that executes the body only when the condition is true. For example:

```
(when (= x 10)
  (print "x is 10")
  (incf x))
```

Expanding when:

151

```
(if (= x 10)
   (progn
      (print "x is 10")
      (incf x)))
```

Continue expanding incf within progn:

```
(if (= x 10)
   (progn
      (print "x is 10")
      (setq x (+ x 1))))
```

Understanding these expansion steps helps in debugging macros. One effective way to observe this expansion is using the macroexpand function:

```
(macroexpand '(incf x))
```

Result:

```
(setq x (+ x 1))
```

For nested expansions:

```
(macroexpand '(with-temp-var (x 10)
               (incf x)
               (print x)))
```

Result:

```
(let ((x 10))
   (incf x)
   (print x))
```

Subsequent invocation of macroexpand further reveals:

```
(macroexpand '(let ((x 10))
               (incf x)
               (print x)))
```

Final result:

```
(let ((x 10))
   (setq x (+ x 1))
   (print x))
```

During macro development, systematically applying macroexpand ensures correct behavior. Expanding macros incrementally aids in identifying issues early, facilitating debugging and refinement.

Experimenting with various macro definitions and their expansions enriches comprehension. Through consistent practice, the intricacies of macro expansion and evaluation become intuitive, allowing for advanced and efficient macro-based solutions. Continuously applying these techniques fosters proficiency in leveraging Lisp's meta-programming capabilities effectively.

6.4 Advanced Macro Techniques

In this section, we delve into advanced macro techniques, building on our foundational understanding of simple macros. These techniques are essential for creating more sophisticated and powerful macros, enabling us to leverage the full potential of Lisp's meta-programming capabilities.

One powerful advanced technique is the use of backquote (or quasiquote) and comma within macros. The backquote facilitates the construction of lists while allowing certain elements to be evaluated.

```
(defmacro example-macro (name)
  '(progn
     (defvar ,name "default value")
     (setf ,name "new value")))
```

In this example, the backquote ("") creates a template for the code to expand. The usage of comma allows the actual value of name to be inserted into the template during macro expansion.

Another advanced technique is the use of gensym to generate unique symbols, ensuring that macro expansions do not accidentally capture or conflict with variables in the context where the macro is used. This is particularly useful in maintaining hygiene in macros.

```
(defmacro safe-let ((var value) &body body)
  (let ((temp-var (gensym)))
    '(let ((,temp-var ,value))
       (let ((,var ,temp-var))
         ,@body))))
```

Here, gensym generates a unique symbol for temp-var, preventing any collision with existing variables named temp-var in the macro user's code.

In scenarios where macros need to manipulate other macros or functions, the macroexpand function becomes extremely useful. macroexpand returns the expanded form of a macro invocation, allowing inspection and debugging of the macro expansion process.

```
(defmacro inspect-macro (form)
  '(let ((expanded-form (macroexpand ',form)))
     (format t "Expanded form: ~a~%" expanded-form)
     ,form))
```

Invoking (inspect-macro (example-macro foo)) would output the expanded form of example-macro, aiding in diagnostics and ensuring correctness of macro behavior.

Additionally, Lisp supports recursive macros which call themselves within their expansions. This allows complex repetitive code generation patterns.

```
(defmacro n-times (n expr)
  (if (= n 0)
      nil
      '(progn
         ,expr
         (n-times ,(- n 1) ,expr))))
```

Using n-times, one can repeat an expression a specified number of times. For example, (n-times 3 (print "Hello")) will expand into three print calls.

Error checking and handling within macros is another critical advanced technique for creating robust and user-friendly macros. One can incorporate assert statements or conditionals to validate macro arguments.

```
(defmacro checked-div (numerator denominator)
  '(progn
     (assert (not (zerop ,denominator)) (nil) "Division by zero")
     (/ ,numerator ,denominator)))
```

The checked-div macro includes an assert statement to ensure that the denominator is not zero, preventing division by zero errors.

Furthermore, macros can be designed to accept keyword arguments, enhancing flexibility and readability.

```
(defmacro customizable-print (&rest args &key (message "Default
    message") (count 1))
  '(dotimes (i ,count)
     (print ,message)))
```

Using customizable-print, one can specify optional :message and :count keywords to control the behavior of the macro, e.g., (customizable-print :message "Hi!" :count 3).

Advanced macros can also leverage pattern matching for more complex code transformations. Pattern matching macros allow for diversified input forms and enable elegant extraction and handling of complex structures. This can be efficiently managed using utility functions such as cl-ppcre:scan for regular expression matching, or more advanced parsing libraries for manipulating the input macro arguments.

Integrating these advanced macro techniques enhances the capability to write efficient, robust, and flexible macros that significantly extend Lisp's functionality. As we move forward, it will be clear how these principles apply in practical applications, including code generation and sophisticated compile-time computations.

6.5   Hygiene in Macros

In Lisp, macros offer unparalleled flexibility and power by allowing programmers to manipulate code structure and generate new code at compile time. However, the use of macros introduces the potential for variable name clashes and unintended capturing of symbols, leading to subtle and hard-to-debug errors. This problem is addressed through the concept of hygiene in macros.

Hygiene in macros ensures that the macro expansion does not inadvertently capture or clash with identifiers in the surrounding code. To illustrate this problem, consider the following macro definition and its potential pitfalls:

```
(defmacro capture-example (variable)
  '(let ((temp ,variable))
     (+ temp 10)))
```

Using this macro in a context where temp is already defined can lead to unexpected behavior:

```
(let ((temp 3))
  (capture-example 5))
```

If the macro is expanded in this context, the temp variable within the macro can unintentionally capture the outer temp. The resulting expan-

155

sion and evaluation would be as follows:

```
(let ((temp 3))
  (let ((temp 5))
    (+ temp 10)))
```

To prevent such name clashes, we employ macro hygiene techniques. One effective approach is to use gensym, a function that generates unique symbols to ensure that the names introduced by the macro do not conflict with any other symbols in the code. Here is an improved version of the previous macro using gensym:

```
(defmacro capture-example (variable)
  (let ((temp-sym (gensym "temp")))
    `(let ((,temp-sym ,variable))
       (+ ,temp-sym 10))))
```

This version ensures that temp-sym is a unique symbol each time the macro is expanded, thus avoiding any potential name clashes. When the macro is expanded, it will look similar to:

```
(let ((temp 3))
  (let ((#:temp1011 5))
    (+ #:temp1011 10)))
```

Here, #:temp1011 represents a unique symbol generated by gensym, which does not clash with the outer temp.

Hygiene not only pertains to avoiding name clashes but also to ensuring that the macro operates correctly in various contexts without unintended side effects. Another common issue is the inadvertent capturing of free variables. Consider the following macro:

```
(defmacro add-x (a)
  `(+ ,a x))
```

Using this macro will cause it to mistakenly capture the nearest x in the surrounding code, leading to unintended results:

```
(let ((x 10)
      (y 5))
  (add-x y)) ;; Evaluates to 15 instead of expected result
```

To preserve the intended free variable behavior, we can use a slightly more advanced technique that involves passing such variables as parameters to macro-generated code:

```
(defmacro add-x (a)
  (let ((x-sym (gensym "x")))
```

```
`(let ((,x-sym x))
   (+ ,a ,x-sym)))))
```

Now, the add-x macro correctly respects the intended scoping rules without capturing erroneous external x:

```
(let ((x 10)
      (y 5))
  (add-x y)) ;; Succesfully evaluates as expected.
```

Some advanced Lisp systems introduce built-in facilities for creating hygienic macros, such as syntax-rules in Scheme or define-syntax in Common Lisp. These constructs provide automatic handling of variable scoping and renaming, reducing the need for explicit gensym usage. Here is a simple example using define-syntax in Scheme:

```
(define-syntax capture-example
  (syntax-rules ()
    ((_ variable)
     (let ((temp variable))
       (+ temp 10)))))
```

This approach utilizes the syntax-rules system to automatically ensure hygiene, making the macro both easier to read and less error-prone.

It is imperative that programmers adopt hygienic practices when designing macros, as failing to do so can lead to unexpected behaviors, difficult-to-trace bugs, and reduced code maintainability. Using techniques like gensym or built-in hygienic macro systems ensures that macros perform their intended tasks without interfering with the surrounding code.

When writing macros, always consider the potential for variable capture and ensure that the hygiene of your macro definitions precludes such pitfalls. This attention to detail will lead to more robust and reliable macro-based solutions within your Lisp programs.

6.6 Macros vs Functions

In Lisp, both macros and functions play essential roles, but they serve distinct purposes and operate at different stages of code execution. Understanding the differences between macros and functions is important for leveraging the full potential of Lisp's metaprogramming capabilities.

Firstly, let's examine the primary distinction: evaluation timing. Functions operate during runtime. When a function is invoked, its arguments are evaluated, and then the function is applied to these evaluated arguments. Macros, on the other hand, operate during compile time (or more accurately, macro expansion time). A macro receives its arguments unevaluated, generates Lisp code, and this generated code is then compiled and run in place of the macro invocation.

Let us consider the syntax and behavior of a function. The following example defines a simple addition function:

```
(defun add (a b)
  (+ a b))
```

Calling (add 1 2) will evaluate 1 and 2 before applying the + operation, producing the expected result, 3.

Now, consider a macro with similar functionality:

```
(defmacro add-macro (a b)
  `(+ ,a ,b))
```

When (add-macro 1 2) is invoked, 1 and 2 are not evaluated initially. Instead, the macro expands into (+ 1 2), which is then compiled. The resulting compiled code is what executes at runtime.

This distinction extends to more complex scenarios, allowing macros to control the flow of evaluation. Consider the following example:

```
(defun increment-list (lst)
  (mapcar #'(lambda (x) (+ x 1)) lst))
```

In this function, mapcar applies an anonymous function that increments each element by 1. Attempting to implement a similar behavior using a macro might look like this:

```
(defmacro increment-list-macro (lst)
  `(mapcar #'(lambda (x) (+ x 1)) ,lst))
```

The macro increment-list-macro expands exactly into the code provided to mapcar, with lst interpolated during the macro expansion.

An essential aspect of macros involves avoiding unnecessary evaluation. Suppose we wished to implement a simple logging mechanism that only logs a message if debugging is enabled:

```
(defvar *debug* t)

(defun debug-log (msg)
  (when *debug*
    (print msg)))
```

Calling (debug-log "This is a log message.") prints the message when
debug is true. However, the parameter msg is always evaluated,
which can be inefficient if the construction of msg is expensive. A macro
version improves this by conditionally evaluating msg:

```
(defmacro debug-log-macro (msg)
  '(when *debug*
     (print ,msg)))
```

With (debug-log-macro "This is a log message."), the macro expansion
ensures msg is only evaluated when *debug* is true, providing a more
optimal solution.

Another critical difference is how they influence code readability and
maintainability. Macros can enable more concise and expressive constructs, but they can also obscure the flow of execution, making debugging more challenging.

To illustrate, consider the following macro that simplifies error checking:

```
(defmacro check-and-do (condition &rest body)
  '(if ,condition
       (progn ,@body)
       (error "Condition failed: ~A" ',condition)))
```

This macro expands into an if statement that either executes the body
if the condition is true or raises an error. For instance:

```
(check-and-do (> 3 2)
  (print "Condition passed."))
```

This code will print "Condition passed." because the condition (> 3 2)
is true. If it were false, an error would be raised. This macro enhances
code readability and reduces repetitive error-handling code blocks.

Lastly, consider macro hygiene. When writing macros, it's vital to prevent name collisions by ensuring that generated symbols are unique.

Lisp provides the gensym function to create unique symbols:

```
(defmacro safe-let ((var val) &body body)
  (let ((temp-var (gensym)))
    `(let ((,temp-var ,val))
       (if ,temp-var
           (let ((,var ,temp-var))
             ,@body)
           (error "Initialization failed")))))
```

This macro defines a safe-let construct, where temp-var is guaranteed to be unique, thus preventing any accidental name clashes within body.

Through these examples, we've seen that macros offer considerable power in controlling code evaluation and formation at compile time. However, their use should be balanced against the potential complexity they introduce, highlighting the importance of clear and maintainable code practices. Functions, executing at runtime, remain essential for straightforward procedural and functional operations, emphasizing evaluation of arguments within their invocation context.

6.7   Code Generation with Macros

Macrology in Lisp allows developers to write code that generates other code, a paradigm known as code generation. Code generation with macros can lead to more concise, readable, and maintainable code by abstracting repetitive patterns and boilerplate code. This section will delve into the mechanics of code generation using macros and explore various techniques and best practices to leverage this feature effectively.

A fundamental example of code generation using macros involves creating a macro that generates a sequence of similar function definitions. Consider a scenario where you need to define multiple functions that differ only slightly in their implementation. Without macros, each function would need its explicit definition, leading to repetitive and error-prone code. Macros can automate this process.

```
(defmacro define-simple-function (name param body)
  `(defun ,name (,param)
     ,body))
```

```
(define-simple-function my-add (x)
  (+ x 5))

(define-simple-function my-sub (x)
  (- x 5))
```

In this example, the define-simple-function macro generates the defun forms for two simple functions, my-add and my-sub. The macro takes the function name, parameter list, and body as arguments and constructs the corresponding function definitions. The backquote `() operator and comma (,) insert the macro arguments into the generated form, enabling the definition of multiple similar functions with minimal redundancy.

Macros also allow for more complex code generation scenarios, such as generating boilerplate code for data structure accessors and mutators. Consider a case where you need to define accessors and mutators for a given data structure:

```
(defmacro define-accessors-and-mutators (struct-name &rest fields)
  (let ((accessors '())
        (mutators '()))
    (dolist (field fields)
      (push '(defun ,(intern (concatenate 'string (symbol-name
                 struct-name) "-" (symbol-name field))) (instance)
                 (getf (cdr instance) ,field)) accessors)
      (push '(defun ,(intern (concatenate 'string "set-" (symbol-name
                 struct-name) "-" (symbol-name field))) (instance value)
                 (setf (getf (cdr instance) ,field) value)) mutators))
    '(progn ,@(nreverse accessors) ,@(nreverse mutators))))

(define-accessors-and-mutators my-struct name age)

(defparameter *example* (list 'my-struct :name "John Doe" :age 30))

(my-struct-name *example*) ; -> "John Doe"
(set-my-struct-age *example* 31)
(my-struct-age *example*) ; -> 31
```

In this macro, define-accessors-and-mutators takes a structure name and a list of fields. It iterates over the fields to generate accessor and mutator functions for each field. The dolist construct iterates over the fields list and pushes the generated forms to the accessors and mutators lists. Finally, all the generated forms are combined into a progn form which is returned by the macro. This approach abstracts away the repetitive code of writing individual accessors and mutators, enabling more maintainable and concise code.

An advanced use of code generation involves creating domain-specific languages (DSLs) within Lisp. By leveraging macros, you can design custom syntax and functionality tailored to specific problem domains. This technique is particularly useful for creating expressive and readable code for complex tasks. Here's a simplified example of creating a small DSL for describing HTML elements:

```
(defmacro html-element (name &rest content)
  `(cons ',name ',content))

(defmacro html (&rest elements)
  `(list ,@elements))

(html
  (html-element :div
    (html-element :p "This is a paragraph within a div.")
    (html-element :span "This is a span within a div.")))
```

In this example, the html-element macro generates cons cells representing HTML elements, while the html macro generates a list of these elements. This small DSL allows for a simple and readable way to describe nested HTML structures directly within Lisp code.

When creating code-generating macros, it is crucial to consider readability, maintainability, and debugging. Generated code can become complex and difficult to debug if not handled carefully. One approach to ensure clarity is to use helper functions and modularize the code generation logic. Here is a refined example using helper functions:

```
(defun generate-accessor (struct-name field)
  `(defun ,(intern (concatenate 'string (symbol-name struct-name) "-"
      (symbol-name field))) (instance)
    (getf (cdr instance) ,field)))

(defun generate-mutator (struct-name field)
  `(defun ,(intern (concatenate 'string "set-" (symbol-name
      struct-name) "-" (symbol-name field))) (instance value)
    (setf (getf (cdr instance) ,field) value)))
```

```
(defmacro define-accessors-and-mutators-v2 (struct-name &rest fields)
  (let ((accessors-mutators '()))
    (dolist (field fields)
      (push (generate-accessor struct-name field) accessors-mutators)
      (push (generate-mutator struct-name field) accessors-mutators))
    `(progn ,@(nreverse accessors-mutators)))))

(define-accessors-and-mutators-v2 my-new-struct id value)

(defparameter *new-example* (list 'my-new-struct :id 101 :value "
    Sample"))

(my-new-struct-id *new-example*) ; -> 101
(set-my-new-struct-value *new-example* "Updated")
(my-new-struct-value *new-example*) ; -> "Updated"
```

In this refined version, generate-accessor and generate-mutator helper functions encapsulate the logic for generating accessor and mutator function forms. The macro define-accessors-and-mutators-v2 utilizes these helper functions to create the complete set of accessors and mutators, enhancing readability and maintainability.

The ability to generate code with macros is a significant feature of Lisp, offering powerful ways to abstract and automate repetitive coding tasks. Proper utilization of this feature can lead to more expressive, concise, and maintainable code while avoiding common pitfalls associated with code complexity and debugging.

6.8   Debugging Macros

Effective debugging of macros in Lisp is crucial given their complexity and the potential for subtle bugs that can be difficult to trace. This section delves into methods and tools for debugging macros, ensuring more straightforward identification and resolution of issues. We will cover common strategies, the use of debugging functions, and practical examples.

One of the first steps in debugging macros is to understand the macro expansion. Macro expansion can be investigated using the macroexpand-1 and macroexpand functions. These tools display the code that a macro generates, allowing you to inspect it for correctness before full evaluation.

```
(defmacro my-add (a b)
  '(+ ,a ,b))

(macroexpand-1 '(my-add 2 3))
```

The output of the above code will be:

```
(+ 2 3)
```

In the example above, the macroexpand-1 function shows the immediate expansion of the my-add macro. For nested macros or macros that expand to other macros, you may use macroexpand, which recursively expands until it reaches a form that is not a macro.

Another strategy is to decompose macros into smaller, verifiable components. By breaking down a complex macro into simpler parts, each part can be individually tested and verified before combining them into a larger macro.

Consider a macro that generates a conditional logging statement:

```
(defmacro log-if (condition message)
  '(when ,condition
     (print ,message)))
```

If this macro does not work as expected, it can be debugged by isolating the individual components. Verify each smaller part, such as the when construct and the print statement, independently before integrating them.

An additional layer of complexity arises from the macro's context. Special attention must be paid to variable scope and symbol resolution. Mismanagement in these areas can lead to issues commonly referred to as macro hygiene problems.

To address hygiene issues, utilize unique symbols within the macro body using the gensym function, which generates a new, unique symbol.

```
(defmacro safe-log (message)
  (let ((msg-sym (gensym "msg")))
    '(let ((,msg-sym ,message))
       (print ,msg-sym))))
```

In the above example, gensym ensures that msg-sym does not inadvertently clash with existing symbols. The generated symbol is unique, minimizing the risk of conflicts.

Printing debug information during macro expansion can also be helpful. This technique involves inserting print statements within the macro definition to display intermediate results:

```
(defmacro debug-add (a b)
  '(let ((result (+ ,a ,b)))
     (print result)
     result))

(macroexpand-1 '(debug-add 4 5))
```

The output will inform you of the generated code:

```
(LET ((RESULT (+ 4 5)))
  (PRINT RESULT)
  RESULT)
```

When debugging more advanced macros, it is often useful to leverage the Lisp environment's integrated debugging tools. Features such as step-through debugging, breakpoints, and inspection functionalities enhance the process of identifying and resolving macro-related issues.

Consider the scenario where a macro generates an entire function definition. It is beneficial to check not only the structural accuracy but also the functional correctness post-expansion:

```
(defmacro create-adder (x)
  '(lambda (y)
     (+ ,x y)))

(defparameter adder-fn (create-adder 10))

(funcall adder-fn 5)
```

Evaluating the expanded form with macroexpand or executing the resulting code with test cases can confirm correct behavior. Furthermore, adding checks or assertions within the macro definition validates assumptions and ensures that edge cases are managed properly:

```
(defmacro create-adder-checked (x)
  (assert (numberp x) (x) "Argument must be a number")
  '(lambda (y)
```

```
(+ ,x y)))
```

Utilizing assertions guarantees that the macro arguments conform to expected types or values, catching issues early in the macro expansion phase.

Lastly, documenting macros thoroughly and providing usage examples allow peers and future users to understand the intended functionality and constraints, which aids in debugging and maintaining these macros. Careful attention to detail and methodical debugging practices ultimately result in robust, reliable macros that can be confidently used in complex Lisp programs.

6.9   Common Macro Pitfalls

Macros in Lisp provide an exceptional level of flexibility and power for code generation and abstraction. However, this capability comes with potential pitfalls that can lead to subtly incorrect code, maintenance difficulties, and performance issues. Understanding these common pitfalls is crucial to avoid introducing bugs or inefficiencies into your programs. The following pitfalls frequently occur when writing macros, and this section aims to make you aware of them, enabling you to write better and more robust macros.

1. Variable Capture and Shadowing:

The most notorious problem with macros is variable capture, where a macro unintentionally captures or modifies a variable from its expansion context. Consider the following macro:

```
(defmacro add-one (x)
  `(+ ,x 1))
```

Using the following code:

```
(let ((x 10))
  (add-one x))
```

The resulting expression after macro expansion is:

```
(+ x 1)
```

Here, x is correctly replaced, but if the macro used a local variable also named x internally, it could lead to conflicts. To prevent this, use gensym to create unique symbols:

```
(defmacro add-one (x)
  (let ((g (gensym)))
    `(let ((,g ,x))
       (+ ,g 1))))
```

This approach generates a unique symbol, avoiding name conflicts.

2. Incorrectly Quoted Code:

Improper usage of quoting and unquoting can lead to incorrect expansions. Consider this macro:

```
(defmacro increment (var)
  `(setq ,var (+ ,var 1)))
```

This macro seems straightforward but could malfunction if not used carefully. For instance:

```
(increment x)
```

This expands correctly to:

```
(setq x (+ x 1))
```

However, if increment is invoked in a more complex expression, such as within nested macros or functions, incorrect quoting can quickly complicate things. Verify each part of the macro, checking which elements should be quoted and which should be evaluated immediately.

3. Evaluation Order:

Macro arguments are not evaluated before being passed to the macro. This characteristic differs from functions where arguments are evaluated first. For example:

```
(defmacro swap (a b)
  `(let ((temp ,a))
     (setq ,a ,b)
     (setq ,b temp)))
```

Using the macro as:

```
(swap x y)
```

The macro expands to:

```
(let ((temp x))
  (setq x y)
  (setq y temp))
```

Here, a and b are inappropriately swapped if they represent more complex expressions. Consider ensuring they are simple variables or ensuring they produce valid results upon expansion.

4. Side Effects:

Be cautious with macros producing side effects, especially when macro arguments have side effects themselves. Consider:

```
(defmacro increment (x)
  '(setq ,x (+ ,x 1)))
```

Invoking increment with an expression, such as:

```
(increment (foo))
```

The expansion expects + to increment (foo), which may produce unintended effects if foo has side effects or returns varying values with each call. Avoid wrapping expressions with side effects directly into macros unless the macro explicitly handles such cases.

5. Complexity and Debuggability:

Macros can obscure the simplicity and clarity of code, particularly when they become overly complex. Balanced usage of macros is advisable, ensuring they remain straightforward and maintainable. For problematic macros, the macro expansion itself can be debugged using:

```
(macroexpand '(your-macro call))
```

Additionally, some implementations provide extended debugging tools to trace or step through macro expansions.

6. Overuse and Poor Abstraction:

Abusing macros by overusing them instead of conventional functions can lead to code that is difficult to maintain or understand. Use macros where they provide clear benefits, primarily for syntactic abstraction or compile-time computations rather than runtime functions. Evaluate whether a more straightforward function can fulfill the needs before resorting to macro solutions.

Through cautious writing, careful expansion tests, and leveraging Lisp's powerful macro expansion tools, these pitfalls can be mitigated, leading to more robust and maintainable code. Be vigilant to identify these issues early in the macro design process.

6.10 Practical Examples of Macros

To fully appreciate the power of macros in Lisp, it is essential to explore practical examples that demonstrate their utility and flexibility. This section will delve into several real-world applications of macros, highlighting how they can simplify complex tasks, enhance code readability, and reduce redundancy.

Consider the classic example of a macro that provides a convenient syntax for when, a commonly used conditional construct in Lisp:

```
(defmacro my-when (condition &body body)
  '(if ,condition
       (progn ,@body)))
```

In this example, the my-when macro takes a condition and a body of code to execute if the condition evaluates to true. The progn function ensures that multiple expressions are evaluated sequentially. Here is how one might use this macro:

```
(my-when (> x 10)
  (format t "x is greater than 10")
  (setq y (* x 2)))
```

This invocation checks if x is greater than 10 and, if so, prints a message and sets the value of y to twice the value of x.

Another practical use case for macros is creating a with-open-file macro that streamlines file operations, ensuring that files are properly closed after operations, preventing resource leaks:

```
(defmacro with-open-file ((var filename &rest options) &body body)
  '(let ((,var (open ,filename ,@options)))
     (unwind-protect
         (progn ,@body)
       (when (and ,var (streamp ,var))
         (close ,var)))))
```

This macro simplifies file handling by taking a variable, a filename, and a list of options for opening the file. It ensures that the file is closed after the body of the macro has been evaluated, even if an error occurs.

Here is an example of using with-open-file:

```
(with-open-file (stream "example.txt" :direction :output)
  (format stream "Hello, file!"))
```

This invocation opens example.txt for writing and ensures that the file is closed after writing the message.

Macros can also help define domain-specific languages (DSLs) within Lisp, making it more expressive and suitable for specific problems. Consider the defparameterised-class macro that facilitates class definitions with default initial values for parameters:

```
(defmacro defparameterised-class (name parameters &body slots)
  '(defclass ,name ()
     ,(loop for param in parameters
            collect '(,param :initarg ,(intern (concatenate 'string ":" (
                      symbol-name param)))
                             :initform nil :accessor ,(intern (
                             concatenate 'string (symbol-name
                             name) "-" (symbol-name param)))
                             ))
     ,@slots))
```

This macro defines a class with given parameters and auto-generates accessor methods for each parameter. Here is an example of how to use this macro:

```
(defparameterised-class my-class (param1 param2)
  ((slot1 :initform 100)
   (slot2 :initform "default")))
```

The resulting class my-class will have param1 and param2 as its parameters, along with slot1 and slot2 as its slots, with auto-generated accessor methods for accessing and modifying these parameters.

Here is how one might instantiate an object and use the accessors:

```
(let ((obj (make-instance 'my-class :param1 42 :param2 "test")))
  (format t "param1: ~A, param2: ~A, slot1: ~A, slot2: ~A~%"
          (my-class-param1 obj)
          (my-class-param2 obj)
          (slot1 obj)
          (slot2 obj)))
```

Macros not only simplify coding but also facilitate building abstractions that tailor the language for specific solutions. The flexibility and power provided allow programmers to create more concise, readable, and maintainable code, illustrating the prowess of Lisp's macro system.

6.11   Introduction to Meta-programming

Meta-programming refers to the practice of writing programs that have the ability to treat other programs as data. This allows programs to read, generate, analyze, or transform other programs, and even modify themselves while running. In the context of Lisp, meta-programming becomes particularly powerful due to the language's homoiconic property, which means that the structure of Lisp code is inherently represented as Lisp data structures.

A key aspect of meta-programming in Lisp is the use of macros, which we have explored extensively in previous sections. Lisp macros enable programmers to extend the language by defining new syntactic constructs in a way that appears seamless in regular code. This ability to create domain-specific languages or to introduce new abstractions without sacrificing performance or readability is a central feature of Lisp's meta-programming capabilities.

To understand meta-programming deeply, it is essential to grasp how Lisp treats code and data interchangeably. In Lisp, the primary data structure is the list, and code itself is written in the form of lists. For example, a function call in Lisp, such as adding two numbers, is written as:

```
(+ 2 3)
```

This expression is both a piece of executable code and a list containing three elements: the symbol $+$, and the numbers 2 and 3. This duality allows Lisp programs to manipulate their own code with ease.

One of the foundational tools for meta-programming in Lisp is the quote function. The quote function prevents its argument from being evaluated, treating it as a data structure instead of executable code. For example:

```
(quote (+ 2 3))
```

This returns the list $(+ 2 3)$ without evaluating it. A shorthand for using quote is the apostrophe ('), making the above example equivalent to:

```
'(+ 2 3)
```

This simple mechanism is the cornerstone of more sophisticated meta-programming techniques. By quoting code, macros can inspect and transform program fragments before they are executed.

Consider a simple macro that swaps the arguments of a function call:

```
(defmacro swap-args (fn a b)
  '(,fn ,b ,a))
```

Here, the backquote (or quasiquote,`) is used to construct a new list in which the unquote operator , is utilized to insert the evaluated results of fn, a, and b. This macro, when called as follows:

```
(swap-args + 2 3)
```

would expand to:

```
(+ 3 2)
```

and consequently evaluate to 5.

Another powerful technique in meta-programming is the use of eval, which takes a piece of quoted code and evaluates it in the current environment. This allows dynamic generation and execution of code, although it must be used with caution due to potential security and maintenance issues. An example of eval in use is:

```
(eval '(+ 2 3))
```

which, unsurprisingly, returns 5.

Meta-programming is not limited to the manipulation of function calls or arithmetic operations. It can be extended to construct entire programs dynamically, implement optimizations, or even to create new control structures. For example, let's create a macro that defines a new looping construct:

```
(defmacro repeat (n &body body)
  '(dotimes (i ,n)
     ,@body))
```

This repeat macro takes a number n and a body of code, and executes the body n times using the dotimes construct. When used as follows:

```
(repeat 3
  (print "Hello"))
```

it expands to:

```
(dotimes (i 3)
  (print "Hello"))
```

which results in printing "Hello" three times.

The power of meta-programming in Lisp allows for extensive customization and extension of the language. It enables the creation of powerful abstractions and domain-specific languages tailored to specific tasks and problem domains. As macros and higher-order functions combine, they offer unparalleled flexibility and expressiveness.

Continuing our exploration of meta-programming, it is crucial to maintain code clarity and ensure that macros are well-documented and tested. Misuse of meta-programming techniques can lead to code that is difficult to read, understand, and maintain. Thus, while meta-programming stands as a powerful tool in a Lisp programmer's toolkit, it also demands a high degree of discipline and insight to wield effectively.

6.12   Best Practices for Writing Macros

When developing macros in Lisp, adopting best practices can significantly enhance code readability, maintainability, and robustness. This section covers essential guidelines to follow, ensuring that macros are well-designed and effectively integrated into your programming projects.

1. Understand When to Use Macros: Before writing a macro, evaluate if a macro is necessary or if a function could suffice. Macros are best utilized when they need to manipulate code forms at compile-time, such as generating new syntax or reusable code templates. If the same functionality can be achieved using functions, prefer functions due to their simplicity and ease of debugging.

2. Preserve Code Clarity: Macros can obscure the flow of code if not written clearly. Strive to make macro definitions transparent and document their behavior thoroughly. Use descriptive names for macros and their arguments. Annotate the purpose and examples of usage within comments.

173

3.   Protect Against Unintentional Variable Capture (Hygiene):
When writing macros, ensure they are 'hygienic' by avoiding
unintentional variable capture. This can be achieved by using Lisp's
gensym function to generate unique symbols. Consider the following
example:

```
(defmacro with-gensyms ((&rest names) &body body)
  "Generate unique symbols for each name in NAMES and bind them
    within BODY."
  (let ((bindings (mapcar (lambda (n)
                           '(,n (gensym)))
                         names)))
   '(let ,bindings ,@body)))

(defmacro my-macro (x)
  (with-gensyms (temp)
   '(let ((,temp ,x))
      (+ ,temp ,temp))))
```

In this example, the with-gensyms macro ensures that the temp variable
inside my-macro does not unintentionally capture or clash with other
variables in the user's code.

4. Use Backquote and Comma for Readability: Lisp's backquote (')
and comma (,) operators simplify the process of generating code structures within macros. The backquote allows embedding code directly,
and commas enable evaluation of expressions within the quoted structure. Example:

```
(defmacro example-macro (name)
  '(defun ,name ()
     (print "Hello, World!")))
```

This macro generates a function definition with the specified name.

5. Test Macros Thoroughly: Macros can be complex and prone to
subtle bugs. Write extensive test cases for your macros to validate
their behavior across diverse scenarios. Testing not only ensures correctness but also aids in documenting expected behavior.

6. Avoid Heavy Computation in Macros: Since macros execute at
compile-time, avoid placing heavy computation or side effects within
them. Perform extensive calculations at runtime within the generated
code rather than the macro itself. This practice keeps compilation times

reasonable and maintains separation between compilation and execution time.

7. Be Explicit About Return Values: Ensure that the code generated by macros returns expected types and values. Implicit and unclear return values can cause unexpected behavior in the macro's usage context.

8. Adhere to Lisp Idioms: Write macros in a way that integrates seamlessly with Lisp idioms and conventions. Follow common naming schemes, argument patterns, and code structure conventions native to Lisp. This harmonization with Lisp's idiomatic usage ensures that other programmers can understand and maintain your macros more easily.

9. Provide Ample Documentation: Document macros thoroughly with docstrings and comments. Outline the macro's purpose, expected arguments, and potential side effects. Provide examples of usage for clarity. Good documentation helps others (and your future self) understand and use the macro correctly.

10. Debug Macros Systematically: Use Lisp's macro expansion capabilities to debug macros systematically. Employ the macroexpand and macroexpand-1 functions to view the expanded forms of macros. This approach facilitates understanding how the macro generates code and identifying potential issues.

```
CL-USER> (macroexpand '(example-macro my-func))
(DEFUN MY-FUNC NIL (PRINT "Hello, World!"))
T
```

This output allows verification of the macro's expansion against the intended generated code.

11. Consider Macro Simplicity Over Cleverness: While macros offer powerful code manipulation capabilities, strive for simplicity over cleverness. Clever macros may leverage obscure behavior for compactness but can be challenging to read, debug, and maintain. Simplicity in macro design ensures that they are accessible and comprehensible to a broader set of programmers.

12. Review and Refactor: Regularly review and refactor macros as part of overall code hygiene. As the codebase evolves, some macros may become outdated or suboptimal. Refactoring macros ensures they remain efficient and aligned with current project requirements.

Following these best practices ensures that the macros you write are effective, maintainable, and beneficial to your Lisp programming endeavors.

Chapter 7

Advanced Data Structures

This chapter delves into advanced data structures in Lisp, covering balanced trees, graphs and their algorithms, priority queues, and heaps. It further explores sets, bags, and variants of linked lists, including tries and suffix trees. Complex hash table implementations and persistent data structures are examined, along with memory-efficient designs. The chapter also addresses the design and custom creation of data structures tailored to specific needs, giving readers the knowledge to implement sophisticated and efficient data management solutions in their Lisp programs.

7.1 Introduction to Advanced Data Structures

When developing effective programs, the choice of data structure is integral to both the performance and maintainability of the software. In Lisp, as with many other languages, advanced data structures provide mechanisms to store, manipulate, and retrieve data with efficiency and precision. This section introduces key concepts and sets the stage for in-depth discussions on various advanced data structures.

Every data structure is designed to handle certain types of operations effectively. These operations generally include insertion, deletion, searching, and traversal. The efficiency of these operations can greatly influence the overall performance of an application. We will explore balanced trees, graphs, heaps, priority queues, sets, bags, linked lists, tries, suffix trees, complex hash tables, and persistent data structures.

```
(defun example-function (data-structure)
  "An example function demonstrating the structure of a Lisp
      function."
  (let ((result nil))
    ;; perform operations on data-structure
    ;; return the result
    result))
```

In Lisp, list processing and functional paradigms emphasize immutability and recursion, characteristics that shape the way data structures are designed and implemented. For instance, tree structures maintain balance properties to ensure logarithmic depth, making operations like search, insertion, and deletion efficient.

Balanced trees, such as AVL trees and Red-Black trees, ensure that no single path in the tree is disproportionately long compared to others, thereby providing logarithmic time complexity for most operations. This section details the intricacies of maintaining balance and the algorithms involved.

```
1  Function InsertNode(node, value):
2      if value < node.value then
3          if node.left = nil then
4              node.left ← new Node(value);
5          else
6              InsertNode(node.left, value);

7      if value > node.value then
8          if node.right = nil then
9              node.right ← new Node(value);
10         else
11             InsertNode(node.right, value);
```

Graphs and their associated algorithms form another cornerstone of sophisticated data structures. Graphs can represent networks of interconnected objects, with widespread applications in social networks, biological networks, and routing algorithms. Both directed and undirected graphs will be analyzed, along with algorithms for traversing and searching graphs, such as Depth-First Search (DFS) and Breadth-First

Search (BFS).

```
(defun breadth-first-search (graph start-node)
  "Perform BFS on GRAPH starting from START-NODE."
  (let ((queue (list start-node))
        (visited '()))
    (loop while queue do
      (let ((node (pop queue)))
        (unless (member node visited)
          (push node visited)
          (dolist (neighbor (get-neighbors graph node))
            (push neighbor queue)))))
    visited))
```

Priority queues and heaps are fundamental in scenarios where the order of processing matters. Priority queues allow elements to be processed based on their priority rather than their insertion order. Heaps, which are a type of complete binary tree, serve as an efficient implementation of priority queues. Operations such as insert, delete, and extract-min (or extract-max) are optimized through the structure of the heap.

```
(defun heap-insert (heap value)
  "Insert VALUE into HEAP, maintaining the heap property."
  (vector-push-extend value heap)
  (heapify-up heap (1- (length heap))))

(defun heapify-up (heap index)
  "Ensure the heap property is maintained from a node to the root."
  (let ((parent (floor (/ (1- index) 2))))
    (when (and (>= index 1)
               (> (aref heap parent) (aref heap index)))
      (rotatef (aref heap parent) (aref heap index))
      (heapify-up heap parent))))
```

This section provides the foundation for understanding the motivations, algorithms, and implementations of various advanced data structures. The subsequent sections elaborate on the specifics, covering implementation details and performance considerations. The correct application of these data structures enhances the efficiency and scalability of Lisp programs, enabling developers to tackle complex data handling with confidence and precision.

7.2   Balanced Trees

Balanced trees are a critical component in the realm of advanced data structures. They ensure that operations such as insertion, deletion, and lookup are performed efficiently by maintaining an optimal height. Among the most notable balanced trees are AVL trees and Red-Black trees. This section elucidates their mechanisms, providing a comprehensive insight into their functions and implementations.

AVL Trees

AVL (Adelson-Velsky and Landis) trees are self-balancing binary search trees. They maintain their balance by enforcing a condition that the height difference (balance factor) of any node's left and right subtrees is not greater than one.

The core operations (insertion and deletion) in an AVL tree involve standard binary search tree operations followed by specific rotations to restore balance if it is disturbed. The types of rotations are:

- **Single Right Rotation (LL Rotation)**

- **Single Left Rotation (RR Rotation)**

- **Left-Right Rotation (LR Rotation)**

- **Right-Left Rotation (RL Rotation)**

Let's consider the implementation details of these rotations.

```
(defun right-rotate (y)
     (let ((x (left y))
           (T2 (right x)))
          (setf (right x) y)
          (setf (left y) T2)
          (setf (height y) (max (height (left y)) (height (right y)) 1))
          (setf (height x) (max (height (left x)) (height (right x)) 1))
          x))

(defun left-rotate (x)
     (let ((y (right x))
           (T2 (left y)))
          (setf (left y) x)
          (setf (right x) T2)
```

```
        (setf (height x) (max (height (left x)) (height (right x)) 1))
        (setf (height y) (max (height (left y)) (height (right y)) 1))
        y))

(defun get-balance (n)
  (if (null n)
      0
      (- (height (left n)) (height (right n)))))
```

The insertion operation in an AVL tree includes calculating the balance factor and performing rotations if the tree becomes unbalanced.

```
(defun avl-insert (node key)
  (if (null node)
      (make-avl-node key)
      (progn
        (if (< key (key node))
            (setf (left node) (avl-insert (left node) key))
            (setf (right node) (avl-insert (right node) key)))))

  (setf (height node) (1+ (max (height (left node)) (height (right
      node)))))

  (let ((balance (get-balance node)))
    (cond ((and (> balance 1) (< key (key (left node))))
           (right-rotate node))
          ((and (< balance -1) (> key (key (right node))))
           (left-rotate node))
          ((and (> balance 1) (> key (key (left node))))
           (progn
             (setf (left node) (left-rotate (left node)))
             (right-rotate node)))
          ((and (< balance -1) (< key (key (right node))))
           (progn
             (setf (right node) (right-rotate (right node)))
             (left-rotate node)))))
  node)
```

Red-Black Trees

Red-Black trees, another type of self-balancing BST, maintain balance with a different approach. They enforce that every node is either red or black, root nodes are black, red nodes must not have red children, and the path from the root to the leaves contains the same number of black nodes.

Red-Black trees involve complex insertion and deletion algorithms. Here, we will present a simplified version of the insertion operation.

Algorithm 3: Red-Black Tree Insertion Algorithm

Input: Insert node into the Red-Black Tree
Output: Balanced Red-Black Tree

1 insert(node);
2 node.color ← RED;
3 **while** *node is not root and parent.color = RED* **do**
4   **if** *parent is the left child of grandparent* **then**
5   uncle ← grandparent.right;
6   **if** *uncle.color = RED* **then**
7   parent.color ← BLACK;
8   uncle.color ← BLACK;
9   grandparent.color ← RED;
10   node ← grandparent;
11   **else**
12   **if** *node is the right child of parent* **then**
13   node ← parent;
14   left-rotate(node);
15   parent.color ← BLACK;
16   grandparent.color ← RED;
17   right-rotate(grandparent);
18   **else**
19   uncle ← grandparent.left;
20   **if** *uncle.color = RED* **then**
21   parent.color ← BLACK;
22   uncle.color ← BLACK;
23   grandparent.color ← RED;
24   node ← grandparent;
25   **else**
26   **if** *node is the left child of parent* **then**
27   node ← parent;
28   right-rotate(node);
29   parent.color ← BLACK;
30   grandparent.color ← RED;
31   left-rotate(grandparent);
32 root.color ← BLACK;

Red-Black trees guarantee $O(\log n)$ time complexity for the fundamental operations. They are often preferred in implementations where rapid insertions and deletions are required due to their smoother and easier to implement balancing techniques compared to AVL trees.

Properties and Applications

Both AVL trees and Red-Black trees are crucial for applications where balanced search operations are paramount. AVL trees are more rigidly balanced, usually resulting in faster lookups, but incur a higher cost in insertions and deletions due to frequent rotations. Conversely, Red-Black trees strike a balance between lookups and structural modifications, making them suitable for real-world applications such as database indexing and memory management.

It is essential to choose the appropriate tree based on specific application needs, performance requirements, and operational efficiency. Understanding these structures' underlying algorithms is fundamental for performance optimization in Lisp programming. Both AVL and Red-Black trees play a pivotal role in enhancing data retrieval speeds and maintaining organized data structures in large-scale systems.

7.3   Graphs and Graph Algorithms

Graphs are an essential data structure in computer science, representing relationships between objects in a highly flexible and dynamic manner. A graph G is defined as a pair (V, E), where V is a set of vertices (or nodes) and E is a set of edges connecting pairs of vertices. Graphs can be classified into several categories based on their properties, such as directed vs. undirected, weighted vs. unweighted, cyclic vs. acyclic, and connected vs. disconnected.

In Lisp, graphs can be represented using various data structures, including adjacency lists, adjacency matrices, and edge lists. The choice of representation depends on the specific requirements of the application and the operations that need to be performed efficiently.

Adjacency List Representation
In an adjacency list representation, each vertex maintains a list of adjacent vertices. This representation is memory-efficient, especially for sparse graphs.

```
(setq *graph* (make-hash-table :test 'equal))

(defun add-edge (graph v1 v2)
  (let ((adj (gethash v1 graph '())))
    (setf (gethash v1 graph) (cons v2 adj))))
```

184

```
(defun add-vertex (graph vertex)
  (setf (gethash vertex graph) '()))

(add-vertex *graph* 'A)
(add-vertex *graph* 'B)
(add-vertex *graph* 'C)
(add-edge *graph* 'A 'B)
(add-edge *graph* 'B 'C)
(add-edge *graph* 'C 'A)
```

Adjacency Matrix Representation

An adjacency matrix uses a 2D array to represent connections between vertices, where each cell (i, j) indicates the presence (and possibly weight) of an edge between vertex i and vertex j. This representation is particularly suitable for dense graphs.

```
(defparameter *size* 3)
(defparameter *matrix* (make-array (list *size* *size*) :
    initial-element 0))

(defun add-edge-matrix (matrix v1 v2)
  (setf (aref matrix v1 v2) 1))

(add-edge-matrix *matrix* 0 1)
(add-edge-matrix *matrix* 1 2)
(add-edge-matrix *matrix* 2 0)
```

Graph Traversal Algorithms

To explore or search through a graph, traversal algorithms such as Depth-First Search (DFS) and Breadth-First Search (BFS) are commonly employed. These algorithms are fundamental for solving problems related to connectivity, pathfinding, and cycle detection.

Depth-First Search (DFS)

DFS explores a graph by starting at a root vertex and recursively visiting adjacent vertices before backtracking. The algorithm can be implemented using recursive function calls or an explicit stack.

```
(defun dfs-util (graph vertex visited)
  (unless (member vertex visited)
    (setf visited (cons vertex visited))
    (dolist (adj (gethash vertex graph))
      (setf visited (dfs-util graph adj visited)))))
```

185

```
    visited)

(defun dfs (graph start)
  (dfs-util graph start '()))
```

```
CL-USER> (dfs *graph* 'A)
(A B C)
```

Breadth-First Search (BFS)

BFS explores a graph level by level, utilizing a queue to manage the frontier of exploration. This algorithm is particularly effective for finding the shortest path in unweighted graphs.

```
(defun bfs (graph start)
  (let ((visited '())
        (queue (list start)))
    (loop
        until (null queue)
        for vertex = (pop queue)
        unless (member vertex visited)
        do (progn
             (setf visited (cons vertex visited))
             (setf queue (append queue (gethash vertex graph)))))
    (nreverse visited)))
```

```
CL-USER> (bfs *graph* 'A)
(A B C)
```

Shortest Path Algorithms

For weighted graphs, finding the shortest path between vertices is a common problem. Dijkstra's algorithm and the Bellman-Ford algorithm are widely used for this purpose.

Dijkstra's Algorithm

Dijkstra's algorithm finds the shortest paths from a source vertex to all other vertices in a graph with non-negative edge weights. It employs a priority queue to efficiently retrieve the next vertex with the smallest tentative distance.

```
(defun dijkstra (graph source)
  (let ((dist (make-hash-table))
        (prev (make-hash-table))
        (pq (make-heap :type '<)))
    (maphash (lambda (vertex _)
               (setf (gethash vertex dist) most-positive-fixnum)
```

186

```
                  (insert-heap pq vertex (gethash vertex dist)))
           graph)
    (setf (gethash source dist) 0)
    (insert-heap pq source 0)
    (loop while (not (heap-empty-p pq))
          for u = (extract-min-heap pq)
          for neighbors = (gethash u graph)
          do (dolist (neighbor neighbors)
               (let* ((v (car neighbor))
                      (weight (cdr neighbor))
                      (alt (+ (gethash u dist) weight)))
                 (when (< alt (gethash v dist))
                 (setf (gethash v dist) alt)
                 (insert-heap pq v alt)
                 (setf (gethash v prev) u)))))
    (values dist prev)))
```

Kruskal's Algorithm

Kruskal's algorithm is used for finding the Minimum Spanning Tree
(MST) of a graph, ensuring that all vertices are connected with the minimum possible total edge weight. It sorts all edges by weight and adds
them one by one to the MST, ensuring no cycles are formed.

```
(defun find (x parent)
  (if (eq (gethash x parent) x)
      x
      (setf (gethash x parent) (find (gethash x parent) parent))))

(defun union (x y parent rank)
  (let ((root-x (find x parent))
        (root-y (find y parent)))
    (unless (eq root-x root-y)
      (if (> (gethash root-x rank) (gethash root-y rank))
          (setf (gethash root-y parent) root-x)
          (progn
            (setf (gethash root-x parent) root-y)
            (when (eq (gethash root-x rank) (gethash root-y rank))
              (setf (gethash root-y rank) (+ (gethash root-y rank) 1))
              ))))))

(defun kruskal (graph)
  (let ((edges (sort (flatten graph) #'car-less-than-car :key #'cdr))
```

```
        (parent (make-hash-table))
        (rank (make-hash-table))
        (mst '()))
  (maphash (lambda (vertex _)
              (setf (gethash vertex parent) vertex)
              (setf (gethash vertex rank) 0))
          graph)
  (dolist (edge edges)
    (let ((u (car edge))
          (v (cdr edge)))
      (unless (eq (find u parent) (find v parent))
        (push edge mst)
        (union u v parent rank))))
  mst))
```

Graphs and their corresponding algorithms are powerful tools that provide solutions to numerous computational problems, from optimization to network analysis. Implementing and understanding these core algorithms in Lisp enables the development of efficient and robust applications in various domains.

7.4   Priority Queues

Priority queues are a fundamental data structure in computer science, widely used in various algorithms such as Dijkstra's shortest path, Huffman coding for data compression, and task scheduling in operating systems. Unlike regular queues where the order of elements is determined by their arrival sequence, priority queues order elements based on their priority. The two common types of priority queue operations are insert (adds an element with a priority) and extract-min or extract-max (removes and returns the element with the highest or lowest priority, respectively).

In Lisp, priority queues can be implemented using different underlying data structures, such as heaps, balanced trees, or even arrays. The choice of the underlying data structure has a significant impact on the efficiency of the priority queue operations. Among these, binary heaps are particularly popular due to their efficiency and simplicity in implementation.

A binary heap can be implemented using an array. This representation ensures efficient insert and extract-min operations, each with a time complexity of $O(\log n)$. Below, we will outline a simple implementation of a min-heap in Lisp, which will serve as the foundation for our priority queue.

```
(defclass min-heap ()
  ((data :initform nil :accessor data)))

(defun parent (index)
  (floor (/ (1- index) 2)))

(defun left-child (index)
  (* 2 (1+ index)))

(defun right-child (index)
  (1+ (* 2 (1+ index))))

(defun heapify-up (heap index)
  (let ((parent-index (parent index)))
    (when (and (>= index 0)
               (< (aref (data heap) index)
                  (aref (data heap) parent-index)))
      (rotatef (aref (data heap) index)
               (aref (data heap) parent-index))
      (heapify-up heap parent-index))))

(defun insert (heap element)
  (vector-push-extend element (data heap))
  (heapify-up heap (1- (length (data heap)))))

(defun heapify-down (heap index)
  (let ((left-index (left-child index))
        (right-index (right-child index))
        (smallest index))
    (when (< left-index (length (data heap)))
      (when (< (aref (data heap) left-index)
               (aref (data heap) index))
        (setf smallest left-index)))
    (when (< right-index (length (data heap)))
      (when (< (aref (data heap) right-index)
               (aref (data heap) smallest))
        (setf smallest right-index)))
```

189

```
    (unless (= index smallest)
      (rotatef (aref (data heap) index)
               (aref (data heap) smallest))
      (heapify-down heap smallest)))))

(defun extract-min (heap)
  (let ((min (aref (data heap) 0)))
    (setf (aref (data heap) 0)
          (aref (data heap) (1- (length (data heap)))))
    (vector-pop (data heap))
    (heapify-down heap 0)
    min))
```

This implementation uses a class min-heap to encapsulate the underlying array, with auxiliary functions to manage the heap's properties. Specifically, the heapify-up function restores the heap invariant by moving an element up the tree, while heapify-down does so by moving an element down.

To demonstrate the usage of our min-heap priority queue, consider the following Lisp script:

```
(defparameter *heap* (make-instance 'min-heap))

(insert *heap* 5)
(insert *heap* 3)
(insert *heap* 8)
(insert *heap* 1)

(format t "Min element: ~a~%" (extract-min *heap*)) ; Should print
    1
(format t "Min element: ~a~%" (extract-min *heap*)) ; Should print
    3
```

Min element: 1
Min element: 3

This script creates an instance of min-heap, inserts several elements, and extracts the minimum element twice, demonstrating that elements are correctly ordered by priority.

In practice, min-heaps effectively support insertion and extraction operations with logarithmic time complexity. For scenarios requiring additional functionality, such as decrease-key operations (useful in algorithms like Dijkstra's), Fibonacci heaps offer more favorable amortized time complexities. Although more complex in implementation, Fibonacci heaps allow for $O(1)$ amortized time complexity for insert and decrease-key operations, while maintaining $O(\log n)$ for extract-min.

Priority queues' flexibility and efficiency make them indispensable in algorithm design and system implementation, enabling the creation of robust and performant solutions.

7.5 Heaps and Heap Operations

A heap is a specialized tree-based data structure that adheres to the heap property. Heaps are commonly used to implement priority queues, which allow for efficient retrieval of the highest (or lowest) priority element. This section explores the various types of heaps, their properties, and fundamental operations.

Definitions and Properties

A heap can be classified as a *min-heap* or a *max-heap*. In a min-heap, the key at the root must be the minimum among all keys present in the heap. Conversely, in a max-heap, the key at the root is the maximum. Heaps must also satisfy the *complete binary tree* property, where all levels, except possibly the last, are fully filled, and the last level has all keys as left as possible.

Consider the following properties of a heap:

- Heap Property: Each parent node i is less than or equal to its children in a min-heap. Mathematically, this is expressed as $A[i] \leq A[2i + 1]$ and $A[i] \leq A[2i + 2]$, where A is the array representing the heap.

- Complete Binary Tree Property: The structure is a complete binary tree with level d containing 2^d nodes, except possibly for the final level.

Basic Operations

Key operations on heaps include insertion, extraction, and deletion. These operations ensure the heap property is maintained and have specific procedures for efficiency.

Insertion Operation

191

The process of inserting a new element into a heap involves adding the element to the end and then restoring the heap property by "bubbling up" the new element to its proper position.

```
(defun heap-insert (heap element)
  (let ((size (length heap)))
    (setf (aref heap size) element)
    (bubble-up heap size)))

(defun bubble-up (heap index)
  (let ((parent (floor (/ (- index 1) 2))))
    (when (and (>= index 0)
               (< (aref heap index) (aref heap parent)))
      (rotatef (aref heap index) (aref heap parent))
      (bubble-up heap parent))))
```

Extraction Operation

Extracting the root element, often referred to as *extract-min* in min-heaps, involves removing the root and replacing it with the last element. The heap property is then restored by "bubbling down" this element.

```
(defun heap-extract-min (heap)
  (let ((min (aref heap 0)))
    (setf (aref heap 0) (aref heap (1- (length heap))))
    (pop heap)
    (bubble-down heap 0)
    min))

(defun bubble-down (heap index)
  (let ((left (1+ (* 2 index)))
        (right (2+ (* 2 index)))
        (smallest index))
    (when (and (< left (length heap))
               (< (aref heap left) (aref heap smallest)))
      (setf smallest left))
    (when (and (< right (length heap))
               (< (aref heap right) (aref heap smallest)))
      (setf smallest right))
    (when (/= index smallest)
      (rotatef (aref heap index) (aref heap smallest))
      (bubble-down heap smallest))))
```

Deletion Operation

Deleting any arbitrary element from the heap involves replacing it with the last element and subsequently performing a bubble-up or bubble-down as required to restore the heap property.

```
(defun heap-delete (heap index)
  (setf (aref heap index) (aref heap (1- (length heap))))
  (pop heap)
  (bubble-up heap index)
  (bubble-down heap index))
```

Heap Construction

Building a heap from an unordered array can be achieved efficiently using a bottom-up approach. This method ensures a time complexity of $O(n)$.

```
(defun build-heap (array)
  (let ((size (length array)))
    (loop for i from (floor (size/2) downto 0)
          do (bubble-down array i))
    array))
```

Heap Applications

Heaps are pivotal in several algorithms due to their efficient support for priority queue operations.

- Heapsort: A sorting algorithm that uses a heap data structure to produce a sorted array. The algorithm outlines how to repeatedly extract the min (or max) and reconstruct the heap.

- Priority Queue: Heaps provide an efficient implementation for priority queues due to the logarithmic time complexity of insertion and extraction operations.

- Graph Algorithms: Algorithms like Dijkstra's shortest path and Prim's minimum spanning tree utilize heaps to optimize their performance.

Heaps, with their structured properties and operations, are indispensable for tasks requiring efficient priority management. Their use in sorting, queuing, and complex graph algorithms demonstrates their utility in various computational problems. This versatility makes understanding and implementing heaps a fundamental skill for proficient Lisp programming.

7.6   Sets and Bag Data Structures

In Lisp programming, sets and bags are fundamental data structures used for grouping items and managing collections. They provide a robust framework for ensuring efficient data operations, particularly when dealing with unique elements or counts of elements.

We begin by defining a set, which is an unordered collection of distinct items. Unlike lists, where order matters and duplicates are allowed, sets guarantee that each element is unique. This property is crucial in applications like membership testing, removing duplicates, and performing set operations such as union, intersection, and difference.

A bag, or multiset, on the other hand, allows for multiple occurrences of the same element. This attribute makes bags suitable for scenarios where the frequency of elements is essential, such as inventory systems or frequency distributions.

Sets in Lisp can be implemented using various techniques, with lists and hash tables being the most common. For instance, a simple list-based implementation of sets relies on the principle that the list does not contain any duplicates. Here's a straightforward example of how to implement and manipulate sets using lists:

```
;; Define a function to check membership in a set
(defun member-set (item set)
   (member item set))

;; Define a function to add an element to a set
(defun add-to-set (item set)
   (if (member-set item set)
       set
       (cons item set)))

;; Define a function to remove an element from a set
(defun remove-from-set (item set)
   (remove item set))

;; Example usage:
(setq my-set '(1 2 3))
```

```
(add-to-set 4 my-set) ;; (4 1 2 3)
(remove-from-set 2 my-set) ;; (1 3)
```

In the code above, member-set checks whether an item is in the set, add-to-set adds an item to the set if it is not already present, and remove-from-set removes the item from the set.

For enhanced performance, particularly with large sets, hash tables are often preferred because of their average constant-time complexity for membership checking, adding, and removing elements. Here's an example of using hash tables to implement sets:

```
;; Define a function to create an empty set
(defun create-set ()
  (make-hash-table :test 'equal))

;; Define a function to check membership in a set
(defun member-set (item set)
  (gethash item set))

;; Define a function to add an element to a set
(defun add-to-set (item set)
  (setf (gethash item set) t))

;; Define a function to remove an element from a set
(defun remove-from-set (item set)
  (remhash item set))

;; Example usage:
(setq my-set (create-set))
(add-to-set 'a my-set)
(add-to-set 'b my-set)
(member-set 'a my-set) ;; t
(remove-from-set 'a my-set)
(member-set 'a my-set) ;; nil
```

In this implementation, a hash table is used to store the elements of the set. Each element is added to the hash table with a default value (T) indicating its presence.

Bags or multisets can be considered an extension of sets, allowing duplicate elements. The key difference is that a bag tracks the count of each element. A common implementation would again utilize hash

195

tables, where the values represent the count of each element. Below is an example:

```lisp
;; Define a function to create an empty bag
(defun create-bag ()
  (make-hash-table :test 'equal))

;; Define a function to add an element to a bag
(defun add-to-bag (item bag)
  (let ((count (gethash item bag 0)))
    (setf (gethash item bag) (1+ count))))

;; Define a function to remove an element from a bag
(defun remove-from-bag (item bag)
  (let ((count (gethash item bag 0)))
    (if (> count 1)
        (setf (gethash item bag) (1- count))
        (remhash item bag))))

;; Define a function to get the count of an element in a bag
(defun count-in-bag (item bag)
  (gethash item bag 0))

;; Example usage:
(setq my-bag (create-bag))
(add-to-bag 'a my-bag)
(add-to-bag 'a my-bag)
(count-in-bag 'a my-bag) ;; 2
(remove-from-bag 'a my-bag)
(count-in-bag 'a my-bag) ;; 1
```

In this bag implementation, add-to-bag increases the count of an item if it already exists, or adds it with a count of 1 if it does not. remove-from-bag decreases the count and removes the item if the count drops to zero, while count-in-bag returns the current count of the item.

Sets and bags are powerful data structures that can be used in a variety of applications. Their efficient implementation and the ability to quickly check membership, add, and remove elements make them indispensable tools in Lisp programming.

196

7.7 Linked Lists and Variants

Linked lists are among the most fundamental data structures in computer science and undoubtedly one of the first topics that in-depth Lisp learners confront. The basic linked list consists of nodes where each node contains data and a reference (or link) to the next node in the sequence. This structure provides a simple yet flexible way to store and manage a collection of elements.

In Lisp, linked lists are idiomatically defined using cons cells. A cons cell is a fundamental building block consisting of two pointers, known as car and cdr. The car pointer typically holds the value or data, while the cdr pointer points to the next cons cell, forming the linked structure. Let us look at a basic example of constructing and manipulating a singly linked list in Lisp:

```
;; Creating a simple linked list with elements 1, 2, and 3
(setq my-list (cons 1 (cons 2 (cons 3 nil))))
```

Navigating or iterating through the linked list can be performed using recursion or iterative loops as follows:

```
;; Recursive function to print each element of the linked list
(defun print-list (lst)
   (when lst
      (print (car lst))
      (print-list (cdr lst))))

(print-list my-list)
```

The output would be:

```
1
2
3
```

This simple implementation underscores the essence of linked lists in Lisp. However, various other forms of linked lists are useful in scenarios requiring enhanced capabilities. These variants include doubly linked lists, circular linked lists, and more complex structures like skip lists.

A *doubly linked list* is a type of linked list where each node maintains references to both the next and the previous nodes, thus enabling bidirectional traversal. To implement doubly linked lists in Lisp, a more elaborate structure is necessary:

```
;; Definition of a doubly linked list node
(defstruct dnode
  value
  previous
  next)

;; Function to create a new doubly linked list node
(defun make-dnode (value &optional previous next)
  (make-dnode :value value :previous previous :next next))

;; Utility function to link two nodes
(defun link-dnodes (node1 node2)
  (setf (dnode-next node1) node2)
  (setf (dnode-previous node2) node1))
```

One significant advantage of doubly linked lists is the ability to traverse the list in reverse, a feature not possible with simple singly linked lists:

```
;; Sample usage
(let ((n1 (make-dnode 1))
      (n2 (make-dnode 2))
      (n3 (make-dnode 3)))
  (link-dnodes n1 n2)
  (link-dnodes n2 n3)
  ;; Traverse forward
  (let ((current n1))
    (while current
      (print (dnode-value current))
      (setf current (dnode-next current))))
  ;; Traverse backward
  (let ((current n3))
    (while current
      (print (dnode-value current))
      (setf current (dnode-previous current)))))
```

The output would be:

```
1
2
3
3
2
1
```

Circular linked lists are another variant where the last node in the sequence points back to the first node, creating a circular structure. This pattern is particularly useful for applications requiring continuous cycling through a list, such as in certain scheduling algorithms:

```
;; Creating a circular singly linked list
(setq circular-list (cons 1 (cons 2 (cons 3 nil))))
(setf (cdr (cdr (cdr circular-list))) circular-list)

;; Function to print elements of a circular linked list with limit
(defun print-circular-list (lst count)
   (loop for i from 1 to count do
       (print (car lst))
       (setf lst (cdr lst))))

(print-circular-list circular-list 9)
```

The output reflects the cyclical nature of the list:

```
1
2
3
1
2
3
1
2
3
```

Skip lists are a more advanced variant employing probabilistic balancing costs. They aim to efficiently provide search, insertion, and deletion operations, mimicking the performance characteristics of balanced trees but with simpler implementation. Skip lists use multiple layers of increasingly sparse linked lists:

```
;; Skip list node definition
(defstruct skip-node
   value
   forward)

;; Function to create a skip list node
(defun make-skip-node (value level)
   (make-skip-node :value value :forward (make-array level :
       initial-element nil)))

;; Example of creating the header node for a skip list of max level 4
(setq header (make-skip-node 'header 4))
```

A skip list node contains an array of forward pointers, where the length of the array corresponds to a level in the skip list.

The efficiency of linked lists and their variants makes them a cornerstone in the management of dynamic sets of data, highly adaptable to the varying needs of complex applications. Whether for simplicity, bidirectional traversal, circular structure, or probabilistic balancing, the array of linked list forms provides powerful tools for sophisticated data manipulation in Lisp programming.

7.8   Tries and Suffix Trees

Tries, also known as prefix trees, are a type of search tree used to store a dynamic set or associative array where the keys are usually strings. Unlike a binary search tree, no node in the tree stores the key associated with that node. Instead, the key is represented by the path from the root to the node. Each edge represents a character of the key, and a node's child corresponds to the possible continuations of the prefix represented by that node.

A suffix tree, on the other hand, is a compressed trie of all suffixes of a given text. It is a powerful tool used particularly in string processing algorithms. The suffix tree for a string S of length n is a rooted directed tree containing all n suffixes of S. It can be constructed in linear time using Ukkonen's algorithm.

To implement a trie in Lisp, we can use associative lists (alists) to store children. Below is a Lisp function to insert a word into a trie:

```
(defun trie-insert (trie word)
  "Insert a word into a trie."
  (if (string= word "")
      (setf (gethash "" trie) t)
    (let* ((first-char (subseq word 0 1))
           (rest-word (subseq word 1))
           (child (gethash first-char trie)))
      (unless child
        (setf child (make-hash-table :test 'equal))
        (setf (gethash first-char trie) child))
      (trie-insert child rest-word))))
```

This function works by recursively inserting characters of the word into the trie. If the word is empty, it marks the end of a word in the trie. Otherwise, it takes the first character, finds or creates the corresponding child node, and recurses on the rest of the word.

To insert the word "hello" into an initially empty trie, we would use:

```
(let ((trie (make-hash-table :test 'equal)))
  (trie-insert trie "hello"))
```

A suffix tree provides a way to efficiently store and query all suffixes of a string. For example, searching for substrings, performing pattern matching, and more complex operations can be done extraordinarily quickly using a suffix tree. The key difference from a trie is compression: nodes with only one child are merged.

To construct a suffix tree, consider the string $S =$ "banana". The suffixes are: "banana", "anana", "nana", "ana", "na", "a". The suffix tree for "banana" would be:

```
    (root)
    /  \
   b    a
  /      \
"anana"   n ...
```

Constructing a suffix tree in Lisp involves more complexity than a trie. One of the most efficient algorithms is Ukkonen's algorithm, which builds the tree in $O(n)$. Below is a simplified version of a suffix tree construction using Ukkonen's algorithm, assuming a basic understanding of the theory behind suffix trees.

```
(defun build-suffix-tree (text)
  (let ((n (length text))
        (root (make-hash-table :test 'equal)))
    (loop for i from 0 below n
       do (add-suffix root (subseq text i)))
    root))

(defun add-suffix (node suffix)
  (loop for i from 0 below (length suffix)
     for char = (subseq suffix i (1+ i))
     do (unless (gethash char node)
          (setf (gethash char node) (make-hash-table :test 'equal)))
       (setf node (gethash char node)))
  (setf (gethash "" node) t))
```

This code builds a basic suffix tree by iteratively adding all suffixes of the input string. Each suffix is added by traversing from the root, creating new nodes as necessary. The leaf nodes (marked by the empty string key) indicate the end of suffixes.

To use this function for the string "banana":

```
(let ((suffix-tree (build-suffix-tree "banana")))
  (print suffix-tree))
```

The resulting suffix tree will provide a powerful tool for various string operations. Both tries and suffix trees are fundamental data structures in computational linguistics, text processing, and bioinformatics. Their efficient querying capabilities make them invaluable for numerous applications.

Comprehending tries and suffix trees not only enhances one's ability to manage and search text data but also forms a rigorous foundation for understanding more sophisticated algorithms in string processing.

7.9   Complex Hash Table Implementations

Hash tables are widely used in Lisp programming for their average-case constant time complexity for search, insertion, and deletion operations. While basic hash tables provide efficient data management, complex hash table implementations accommodate various special requirements such as handling collisions, providing dynamic resizing, supporting concurrent access, and improving memory efficiency.

Collision Handling: A primary concern in hash table implementations is handling collisions, which occur when multiple keys hash to the same index. Two common techniques for collision resolution are chaining and open addressing.

Chaining involves maintaining a list of all elements that hash to the same index. This list can be implemented using a linked list or more advanced data structures like balanced trees for better performance in high collision scenarios.

```
(defun make-hash-table-with-chaining (size)
  (make-array size :initial-element nil))

(defun hash-function (key size)
  (% (sxhash key) size))
```

202

```
(defun insert-with-chaining (key value table)
  (let* ((index (hash-function key (length table)))
         (bucket (aref table index)))
    (setf (aref table index) (cons (cons key value) bucket))))
```

In insert-with-chaining, elements are inserted at the head of the list, ensuring constant time insertion.

Open addressing handles collisions by probing alternative locations in the array. Common probing techniques include linear probing, quadratic probing, and double hashing.

```
(defun find-slot (table key)
  (let ((size (length table))
        (index (hash-function key (length table)))
        (i 0))
    (loop until (or (null (aref table index)) ;; Empty slot found
                    (eql (car (aref table index)) key)) ;; Key found
          do (setf index (% (+ index (expt i 2)) size)
                   i (1+ i)))
    index))

(defun insert-with-quadratic-probing (key value table)
  (let ((index (find-slot table key)))
    (setf (aref table index) (cons key value))))
```

find-slot illustrates quadratic probing to find an open slot, ensuring fewer collisions than linear probing.

Dynamic Resizing: Efficient hash table implementations support dynamic resizing, typically doubling the table size upon reaching a certain load factor. Resizing involves rehashing all existing elements into the new table to maintain the distribution of keys.

```
(defun resize-hash-table (table)
  (let* ((new-size (* 2 (length table)))
         (new-table (make-hash-table-with-chaining new-size)))
    (loop for bucket across table
          when bucket
          do (loop for (key . value) in bucket
                   do (insert-with-chaining key value new-table)))
    new-table))

(defun ensure-capacity (table threshold)
```

```
(when (> (/ (hash-table-count table) (length table)) threshold)
  (resize-hash-table table)))
```

resize-hash-table creates a new larger table and rehashes elements from the old table, while ensure-capacity performs resizing when the load factor exceeds a defined threshold.

Concurrent Access: In multi-threaded environments, synchronizing access to hash tables avoids race conditions. Common techniques include using locks or employing lock-free data structures such as ConcurrentHashMap.

```
(defvar *lock* (make-lock))

(defun insert-concurrently (key value table)
  (with-lock-held ((*lock*))
    (insert-with-chaining key value table)))

(defun lookup-concurrently (key table)
  (with-lock-held ((*lock*))
    (let ((index (hash-function key (length table))))
      (assoc key (aref table index)))))
```

Incorporating with-lock-held ensures exclusive access to the hash table during insertion and lookup operations.

Memory Efficiency: Memory-efficient implementations can optimize space usage while maintaining performance. Techniques like shared buckets and compact key representation can be critical in environments with limited memory.

```
(defun compact-representation (key)
  ;; Use a more compact representation for keys if possible
  ;; Example for demonstration purposes only
  (cond ((stringp key) (intern (string key)))
        (t key)))

(defun insert-with-compaction (key value table)
  (let ((compact-key (compact-representation key)))
    (insert-with-chaining compact-key value table)))
```

By compacting keys, insert-with-compaction reduces memory usage, especially for frequently occurring keys.

Understanding and implementing complex hash table strategies allow for optimal performance and resource management in Lisp applications, addressing the specific requirements of diverse computing environments.

7.10   Persistent Data Structures

Persistent data structures maintain previous versions of themselves when modified. Functional programming paradigms often leverage these structures due to their immutability and referential transparency properties. This section will delve into the principles, implementations, and benefits of persistent data structures in Lisp.

Definition and Properties

A data structure is termed persistent if existing versions remain unaltered after any modifications. This property can be divided into:

- **Partial Persistence**: Only the newest version can be modified, while older versions remain immutable and accessible.

- **Full Persistence**: All versions of the data structure, both past and present, can be accessed and modified.

The essential properties include:

- Immutability: Structural invariants remain intact across versions.

- Sharing: Common parts of the data structure are shared among versions, optimizing space usage.

Implementation Techniques

Persistent data structures are typically implemented using either path copying or fat nodes.

Path Copying

Path copying involves creating copies of nodes that lie on the path from the root to the modified node, ensuring that shared substructures remain unchanged. Consider a simple example of updating a binary search tree (BST):

```
(defstruct node key left right)
```

```
(defun insert (x tree)
  (if (null tree)
      (make-node :key x)
      (if (< x (node-key tree))
          (make-node :key (node-key tree)
                     :left (insert x (node-left tree))
                     :right (node-right tree))
          (make-node :key (node-key tree)
                     :left (node-left tree)
                     :right (insert x (node-right tree))))))
```

Here, insert function copies nodes along the path while updating a value.

Fat Nodes

Fat nodes store historical modifications at each node, often with versions encoded as a series of changes. Consider the following representation where each node maintains an array of modifications:

```
(defstruct fat-node key (mods nil))

(defun insert-fat (x tree version)
  (if (null (node-key tree))
      (make-fat-node :key x)
      (let ((mods (node-mods tree)))
        (if (< x (node-key tree))
            (setf (node-mods tree)
                  (append mods (list (make-mod :version version :left
                                (insert-fat x (node-left tree version)))))))
        (if (> x (node-key tree))
            (setf (node-mods tree)
                  (append mods (list (make-mod :version version :
                       right (insert-fat x (node-right tree version)))))
                  )
        tree)))
```

Fat nodes allow tracking of changes with appended versions, facilitating full persistence.

Benefits of Persistent Data Structures

Persistent data structures offer several crucial benefits:

- Version Control: Effective management of historical states, essential in applications like undo systems, versioned data stores, and computational imaging.

- Thread Safety: Immutability ensures that concurrent threads can operate on shared data structures without synchronization mechanisms.

- Functional Programming Support: Persistent data structures inherently align with the principles of functional programming languages by maintaining immutability.

Persistent Data Structures in Lisp

Lisp's versatility in list manipulation aligns well with persistent data structures.

Persistent Lists

Consider a simple example of a persistent singly linked list where modifications yield a new list:

```
(defun plist-cons (x plist)
  (cons x plist))

(defun plist-get (p index)
  (nth index p))
```

Here, plist-cons adds an element to the persistent list, while plist-get retrieves an element by index. The original list remains accessible after the addition.

Persistent Arrays

Persistent arrays can be implemented using the vector data structure along with version tracking, as illustrated:

```
(defstruct pvector (array #(0 0 0 0)) versions)

(defun pvector-set (vec index value version)
  (let ((new-array (copy-seq (pvector-array vec))))
    (setf (elt new-array index) value)
    (make-pvector :array new-array :versions (append (
      pvector-versions vec) (list version)))))
```

Using pvector-set, arrays maintain immutability by copying and modifying the array, then appending a new version.

Persistent data structures in Lisp allow robust versioning, serialization, and backward/forward compatibility. These characteristics make them indispensable for modern software systems requiring consistent and reliable state management.

7.11   Memory-efficient Data Structures

Memory efficiency is a critical consideration in the design and implementation of data structures, especially in environments where resource constraints are significant.   This section evaluates various memory-efficient data structures, addressing their design principles and implementation strategies, with a particular focus on Lisp. Specific attention will be given to succinct and compact data structures, as well as techniques for reducing memory overhead.

The first step in understanding memory-efficient data structures is to recognize the impact of metadata and pointer overheads. Every node in a conventional linked data structure, such as a linked list or tree, typically includes additional memory to store pointers and possibly other metadata. This overhead can be significant, particularly in large data sets.

Succinct Data Structures offer an effective solution by storing data in a compact form while still allowing efficient access and manipulation. These structures use the minimum possible space within a constant factor of the optimal. For example, a bit vector often models succinct data structures, allowing operations such as rank and select to be implemented efficiently.

Consider implementing a succinct bit vector in Lisp. Below is a sample implementation using Common Lisp:

```
(defun bitvector-rank (bitvector i)
  "Calculate the number of 1s in the bitvector up to position i."
  (let ((count 0))
    (dotimes (index (1+ i) count)
      (when (char= (aref bitvector index) #\1)
        (incf count)))))

(defun bitvector-select (bitvector count)
  "Find the position of the count-th 1 in the bitvector."
  (let ((occurrences 0))
    (dotimes (index (length bitvector))
```

```
(when (char= (aref bitvector index) #\1)
  (incf occurrences))
(when (= occurrences count)
  (return index)))))
```

```
CL-USER> (bitvector-rank "101010111" 4)
3
CL-USER> (bitvector-select "101010111" 3)
4
```

For further space optimization, compressed tries are another memory-efficient data structure. Traditional tries store one character per node, but compressed tries merge chains of single-child nodes into a single node. This compression can save a significant amount of memory, especially with long strings containing common prefixes.

Below is an example code that demonstrates the insertion and lookup functions in a compressed trie:

```
(defstruct comp-trie
  char
  children
  end-of-word)

(defun insert (root word)
  (let ((current-node root)
        (word-length (length word)))
    (loop for i from 0 to (1- word-length) do
      (let* ((char (char word i))
             (child (assoc char (comp-trie-children current-node))
                    :test 'char=))
        (if child
            (setf current-node (cdr child))
            (let ((new-node (make-comp-trie :char char :children
                            nil :end-of-word nil)))
              (push (cons char new-node) (comp-trie-children
                    current-node))
              (setf current-node new-node)))))
    (setf (comp-trie-end-of-word current-node) t)))

(defun lookup (root word)
  (let ((current-node root)
        (word-length (length word)))
    (loop for i from 0 to (1- word-length) always
      (let* ((char (char word i))
```

```
                    (child (assoc char (comp-trie-children current-node))
                         :test 'char=))
            (if child
                (setf current-node (cdr child))
                (return nil)))
        finally (return (comp-trie-end-of-word current-node)))))
```

```
CL-USER> (defvar *root* (make-comp-trie :char nil :children nil :end-of-word nil))
*ROOT*
CL-USER> (insert *root* "lisp")
NIL
CL-USER> (insert *root* "list")
NIL
CL-USER> (lookup *root* "lisp")
T
CL-USER> (lookup *root* "lis")
NIL
```

Other memory-efficient structures like chunked linked lists combine arrays and linked lists to reduce the space overhead and improve cache performance. A chunked linked list divides the data into chunks of contiguous memory (arrays) linked together, which helps to reduce the number of pointers while maintaining the flexibility of a linked list.

In Lisp, a simple chunked linked list implementation can be constructed as follows:

```
(defparameter +chunk-size+ 4)

(defun make-chunked-list ()
  (list :chunks nil
        :size 0))

(defun chunked-list-insert (chunklist value)
  "Insert value into chunked list."
  (let* ((chunks (first chunklist))
         (current-size (second chunklist))
         (last-chunk (first chunks)))
    (if (or (null last-chunk) (>= (length last-chunk) +chunk-size+))
        (push (list value) chunks)
      (push value last-chunk))
    (incf current-size)
    (setf (second chunklist) current-size)))

(defun chunked-list-get (chunklist index)
  "Retrieve value at given index in a chunked list."
  (let ((current-index 0))
```

```
(dolist (chunk (first chunklist))
  (let ((chunk-size (length chunk)))
    (when (<= current-index index (+ current-index chunk-size
        -1))
      (return (nth (- index current-index) chunk)))
    (incf current-index chunk-size)))))
```

```
CL-USER> (defvar *chlist* (make-chunked-list))
*CHLIST*
CL-USER> (chunked-list-insert *chlist* 1)
(1)
CL-USER> (chunked-list-insert *chlist* 2)
(1 2)
CL-USER> (chunked-list-insert *chlist* 3)
(1 2 3)
CL-USER> (chunked-list-insert *chlist* 4)
(1 2 3 4)
CL-USER> (chunked-list-insert *chlist* 5)
((5) (1 2 3 4))
CL-USER> (chunked-list-get *chlist* 4)
5
```

Another critical aspect of memory efficiency is the use of data encoding techniques which optimize memory utilization. For instance, Huffman Coding is a widely used method for lossless data compression, reducing the memory footprint by assigning short binary codes to frequently used characters and longer codes to less frequent characters.

Adaptive approaches continuously remain effective for varying data patterns. Techniques like dynamic unrolling and space-efficient sequential representations align with modern processors' cache hierarchies, optimizing both memory usage and speed. These techniques often require a detailed understanding of both data retrieval patterns and underlying hardware characteristics.

Memory pool allocation effectively manages memory usage in scenarios where objects of similar sizes are frequently created and destroyed. This technique involves allocating a large block of memory and subdividing it into smaller chunks as needed. It reduces fragmentation and overhead associated with individual allocation and deallocation actions and can significantly improve performance in specific applications.

Here is a conceptual overview of memory pool allocation in Lisp:

```
(defparameter *memory-pool* (make-array 1000))

(defun allocate-from-pool (size)
  "Allocate memory from the pool."
  (let ((block (make-array size :initial-element nil)))
```

211

```
;; In practice, allocation logic will be more complex
block))

(defun free-to-pool (block)
  "Free the allocated block back to the pool."
  (fill block nil))
```

By carefully structuring and utilizing memory-efficient data structures, Lisp programmers can manage large data sets effectively, reduce memory overhead, and enhance the overall performance of their applications. The strategies discussed, from succinct data structures to advanced memory pooling techniques, collectively contribute to the efficient management of memory resources.

7.12   Custom Data Structure Design

Creating custom data structures in Lisp involves a thorough understanding of both abstract data types (ADTs) and the specifics of Lisp's features, such as first-class functions and dynamic typing. Custom data structure design can maximize efficiency and tailor data management to specific application needs. This section will cover the essential steps to design, implement, and utilize custom data structures in Lisp, including defining the structure, writing accessor and mutator functions, and ensuring efficient memory usage.

Defining the Data Structure: A custom data structure in Lisp is often defined using the defstruct macro. This macro allows for the creation of a structure with named fields. For example, consider a custom data structure for a point in a 2D space:

```
(defstruct point
  x
  y)
```

This creates a new data type point with fields x and y. Instantiating this structure can be done as follows:

```
(let ((p (make-point :x 3 :y 4)))
  (format t "Point: (~A, ~A)~%" (point-x p) (point-y p)))
```

Point: (3, 4)

212

Accessor and Mutator Functions: Lisp's defstruct automatically generates accessor functions for each field. For more complex operations, custom accessor and mutator functions can be defined. For instance, if additional validation is needed when setting a point's coordinates, we can write:

```
(defun set-point-x (p new-x)
  (assert (numberp new-x) (new-x) "New x coordinate must be a
      number.")
  (setf (point-x p) new-x))

(defun set-point-y (p new-y)
  (assert (numberp new-y) (new-y) "New y coordinate must be a
      number.")
  (setf (point-y p) new-y))
```

The use of assertions ensures that the fields are set with valid data types, thus maintaining data integrity.

Algorithm Integration: Incorporating algorithms into custom structures often involves designing specific methods to manipulate the new data type. Consider a custom structure for a binary tree node:

```
(defstruct tree-node
  value
  left
  right)
```

A function to insert a value into the binary tree can be implemented as follows:

```
(defun insert-tree-node (node value)
  (if node
      (if (< value (tree-node-value node))
          (setf (tree-node-left node)
                (insert-tree-node (tree-node-left node) value))
          (setf (tree-node-right node)
                (insert-tree-node (tree-node-right node) value)))
      (make-tree-node :value value)))
```

This function provides a recursive mechanism to insert values, ensuring that the binary tree maintains its property.

Memory Efficiency and Persistence: One aspect of custom data structure design is efficient memory management. This can be achieved by minimizing memory allocation and reusing existing structures. In Lisp, persistent data structures allow the creation of new versions of a data structure that share most of their parts with the old version. This is especially useful in functional programming paradigms.

Consider the example of a persistent list implemented as a custom data structure:

```
(defstruct persistent-list
  head
  tail)

(defun cons (head tail)
  (make-persistent-list :head head :tail tail))

(defun head (plist)
  (persistent-list-head plist))

(defun tail (plist)
  (persistent-list-tail plist))
```

Using the cons function constructs a new list without altering the original, maintaining persistence by sharing the tail of the list between versions.

Design Considerations: Designing custom data structures requires careful consideration of the intended use cases and performance characteristics. Key components of the design process include:

- **Data Integrity:** Ensure that the data structure maintains validity constraints, such as type assertions and value ranges.

- **Efficiency:** Optimize for both time and space complexity. Lazy evaluation and memoization may be employed where appropriate.

- **Usability:** Provide a clear, intuitive interface for using the data structure. This involves defining idiomatic accessor and mutator functions.

- **Extensibility:** Allow for future extensions or variations of the data structure without major overhauls to the codebase. Leveraging Lisp's macro system can facilitate this.

214

Custom data structures constructed with the above considerations in mind can result in robust, efficient, and maintainable Lisp programs. Ultimately, the adaptability provided by custom-designed data structures enables the programmer to meet specific application requirements effectively.

Chapter 8

Input/Output and File Handling

This chapter covers the essentials of input/output operations and file handling in Lisp. It begins with basic input and output functions before moving on to file streams, including reading from and writing to files. Binary file handling and formatted output are discussed, along with strategies for managing large files and handling I/O errors. The chapter also introduces network I/O basics and examines popular libraries for advanced I/O operations. Best practices for efficient and effective I/O and file handling are provided to ensure robust program design.

8.1   Introduction to Input/Output in Lisp

Input/Output (I/O) operations are fundamental for any programming language, enabling interaction with users, files, and other systems. In Lisp, I/O operations are designed to be flexible and powerful, allowing programmers to handle a variety of data sources and sinks efficiently. This section introduces the core concepts and functionalities related to basic I/O in Lisp, setting the stage for more advanced discussions in subsequent sections.

Lisp supports both interactive and non-interactive I/O. Interactive I/O involves direct communication with the user through the command line or

other interfaces, while non-interactive I/O generally involves file operations or network interactions where the data flows between the program
and various non-human endpoints.

Interactive Input

Interactive input in Lisp is carried out using the read function. This function reads an S-expression (symbolic expression) from the standard
input, evaluates it, and returns the result. Other interactive input functions, such as read-line, allow for reading text line-by-line.

```
;; Example of using read to capture user input
(defun get-user-input ()
  (format t "Enter an S-expression: ")
  (let ((input (read)))
    (format t "You entered: ~A~%" input)))

(get-user-input)
```

When executed, this code will prompt the user for an S-expression and
then print the entered expression.

```
Enter an S-expression: (+ 1 2)
You entered: (+ 1 2)
```

Interactive Output

For interactive output, Lisp provides several functions such as print,
princ, prin1, and format. These functions allow for varying levels of
output formatting and control.

```
;; Examples of different output functions
(defun demonstrate-output ()
  (let ((a 42)
        (b "Hello, world!"))
    (print a) ;; Prints with a newline and returns the value
    (princ b) ;; Prints without newline or extra formatting
    (prin1 a) ;; Prints using the READable representation
    (format t "~%Formatted output: ~a and ~a~%" a b))) ;;
      Formatted output

(demonstrate-output)
```

```
42
Hello, world!42
Formatted output: 42 and Hello, world!
```

Non-Interactive Input and Output

Non-interactive I/O generally deals with file operations. Lisp provides several functions and macros to handle file I/O efficiently. The with-open-file macro is frequently used for opening files in a safe manner, ensuring that files are closed properly even if an error occurs during processing.

```
;; Reading from a file using with-open-file
(defun read-from-file (filename)
  (with-open-file (stream filename)
    (loop for line = (read-line stream nil nil)
          while line
          do (print line))))

;; Writing to a file using with-open-file
(defun write-to-file (filename content)
  (with-open-file (stream filename :direction :output :if-exists :
      supersede)
    (write-line content stream)))
```

In these examples, read-from-file opens a file in read mode and prints each line until the end-of-file (EOF) is reached. The write-to-file function demonstrates how to open a file in write mode and write a string of text to it.

Streams in Lisp

Streams are a central concept in Lisp I/O, representing sources and destinations for data. There are several types of streams: *input streams*, *output streams*, *bidirectional streams*, and *broadcast streams*, among others. Input streams are used for reading data, while output streams are used for writing data.

```
;; Example of using streams
(defun stream-examples ()
  (let ((input-stream (make-string-input-stream "Example input"))
        (output-stream (make-string-output-stream)))
    (format t "Input Stream Content: ~A~%" (read-line input-stream)
      )
    (write-line "Output goes here" output-stream)
    (format t "Output Stream Content: ~A~%" (
        get-output-stream-string output-stream)))))
```

Here, make-string-input-stream creates an input stream from a string and make-string-output-stream creates an output stream that can later be converted back to a string using get-output-stream-string.

Understanding these foundational concepts allows Lisp programmers to handle a wide range of I/O tasks efficiently and prepares them for more complex scenarios involving advanced I/O operations and error handling.

8.2   Basic Input and Output

In this section, we delve into the foundational aspects of handling basic input and output (I/O) operations in Lisp. Mastery of these operations is essential for building interactive programs and for tasks involving user input or displaying results.

Lisp provides a set of functions specifically designed for these purposes. The central concept revolves around reading data from standard input (typically the keyboard) and writing data to standard output (typically the screen).

Reading Input

The primary function for reading input from the user is read. This function reads an input expression and returns it as a Lisp object. This functionality is pivotal when the user needs to provide data at runtime.

```
(setq user-input (read))
```

In this example, user-input will hold the value entered by the user until the next expression is read.

read-line is another useful function designed for reading a line of text as a string. This function reads characters from the input stream until it encounters a newline character.

```
(setq user-input-line (read-line))
```

Writing Output

For output operations, the print and format functions are extensively utilized.

print is the simplest output function. It outputs the printed representation of an object to standard output, followed by a newline.

```
(print "Hello, World!")
```

220

The format function is more sophisticated and versatile, allowing customized formatting of output.

```
(format t "Hello, ~a!~%" "World")
```

Here, ~a is a directive that formats its corresponding argument as an aesthetic representation, and ~% introduces a newline. The t argument directs the formatted output to the standard output stream.

Interactive Input and Output

Combining reading and writing operations facilitates interactive programs. Consider a small program that asks for the user's name and greets them:

```
(format t "What is your name?~%")
(setq name (read-line))
(format t "Hello, ~a!~%" name)
```

(format t "What is your name? %") outputs the prompt, (setq name (read-line)) reads the user's input, and (format t "Hello, ~a! %") finally, outputs a greeting using the input name.

I/O with Numbers

Lisp effortlessly handles numeric input and output. Reading a number uses the same read function but expects a numeric input.

```
(setq user-number (read))
```

Here's an example where the program reads a number, doubles it, and prints the result:

```
(format t "Enter a number:~%")
(setq number (read))
(format t "Twice your number is ~d~%" (* 2 number))
```

In the above example, the * function multiplies the given number by two, and ~d in the format function is a directive for formatting integers.

Error Handling During I/O

When dealing with I/O operations, effective handling of unexpected inputs or errors is crucial. Lisp provides error handling constructs such as ignore-errors and handler-case.

ignore-errors can be used to run a code block and suppress any errors that occur.

```
(setq number
  (ignore-errors
    (read)))
```

For more fine-grained error control, handler-case can be used to manage specific errors.

```
(handler-case
    (progn
      (format t "Enter a number:~%")
      (setq number (read))
      (format t "You entered: ~d~%" number))
  (error (e)
    (format t "An error occurred: ~a~%" e)))
```

The handler-case block specified above attempts to read and print a number. If an error occurs during input, it catches the error and describes it.

Effective use of these basic input and output operations forms the bedrock of user interaction in Lisp programs. Familiarity with these functions empowers the programmer to construct interactive, robust, and user-friendly applications.

8.3   File Streams

File streams in Lisp provide a powerful and flexible mechanism for reading from and writing to files. A stream is an abstraction that represents a source or destination of data. When working with file streams, Lisp provides several built-in functions to open, read, write, and close files efficiently. This section delves into the specifics of handling file streams in Lisp, ensuring that your program can manage external data inputs and outputs seamlessly.

To begin with, file streams are created using the open function. This function requires at least one argument: the name of the file to open. Optional arguments include the :direction keyword, which specifies the intended use of the file stream, such as :input for reading, :output for writing, or :io for both reading and writing.

```
;; Open a file for reading
```

```
(defparameter *input-stream* (open "input.txt" :direction :input))

;; Open a file for writing
(defparameter *output-stream* (open "output.txt" :direction :output)
  )

;; Open a file for both reading and writing
(defparameter *io-stream* (open "data.txt" :direction :io))
```

Once a stream is open, various functions are available to read from and write to the stream. For reading from a stream, functions such as read-char, read-line, and read can be utilized. read-char reads a single character from the stream, read-line reads an entire line, and read is used for reading Lisp objects.

```
;; Read a single character
(defparameter *char* (read-char *input-stream*))

;; Read a single line
(defparameter *line* (read-line *input-stream*))

;; Read a Lisp object
(defparameter *object* (read *input-stream*))
```

Writing to a stream can be accomplished using functions such as write-char, write-line, and princ or print. write-char writes a single character to the stream, while write-line writes a complete line. The princ and print functions are used to output Lisp objects.

```
;; Write a single character
(write-char #\A *output-stream*)

;; Write a single line
(write-line "Hello, World!" *output-stream*)

;; Write a Lisp object
(princ '(1 2 3) *output-stream*)
(print '(a b c) *output-stream*)
```

It's crucial to ensure that any open streams are properly closed after operations to free system resources. This is done using the close function. The use of the with-open-file macro simplifies the process by automatically closing the file stream when the block of code completes, even if an error occurs within the block.

```
;; Close streams manually
(close *input-stream*)
(close *output-stream*)
(close *io-stream*)

;; Using with-open-file macro
(with-open-file (stream "output.txt" :direction :output)
  (write-line "This line will be written to the file." stream))
```

In addition to the standard open function, Lisp provides options for handling binary files and handling common issues, such as file-not-found errors. When opening binary files, the :element-type keyword is often used, for example, with (unsigned-byte 8) for byte-wise operations.

```
;; Open a binary file for reading
(defparameter *binary-input-stream* (open "binary.dat"
                                          :direction :input
                                          :element-type '(
                                              unsigned-byte 8)))

;; Read bytes from the binary file
(defparameter *byte* (read-byte *binary-input-stream*))

;; Close the binary stream
(close *binary-input-stream*)
```

Error handling while dealing with file streams can be efficiently managed using condition handling in Lisp. For example, the handler-case construct allows you to handle and recover from errors such as attempting to open a non-existent file.

```
(handler-case
    (with-open-file (stream "non-existent-file.txt" :direction :input)
      (read-line stream))
  (file-error (e)
    (format t "Error opening file: ~A~%" e)))
```

Overall, mastering file streams in Lisp requires a thorough understanding of how to create, manipulate, and close streams effectively. Proficiency in using functions for reading and writing data, along with proper error handling practices, ensures robust and reliable I/O operations in your Lisp programs.

8.4 Reading from Files

Reading from files in Lisp is a fundamental operation that allows programs to ingest external data for processing. This section will detail the mechanisms for opening, reading, and closing files, as well as strategies for handling different file structures and sizes. We will delve into specific functions provided by Lisp for file reading and demonstrate with examples to ensure clarity.

Lisp provides several built-in functions to facilitate reading from files, the most commonly used of which include open, read, read-line, and close. Understanding how to use these functions effectively is crucial for any Lisp programmer.

- open: Opens a file stream.

- read: Reads the next object from a stream.

- read-line: Reads a line of text from a stream.

- close: Closes a file stream.

To read from a file in Lisp, one typically follows these steps:

- Open the file using open.

- Read the file content using read or read-line.

- Process the read data as needed.

- Close the file using close to free system resources.

```
;; Opening a file for reading
(let ((stream (open "example.txt" :direction :input)))
  ;; Ensure the stream is successfully opened
  (when stream
    (unwind-protect
      (loop for line = (read-line stream nil)
            while line
            do (print line))
```

```
;; Ensure the stream is closed
(close stream))))
```

The above example demonstrates opening a file named example.txt for reading. The open function is called with the file name and the keyword argument :direction :input, indicating that the file will be read. The let construct binds the returned stream to the variable stream.

The when expression checks if the open call was successful. If the file is successfully opened, the code enters the unwind-protect block. Here, we use a loop construct to read each line from the file with read-line. The print function outputs each line to the standard output. Finally, the close function ensures that the stream is closed properly, even if an error occurs within the unwind-protect block.

read-line reads a line from the stream, returning a string for each line read. If the end of the file is reached, read-line returns nil.

For programs needing to read entire files into memory, with-open-file is a more robust and concise method, abstracting the file open and close operation:

```
(with-open-file (stream "example.txt" :direction :input)
  (loop for line = (read-line stream nil)
        while line
        do (print line)))
```

The with-open-file macro automatically handles the stream open and close operations, reducing boilerplate code. In this example, stream management and error handling are implicit, resulting in cleaner and more maintainable code.

While reading structured data, such as Lisp objects, the read function is appropriate. It reads the next Lisp object from the stream, which could be a number, symbol, list, or any valid Lisp expression.

```
(with-open-file (stream "data.lisp" :direction :input)
  (loop for obj = (read stream nil)
        while obj
        do (print obj)))
```

Here, the read function is used within a loop to read each Lisp object from data.lisp. This approach is useful when dealing with files that contain serialized Lisp expressions, enabling direct evaluation or manipulation of the read data.

226

Reading large files or files that do not fit into memory requires a different strategy to ensure efficiency. By processing the file incrementally, memory consumption is kept in check:

```
(defun process-large-file (filename)
  (with-open-file (stream filename :direction :input)
    (loop for line = (read-line stream nil)
          while line
          do (progn
               ;; Process each line here
               (print (length line))))))
```

In this example, process-large-file reads a file named filename line by line, processing each line individually. This method, combined with efficient in-memory data structures, facilitates the handling of large files without exhausting system resources.

Error handling during file reading is critical for robust software. Lisp provides mechanisms such as handler-case and ignore-errors to manage unexpected conditions:

```
(defun safe-read-file (filename)
  (ignore-errors
    (with-open-file (stream filename :direction :input)
      (loop for line = (read-line stream nil)
            while line
            do (print line)))))
```

The safe-read-file function demonstrates how ignore-errors can be used to handle potential errors gracefully. If an error occurs, the operation is aborted, and the program continues execution, ensuring the file stream is appropriately closed.

Mastering the basics of reading from files in Lisp provides a solid foundation for advanced input/output operations. Combining these techniques with efficient data processing approaches ensures that programs remain performant and reliable when working with various data sources.

8.5   Writing to Files

Writing data to files in Lisp involves creating or opening a file stream for output, directing the desired data to that stream, and closing the stream afterward. This ensures that data is written to the file accurately and that system resources are managed efficiently.

To write to a file in Lisp, the with-open-file macro is commonly used. This macro ensures that a file stream is properly opened and closed, even if an error occurs during file operations. The with-open-file macro uses the following syntax:

```
(with-open-file (stream filename :direction :output :if-exists :supersede
    :if-does-not-exist :create)
  ;; body
  )
```

- stream is the variable that will be bound to the newly created stream.

- filename is the name of the file to write to.

- :direction specifies that the file is opened for output with the keyword :output.

- :if-exists determines what action to take if the file already exists. Common values include:

    - :supersede to replace the existing file,
    - :append to append to the existing file,
    - :overwrite to overwrite the file from the beginning.

- :if-does-not-exist specifies what to do if the file does not exist. The keyword :create is typically used to create the file.

Within the body of the with-open-file macro, the stream variable refers to the open file stream. Data is written to the file using the write-line and format functions.

The write-line function writes a string to the output stream followed by a newline:

```
(write-line "This is a sample line of text." stream)
```

Below is a complete example that demonstrates writing multiple lines to a file named "output.txt":

```
(with-open-file (stream "output.txt" :direction :output :if-exists :
    supersede :if-does-not-exist :create)
  (write-line "Line 1: This is the first line." stream)
  (write-line "Line 2: This is the second line." stream)
  (write-line "Line 3: This is the third line." stream))
```

Executing the above code will result in the creation of a file named "output.txt" containing the following content:

```
Line 1: This is the first line.
Line 2: This is the second line.
Line 3: This is the third line.
```

For more complex output requirements, the format function provides versatile capabilities to produce formatted text. The format function uses format directives to control the output:

```
(format stream "~A ~D ~%~A" "Value:" 42 "Another string")
```

In this example:

- A ensures that the argument is printed using its aesthetic representation.

- D prints the argument as a decimal number.

- % outputs a newline.

The output of the above format statement written to the stream would be:

```
Value: 42
Another string
```

Writing binary data to files is also possible in Lisp by setting the :element-type in with-open-file. The :element-type keyword specifies the type of elements to be read from or written to the file. For example, to write bytes to a file:

```
(with-open-file (stream "binary-output.dat" :direction :output :
    element-type '(unsigned-byte 8) :if-exists :supersede :
    if-does-not-exist :create)
  (write-byte 120 stream) ; Write the byte value 120 to the output
    stream.
  (write-byte 255 stream) ; Write the byte value 255 to the output
    stream.
```

```
 (write-byte 0 stream)) ; Write the byte value 0 to the output stream
```

The write-byte function writes a single byte to the binary file stream. The above code creates the file "binary-output.dat" with the specified bytes written to it.

Managing resources and ensuring data integrity is crucial during file operations. Thus, the with-open-file macro is highly recommended as it handles the opening and closing of file streams efficiently.

8.6 Binary File Handling

In Lisp, handling binary files requires a different approach compared to text files due to the need to manipulate raw bytes rather than encoded characters. This section will detail how to open, read, write, and manipulate binary files using Lisp's built-in functions. Understanding binary file operations is essential for applications involving non-textual data such as images, executable files, or serialized objects.

Opening Binary Files: To work with binary files, you typically use the open function with the appropriate parameters. When opening a file for binary operations, the :element-type keyword is critical. This keyword allows you to specify the type of data elements to be read or written, which is crucial for handling binary data correctly. For binary files, you generally set the :element-type to '(unsigned-byte 8).

```
(defvar *input-stream* (open "example.bin" :direction :input :
    element-type '(unsigned-byte 8)))
(defvar *output-stream* (open "output.bin" :direction :output :
    element-type '(unsigned-byte 8)))
```

Reading Binary Data: The read-byte function is used to read bytes from a binary input stream. It reads a single byte and returns it as an integer between 0 and 255. For reading multiple bytes, you may use the read-sequence function, which reads a specified sequence of bytes into a Lisp array.

```
(let ((byte (read-byte *input-stream*)))
  (format t "Read byte: ~a~%" byte))

(let ((buffer (make-array 1024 :element-type '(unsigned-byte 8))))
```

```
(read-sequence buffer *input-stream*)
(format t "Buffer content: ~a~%" buffer))
```

Writing Binary Data: To write binary data to an output stream, you use the write-byte function, which writes a single byte. Similarly, write-sequence can be used for writing multiple bytes from an array at once.

```
(write-byte 255 *output-stream*)

(let ((data (make-array 1024 :initial-element 0 :element-type '(
    unsigned-byte 8))))
  (write-sequence data *output-stream*))
```

File Positioning: To manipulate the position within a file, Lisp provides the file-position function. This function can be used to query the current position or set a new position within the file, enabling more complex I/O operations such as random access.

```
(format t "Current position: ~a~%" (file-position *input-stream*))
(file-position *input-stream* 128)
(format t "New position: ~a~%" (file-position *input-stream*))
```

Closing Binary Files: After completing read/write operations, it is crucial to close the binary file streams to release system resources. The close function is used for this purpose.

```
(close *input-stream*)
(close *output-stream*)
```

Error Handling: Handling potential errors gracefully is vital in binary file operations to ensure robust and error-resistant code. Common errors include attempts to read beyond the end of a file or write errors due to insufficient disk space. These can be managed using Lisp's condition system.

```
(handler-case
    (let ((byte (read-byte *input-stream*)))
      (format t "Read byte: ~a~%" byte))
  (end-of-file (e)
    (format t "Reached end of file: ~a~%" e))
  (file-error (e)
    (format t "File error: ~a~%" e)))
```

Practical Use Case: Consider the following example that demonstrates a basic scenario of reading an entire binary file into a buffer, processing the buffer, and then writing it to another file. This showcases a practical application of the concepts discussed.

```
(defun process-binary-file (input-filename output-filename)
  (let ((buffer (make-array 1024 :element-type '(unsigned-byte 8))))
    (with-open-file (input-stream input-filename
                     :direction :input
                     :element-type '(unsigned-byte 8))
      (with-open-file (output-stream output-filename
                       :direction :output
                       :element-type '(unsigned-byte 8)
                       )
        (loop while (plusp (read-sequence buffer input-stream))
              do (progn
                   ;; Process the buffer data here
                   (write-sequence buffer output-stream)))))))

(process-binary-file "example.bin" "output.bin")
```

In this example, the process-binary-file function reads chunks of 1024 bytes from the input file, processes them (where a comment indicates that processing would occur), and writes the processed data to the output file.

Understanding and effectively using binary file handling in Lisp opens possibilities for a wide range of applications involving binary data management. This section aims to provide a comprehensive foundation in binary file operations, ensuring program robustness and efficiency.

8.7 Formatted Output

Formatted output in Lisp allows for the creation of text that is structured and aesthetically pleasing, which can be crucial for generating reports, logs, and any kind of user-facing display. Lisp provides several mechanisms to format text output, with the format function being one of the most versatile and widely used.

The format function operates similarly to formatted output functions in other programming languages, such as printf in C or sprintf in Python. The general form of the format function is:

> (format destination control-string &rest arguments)

destination specifies where the output should be directed. It can be a stream, a string (when nil is passed, the output is returned as a string), or t for standard output. The control-string contains the text to be printed along with special tokens (format directives) that are replaced by the values of corresponding arguments.

Here are some common format directives:

- a: Aesthetic representation (prints the argument as is).

- s: Standard representation (prints the argument in a readable format for Lisp objects).

- d: Decimal representation (prints an integer in decimal notation).

- f: Fixed-point notation (prints a floating-point number).

- %: Inserts a newline.

- { }: Iteration construct (used for printing elements of a list or array).

Consider an example where we wish to format output to display a list of students and their grades neatly:

```
(defun print-student-grades (students)
  "Prints the list of students and their grades."
  (format t "Student Name Grade~%")
  (format t "--------------------~%")
  (dolist (student students)
    (destructuring-bind (name grade) student
      (format t "~a~20t~a~% " name grade))))
```

print-student-grades function takes a list of students, each represented as a cons cell with the student's name and grade. It uses 20t to align the grades in a column that starts at the 20th character column. The use of % ensures each student's information is printed on a new line.

```
> (print-student-grades '(("Alice" "A") ("Bob" "B") ("Carol" "C")))
Student Name    Grade
--------------------
Alice           A
Bob             B
Carol           C
```

The t directive is used for tabulation, and its usage can significantly improve the readability of the output, especially when dealing with tabular data.

For more complex formatting, such as aligning columns of numbers or dates, Lisp's format function supports precise control over width, padding, and justification.

Here's an example that demonstrates numerical formatting:

```
(defun print-numerical-data (data)
  "Prints numerical data with headers."
  (format t "~%Number Square Cube~%")
  (format t "-------- -------- ---------~%")
  (dolist (num data)
    (format t "~4d~10d~10d~%" num (* num num) (* num num num
      )))))
```

```
> (print-numerical-data '(2 3 4 5))
Number    Square    Cube
--------  --------  --------
  2         4         8
  3         9        27
  4        16        64
  5        25       125
```

In this example, the numbers are printed in aligned columns with a width of 4 for the number itself and a width of 10 for its square and cube, ensuring clear and consistent formatting.

When dealing with floating-point numbers, the f directive allows specification of the number of digits after the decimal point. For example:

```
(defun print-floats (floats)
  "Prints a list of floating-point numbers formatted to 2 decimal
      places."
  (dolist (num floats)
    (format t "~6,2f~%" num)))
```

```
> (print-floats '(3.14159 2.71828 1.61803))
3.14
2.72
1.62
```

The 6,2f directive specifies that the floating-point number should be printed in a field of width 6, with 2 digits after the decimal point.

Formatted output is an essential tool in a Lisp programmer's toolkit, enabling the creation of professional and easily readable text outputs for a wide range of applications. Stringent control over formatting ensures that data is presented in an orderly and comprehensible manner.

8.8 Handling Large Files

Handling large files efficiently is crucial for many real-world Lisp applications. When working with large data sets, it's essential to write code that minimizes memory usage and processing time while maximizing performance. Several strategies can be employed to handle large files, including buffered reading and writing, using efficient data structures, and leveraging external libraries for optimization.

Buffered I/O is one of the fundamental techniques for managing large files. Instead of reading or writing data one byte at a time, which is inefficient, buffered I/O allows us to process chunks of data, thus reducing the number of I/O operations and enhancing performance.

```
(defun read-large-file-buffered (file-path buffer-size)
  (with-open-file (stream file-path :direction :input)
    (let ((buffer (make-array buffer-size :element-type 'character)))
      (loop for num-chars = (read-sequence buffer stream)
            while (> num-chars 0)
            do (process-chunk buffer num-chars)))))
```

In this example, the read-large-file-buffered function reads chunks of a file in sizes defined by buffer-size. The function process-chunk would handle the actual processing of each chunk read from the file. This method ensures that memory usage is kept in check by not loading the entire file into memory at once.

Similarly, buffered writing can be used to efficiently write large amounts of data to a file:

```
(defun write-large-file-buffered (file-path data buffer-size)
  (with-open-file (stream file-path :direction :output
                                    :if-exists :supersede
                                    :if-does-not-exist :create)
    (loop for start-pos from 0 below (length data) by buffer-size
          for end-pos = (min (+ start-pos buffer-size) (length data))
          do (write-sequence (subseq data start-pos end-pos) stream))
    ))
```

This function, write-large-file-buffered, writes the data to a file in chunks of size buffer-size, ensuring that the memory remains manageable even with large datasets.

Memory mapping is another technique for handling large files efficiently. When using memory mapping, a file is mapped directly into memory, allowing you to access it as if it were a part of your program's memory. This can significantly speed up file access, especially for read-heavy operations. In Common Lisp, this can be achieved using the mmap library.

```
(ql:quickload "mmap")
(use-package :mmap)

(defun read-large-file-mmap (file-path)
  (let ((mapped-file (mmap:file-map file-path :direction :input)))
    (unwind-protect
        (process-mapped-file mapped-file)
      (mmap:unmap mapped-file))))
```

In this example, the read-large-file-mmap function demonstrates how to memory-map a file for reading using the Mmap library. The function process-mapped-file would then handle the processing of the data as if it were loaded into memory.

Using streams wisely is also essential for handling large files in a resource-conscious manner. When dealing with multiple large files or streams of data, it's crucial to ensure that open file descriptors are managed correctly to avoid resource leaks. Properly closing files after use and handling potential exceptions using unwind-protect can prevent such issues:

```
(defun process-multiple-large-files (file-paths)
  (dolist (file-path file-paths)
    (with-open-file (stream file-path :direction :input)
      (unwind-protect
          (process-file-stream stream)
        (close stream)))))
```

The above example uses with-open-file to open each file and ensures that the file is closed properly after processing, even if an error occurs during the file processing.

Efficiently handling large files in Lisp also involves considering appropriate data structures and algorithms suited for large data sets. Algorithms that minimize memory usage and data structures that allow for efficient access and manipulation can significantly improve performance. For example, lazy sequences can be used to process large data sets incrementally:

```
(defun lazy-file-lines (file-path)
  (lambda ()
    (with-open-file (stream file-path :direction :input)
      (loop while (read-line stream nil 'eof)
        collect it))))
```

In the lazy-file-lines function, lines from the file are read lazily, meaning that each line is processed only as needed rather than reading the entire file into memory.

When dealing with exceptionally large files or data sets that do not fit into main memory, external tools and libraries can be leveraged to perform out-of-core processing. Libraries like SB-SYS can assist in managing system-level operations more effectively, including the use of specialized buffers and memory management techniques.

Efficiently handling large files requires a good understanding of both the Lisp programming language and the system-level operations of the platform on which the code is running. Careful attention to memory management, data processing strategies, and proper use of available libraries can ensure robust and efficient handling of large datasets in Lisp.

8.9 Managing File I/O Errors

Effective error handling is essential in robust file I/O operations to ensure your Lisp programs behave predictably under various conditions. This section covers the techniques for detecting and managing errors during file input and output operations.

Error handling in Lisp is generally managed using the handler-case and ignore-errors macros. These constructs allow you to define how your program should respond to different types of errors.

handler-case allows precise control over error handling. Here is an example of how to use it for file I/O operations:

```
(defun read-file-and-handle-errors (filename)
```

237

```
(handler-case
    (with-open-file (stream filename :direction :input)
        (loop for line = (read-line stream nil nil)
            while line
            collect line))
    (file-error (e)
      (format t "An error occurred while opening the file: ~a~%" e))))
```

In this example, handler-case attempts to open the file specified by filename for reading. If a file-error occurs (such as if the file does not exist), the handler prints an error message using format.

When handling multiple error types, you can specify more than one clause in handler-case:

```
(defun read-file-and-handle-multiple-errors (filename)
  (handler-case
      (with-open-file (stream filename :direction :input)
          (loop for line = (read-line stream nil nil)
              while line
              collect line))
      (file-error (e)
        (format t "File error: ~a~%" e))
      (end-of-file (e)
        (format t "Unexpected end of file: ~a~%" e))))
```

In this case, we handle both file-error and end-of-file errors separately, providing a clearer diagnostic message depending on the error type encountered.

The ignore-errors macro offers a simpler way to catch errors, returning nil if an error occurs and suppressing any signaling of the error.

```
(defun read-file-ignore-errors (filename)
  (ignore-errors
    (with-open-file (stream filename :direction :input)
      (loop for line = (read-line stream nil nil)
          while line
          collect line))))
```

This example uses ignore-errors to silently catch any errors that arise during the file reading process. Although it simplifies error handling, it reduces the specificity and visibility of errors, which might not always be desirable.

When working with file streams, you must handle potential errors such as file-error, end-of-file, and read-error. Additionally, guarding against unforeseen errors ensures your program can close file streams properly, thus avoiding resource leaks.

Ensuring proper cleanup often involves utilizing the unwind-protect construct, which guarantees that cleanup code is executed regardless of whether an error occurs.

```
(defun safe-read-file (filename)
  (let ((stream (open filename :direction :input)))
    (unwind-protect
        (loop for line = (read-line stream nil nil)
              while line
              collect line)
      (when stream (close stream)))))
```

In this snippet, unwind-protect ensures that the file stream is closed even if an error occurs within the loop. This approach prevents resource leaks by guaranteeing that the close function is called.

Managing file I/O errors effectively ensures that your programs are resilient and can handle various unexpected situations gracefully, maintaining robust and predictable behavior during execution.

8.10   Network I/O Basics

Understanding Network I/O (Input/Output) opens up the avenue to seamlessly incorporate network communication within Lisp programs. This section covers the fundamental concepts and techniques required to utilize network functionality effectively.

Lisp provides an array of tools and libraries to handle network operations. These tools enable programs to communicate over network protocols such as TCP (Transmission Control Protocol) and UDP (User Datagram Protocol). We will explore the primary library, usocket, which facilitates these operations in a standardized and cross-platform manner.

To begin, ensure that the usocket library is installed and loaded in your Lisp environment. This can be achieved by adding the following lines to your Lisp setup if they are not already present:

```
(ql:quickload "usocket")
```

usocket provides a high-level abstraction of socket programming, allowing for effective network communication without delving deeply into OS-specific socket APIs. Let's delve into creating a simple server and client to illustrate the basic concepts.

Creating a TCP Server

A server waits for incoming connections on a specified port and handles these connections. The following example demonstrates how to create a simple TCP server using usocket:

```
(defpackage :my-server
  (:use :cl :usocket))

(in-package :my-server)

(defun start-server ()
  (let ((socket (socket-listen "127.0.0.1" 4000 :reuse-address t :backlog
      5)))
    (loop
      (let ((client (socket-accept socket)))
        (handle-client client)))))

(defun handle-client (client)
  (unwind-protect
      (let ((stream (socket-stream client)))
        (loop for line = (read-line stream nil)
            while line
            do (format stream "You said: ~a~%" line)))
    (socket-close client)))
```

In this example, the start-server function initiates the server, binding it to 127.0.0.1 on port 4000. The socket-listen function creates a listening socket with a specified backlog. The server enters an infinite loop where it accepts incoming client connections using socket-accept. Each client connection is handed off to the handle-client function.

The handle-client function reads lines from the client, echoing each received line prefixed with "You said: ". The unwind-protect form ensures that the client's socket is closed properly, even if an error occurs.

Creating a TCP Client

240

A client connects to the server and communicates by sending and receiving data. The following example demonstrates how to create a TCP client:

```
(defpackage :my-client
  (:use :cl :usocket))

(in-package :my-client)

(defun start-client ()
  (let* ((socket (socket-connect "127.0.0.1" 4000))
         (stream (socket-stream socket)))
    (unwind-protect
        (progn
          (format stream "Hello, Server!~%")
          (force-output stream)
          (loop for line = (read-line stream nil)
                while line
                do (format t "~a~%" line)))
      (socket-close socket))))
```

The start-client function connects to the server at 127.0.0.1 on port 4000 using socket-connect. It then sends a greeting message to the server. The client enters a loop, reading responses from the server and printing them to the terminal. The unwind-protect form ensures proper closing of the socket upon completion.

Error Handling in Network I/O

Proper error handling is crucial for robust network applications. Network operations can fail due to various reasons such as network unavailability, server overload, or unexpected disconnections. Using condition handling constructs like handler-case or ignore-errors helps manage these scenarios gracefully.

For instance, enhancing the server's client handling with error management:

```
(defun handle-client (client)
  (unwind-protect
      (handler-case
          (let ((stream (socket-stream client)))
            (loop for line = (read-line stream nil)
                  while line
```

```
        do (format stream "You said: ~a~%" line)))
    (error (e)
        (format t "Error handling client: ~a~%" e)))
  (socket-close client)))
```

The handler-case construct captures any error occurring within the client handling logic, printing an error message before closing the client's socket.

Using UDP for Datagram-based Communication

TCP provides a reliable, connection-oriented communication, but sometimes, a connectionless protocol like UDP is more suitable. UDP is often used for applications requiring fast, lossy transmission, such as streaming services or real-time games.

Creating and handling UDP sockets in usocket involves using socket-send and socket-receive functions:

```
(defpackage :my-udp-client
  (:use :cl :usocket))

(in-package :my-udp-client)

(defun start-udp-client ()
  (let ((socket (socket-datagram-listen :local-port 5000)))
    (unwind-protect
        (progn
          (socket-send socket "Server" "127.0.0.1" 6000)
          (multiple-value-bind (data addr port)
              (socket-receive socket)
            (format t "Received from ~a: ~a~%" addr data)))
      (socket-close socket))))
```

The socket-datagram-listen function creates a UDP socket listening on port 5000. The client sends a datagram to the server at 127.0.0.1 on port 6000 using socket-send. It then waits to receive a response with socket-receive, printing the received data.

Understanding these foundational concepts of Lisp network I/O equips you with the ability to integrate network communication into your Lisp applications robustly and efficiently.

8.11 Libraries for Advanced I/O Operations

Advanced I/O operations in Lisp can be greatly facilitated by leveraging robust libraries designed to encompass a wide range of functionalities, extending beyond the basic I/O and file handling offered by the standard system.

CL-FAD (Common Lisp File and Directory) provides extensive high-level functionalities for file and directory manipulation including symbolic links handling, directory traversal, and obtaining file metadata. Below, we delve into the primary features of CL-FAD and how to effectively utilize them in your Lisp applications.

To begin using CL-FAD, you need to load the library:

```
(ql:quickload "cl-fad")
```

```
To load "cl-fad":
  Load 1 ASDF system:
    cl-fad
; Loading "cl-fad"
  ...
```

Directory Traversal

One of the strengths of CL-FAD is simplified directory traversal. The function cl-fad:walk-directory is precisely tailored for this purpose. It walks through a specified directory, calling a provided function on each file and subdirectory encountered.

```
(cl-fad:walk-directory "/path/to/directory"
  (lambda (path)
    (format t "~a~%" path)))
```

This code traverses the specified directory, printing the pathname of each file and subdirectory.

File Metadata

Retrieving detailed file metadata is another essential functionality. The function cl-fad:file-properties returns attributes such as file type, last-modified date, and size.

```
(let ((properties (cl-fad:file-properties "/path/to/file")))
  (format t "File Type: ~a~%" (cl-fad:file-info-type properties))
  (format t "Last Modified: ~a~%" (cl-fad:file-info-last-modified
      properties))
  (format t "File Size: ~a bytes~%" (cl-fad:file-info-size properties)))
```

Here, the code fetches and prints the type, last modified timestamp, and size of the specified file.

Symbolic Links

Managing symbolic links is facilitated through functions such as cl-fad:make-link and cl-fad:follow-link.

Create a symbolic link using:

```
(cl-fad:make-link "/path/to/target" "/path/to/link")
```

To resolve the actual path of a symbolic link, use:

```
(let ((resolved-path (cl-fad:follow-link "/path/to/link")))
  (format t "Resolved Path: ~a~%" resolved-path))
```

Higher-Level I/O Libraries

Beyond CL-FAD, other libraries such as BORDEAUX-THREADS and USOCKET extend the capabilities for handling complex I/O tasks including concurrent I/O operations and network I/O.

Bordeaux-Threads provides a portable, standardized interface for multi-threading operations compatible across various Lisp implementations. This is crucial when dealing with I/O-bound tasks that need parallel execution. Here is an example using bordeaux-threads for handling multiple file read operations:

```
(ql:quickload "bordeaux-threads")
```

```
To load "bordeaux-threads":
  Load 1 ASDF system:
    bordeaux-threads
; Loading "bordeaux-threads"
...
```

Launching multiple threads using bordeaux-threads:

```
(let ((filenames '("file1.txt" "file2.txt" "file3.txt")))
  (mapcar (lambda (filename)
            (bt:make-thread
             (lambda ()
               (with-open-file (stream filename)
                 (loop for line = (read-line stream nil)
                       while line
                       do (format t "~a~%" line))))))
```

```
           filenames))
```

This example illustrates creating multiple threads, each tasked with reading and printing lines from different files.

Network I/O

For network I/O, USOCKET provides a comprehensive suite of functions for socket-based communication, making it feasible to handle networking tasks in your applications.

```
(ql:quickload "usocket")
```

```
To load "usocket":
  Load 1 ASDF system:
    usocket
; Loading "usocket"
...
```

Creating a TCP server:

```
(defun start-tcp-server (port)
  (let ((server (usocket:socket-listen "127.0.0.1" port)))
    (unwind-protect
         (loop
            (let ((client (usocket:socket-accept server)))
              (bt:make-thread
               (lambda ()
                 (unwind-protect
                      (let ((stream (usocket:socket-stream client)))
                        (format t "Accepted connection from ~a~%"
                                (usocket:peer-address client))
                        (do ((line (read-line stream nil) (read-line
                             stream nil)))
                            ((null line))
                          (format t "Received: ~a~%" line)))
                   (usocket:socket-close client))))))
      (usocket:socket-close server))))
```

This function initializes a TCP server that listens for connections on the specified port. Each client connection is handled in a separate thread, reading and printing lines received from the client.

Each of the highlighted libraries ensures that Lisp programmers can handle advanced I/O operations efficiently, leveraging the power and flexibility of Lisp.

8.12   Best Practices for I/O and File Handling

Effective input/output (I/O) operations and file handling are essential for creating robust and performant Lisp programs. Adhering to best practices can lead to more maintainable, extendable, and efficient code. This section discusses various strategies and guidelines that can be employed to improve the quality of I/O and file processing in Lisp.

First, it is crucial to ensure that all file operations are enclosed in appropriate error-handling mechanisms. This helps in managing unexpected scenarios, such as missing files or permission errors, and allows for graceful program termination or recovery. Lisp provides constructs such as handler-case and ignore-errors for this purpose.

```
(handler-case
    (with-open-file (stream "example.txt" :direction :input)
      (loop for line = (read-line stream nil)
            while line do (format t "~a~%" line)))
  (file-error (e)
    (format t "An error occurred: ~a~%" e)))
```

It is also recommended to use the with-open-file macro for file operations. This macro ensures that files are properly closed after their operations are completed, even if an error occurs during the operation. This helps in preventing resource leaks which can lead to file descriptor exhaustion or other system resource constraints.

```
(with-open-file (stream "data.txt" :direction :output :if-exists :
    supersede)
  (format stream "This is an example text written to the file.~%"))
```

When dealing with large files, it is efficient to process files in chunks rather than reading the entire file into memory. This approach minimizes memory usage and can significantly enhance performance for very large datasets.

```
(with-open-file (stream "largefile.txt" :direction :input)
  (loop for block = (make-array 1024 :element-type 'character)
        for bytes-read = (read-sequence block stream)
        while (> bytes-read 0) do
        (process-block block bytes-read)))
```

Proper buffering of I/O operations can also boost performance. By default, Lisp streams are usually buffered, but it can be beneficial to understand and manually adjust the buffer sizes when dealing with high-volume or real-time data streams to avoid frequent I/O operations, which are often expensive.

Consider the format string and escape sequences properly while dealing with formatted outputs. Using format in Lisp can be powerful, but it requires careful construction of format strings to avoid runtime errors and ensure the output is as expected.

```
(format t "~{~a ~}" '(1 2 3 4 5))
```

To ensure the portability and reliability of code, it is good practice to handle different character encodings and newline representations explicitly. Functions like read-line and write-line might need special consideration of encoding formats—UTF-8, ASCII, etc.—to avoid issues when files are shared across different environments.

Prevent and manage I/O errors by validating inputs and outputs appropriately. Before performing file operations, check for file existence and permissions to avoid runtime errors using functions such as probe-file and file-write-date.

```
(defun safe-open-file (filename mode)
  (if (probe-file filename)
      (with-open-file (stream filename :direction mode)
        stream)
      (error "File ~a does not exist" filename)))
```

Concurrent file access scenarios need synchronization mechanisms to prevent race conditions and ensure data consistency. Use locks or other concurrency control structures provided by Lisp to manage simultaneous file access effectively.

```
(defvar *file-lock* (make-lock "File Lock"))

(defun read-shared-file (filename)
  (with-lock-held (*file-lock*)
    (with-open-file (stream filename :direction :input)
      (loop for line = (read-line stream nil)
            while line collect line))))
```

Finally, always document and comment on the file processing functions to make the code more understandable and maintainable. Clear documentation helps other developers (or future you) comprehend the intent and functionality of the code, reducing the maintenance burden and enabling easier debugging or extension.

Adopting these best practices for I/O and file handling in Lisp can lead to more stable, readable, and efficient codebases, contributing to the overall quality and robustness of software projects.

Chapter 9

Error Handling and Debugging

This chapter focuses on error handling and debugging techniques in Lisp. It covers the different types of errors and introduces the condition system for catching and throwing errors. Readers will learn about using 'handler-bind' and 'restart', creating custom conditions, and basic debugging practices. The chapter also explores the use of the debugger, setting breakpoints, step-through debugging, and inspecting and modifying program state. Popular debugging tools and best practices are discussed to equip readers with the skills necessary for effective error management and troubleshooting in Lisp programs.

9.1 Introduction to Error Handling

In Lisp programming, as in many other languages, error handling is a crucial aspect of robust software development. Proper error handling ensures that programs can gracefully handle unexpected situations, maintain functionality, and provide meaningful feedback to the user. This section delves into the fundamental concepts of error handling in Lisp, laying the groundwork for more advanced techniques discussed in subsequent sections.

Lisp, with its rich history and dynamic nature, has developed sophisticated mechanisms for error detection and recovery. The central components that facilitate error handling in Lisp are conditions, handlers, and restarts. These components work together to create a flexible and powerful system for managing errors and other exceptional situations.

A condition is an object that represents an exceptional situation, such as an error or a warning. This object contains information about the nature of the problem. Conditions are classified into various types, allowing developers to define and handle specific conditions based on their program's requirements.

A handler is a function designed to manage particular conditions. When a condition is signaled, the Lisp runtime searches for an appropriate handler to invoke. Handlers can perform various actions, such as logging the error, prompting the user, or attempting a recovery strategy.

Restarts provide a mechanism for resuming execution after an error condition has been handled. They act as predefined recovery strategies that handlers can invoke, allowing the program to continue its execution from a specific state. Restarts enable developers to separate error detection from error recovery, creating a more modular and maintainable codebase.

To get a firm grasp on these concepts, consider the following example of basic error signaling and handling using Lisp's condition system. The example demonstrates how a simple condition can be signaled and handled within a controlled environment.

```
(defun divide (numerator denominator)
  (if (zerop denominator)
      (error 'division-by-zero :numerator numerator :denominator
          denominator)
      (/ numerator denominator)))

(define-condition division-by-zero (error)
  ((numerator :initarg :numerator :reader numerator)
   (denominator :initarg :denominator :reader denominator))
  (:report (lambda (condition stream)
              (format stream "Cannot divide ~A by ~A"
                  (numerator condition)
                  (denominator condition)))))

(handler-case
    (write-line (format nil "~A" (divide 10 0)))
  (division-by-zero (e)
```

```
(format t "~&Caught a division by zero error: ~A~%" e)))
```

In the divide function, we check if the denominator is zero. If it is, an error is signaled using the error function, creating an instance of the division-by-zero condition. The division-by-zero condition is defined using define-condition, specifying the slots numerator and denominator, and a custom report method for displaying a descriptive message.

The handling of this condition is performed using handler-case. If a division-by-zero condition is signaled within the handler-case form, the handler for division-by-zero captures the condition object e and prints a message.

Programs often need more sophisticated error handling scenarios, involving multiple condition types and various handling strategies. Lisp's condition system supports this flexibility, enabling developers to define an array of condition types and corresponding handlers.

Understanding the careful balance between signaling conditions and handling them correctly is essential for writing fault-tolerant Lisp programs. Robust error handling not only aids in maintaining program stability but also enhances user experience by providing clear and actionable feedback during exceptional scenarios.

Advanced techniques, including using handler-bind for more control over condition handling and employing restarts for flexible recovery strategies, are discussed in subsequent sections. Mastery of these concepts will enable you to develop Lisp programs that are both resilient and user-friendly.

9.2 Types of Errors in Lisp

Understanding the types of errors that can occur in Lisp is critical for effective debugging and error handling. In Lisp, errors are categorized into several types, which correspond to different conditions that the system can signal. This section will delve into the most common types of errors, including syntax errors, runtime errors, and logical errors.

Syntax Errors: Syntax errors occur when the source code is not correctly formed according to the rules of the Lisp language. For instance, missing parentheses or invalid special symbols will result in syntax errors. Here is an example of a syntax error:

```
(defun add (a b)
  (+ a b)) ; Missing closing parenthesis
```

Attempting to compile or interpret the above code will produce a syntax error message indicating that the parentheses are mismatched.

Runtime Errors: These errors occur during the execution of a Lisp program. They usually result from invalid operations, such as attempting to access an element out of the bounds of a list, divide by zero, or call a function with incorrect arguments. Here's an example:

```
(defun divide (x y)
  (/ x y))

(divide 10 0) ; Division by zero
```

Executing (divide 10 0) would result in a runtime error because dividing by zero is not a valid operation. Lisp systems signal these errors using specific conditions, such as division-by-zero.

Logical Errors: Logical errors are more subtle and occur when the code does not perform the expected task, even though it runs without syntax or runtime errors. These errors often arise from mistakes in the algorithm or incorrect assumptions about the input data. Consider the following example:

```
(defun factorial (n)
  (if (<= n 1)
      1
      (* n (factorial (- n 1)))))

(factorial -5) ; Incorrect handling of negative numbers
```

While this code correctly computes the factorial for non-negative integers, it fails to handle negative inputs appropriately, thus leading to an infinite recursion and a potential stack overflow.

Type Errors: Type errors occur when an operation is performed on an argument of an incompatible type. In strongly typed Lisp implementations, such arguments cause immediate failure. For instance:

```
(defun concatenate (a b)
  (concatenate 'string a b))

(concatenate 'hello " world") ; Attempt to concatenate a symbol with
```

```
a string
```

The above code attempts to concatenate a symbol ('hello) with a string, which results in a type error since 'hello is not a string.

Name Errors: Name errors occur when referencing undefined variables or functions. These errors are usually straightforward to detect and fix since Lisp provides clear messages indicating the non-existence of the specified name. For instance:

```
(print (undefined-variable))
```

This results in a name error, indicating that undefined-variable is not defined.

Memory Errors: These errors are related to invalid memory access, which is rare in modern high-level Lisp implementations due to automatic memory management and garbage collection routines. However, when interfacing with lower-level system constructs or foreign functions, such issues might arise.

Identifying and categorizing errors appropriately is the first step toward constructing robust error handling mechanisms in Lisp programs. Comprehensive understanding of these error types enables the programmer to anticipate potential issues and implement strategies to mitigate their impact.

9.3 Catching and Throwing Errors

In Lisp, the mechanisms for error handling revolve around the concepts of *catching* and *throwing* errors using the condition system. This section will elucidate the fundamental aspects of catching and throwing errors. Understanding these concepts is crucial for the development of robust and fault-tolerant Lisp applications.

Throwing Errors In Lisp, the signal function is used to throw an error. When signal is called, it initiates the search for a suitable handler that can process the condition. The typical syntax for signaling an error is:

```
(signal condition-type format-string &rest format-arguments)
```

Here, condition-type is a symbol representing the type of the condition being signaled. format-string is a control string for formatting the error message, and format-arguments are the arguments used to replace the placeholders in format-string. For example:

```
(signal 'simple-error "An error occurred: ~A" "Invalid input")
```

The above expression creates and signals a condition of type simple-error. It includes a formatted error message stating "An error occurred: Invalid input".

Catching Errors   To handle conditions once they are signaled, Lisp provides the handler-case construct. handler-case enables the specification of handlers for particular types of conditions. The syntax for handler-case is as follows:

```
(handler-case expression
  (condition-type (variable)
    handler-body))
```

An expression is evaluated within the handler-case. If it successfully completes without signaling a condition, its result is returned. However, if a condition of condition-type arises, the corresponding handler-body is executed with variable bound to the condition. For example:

```
(defun divide (numerator denominator)
  (handler-case (/ numerator denominator)
    (division-by-zero (e)
      (format t "Cannot divide by zero!~%")
      nil)))
```

This function attempts to divide numerator by denominator. If a division-by-zero condition is signaled, the handler prints a message and returns nil.

Common Use Cases   Catching and throwing errors are often employed in various scenarios such as:

- **Resource Management**: Ensuring that resources like files or network connections are correctly released, even when errors occur.

- **Data Validation**: Checking input data for correctness and signaling errors when data does not conform to expected formats.

254

- **Control Flow**: Changing the normal flow of execution in response to exceptional conditions.

Combining signal **and** handler-case   The true power of the condition system is evident when combining signal and handler-case to create customized error-handling logic. One can even invoke specific recovery strategies based on the type of error encountered. For illustrative purposes, consider this enhanced example:

```
(defun fetch-data (source)
  (handler-case
      (progn
        (check-source source)
        (retrieve-data source))
    (source-not-found (e)
      (format t "Source not found: ~A~%" (
         simple-condition-format-arguments e))
      (use-alternative-source))
    (network-error (e)
      (format t "Network error occurred. Retrying...~%")
      (retry-fetch source)))))
```

In the above function, fetch-data attempts to check the validity of source and retrieve data. If a source-not-found condition is signaled, it handles it by notifying the user and switching to an alternative source. If a network-error occurs, it will attempt to retry the fetch operation.

Propagating Conditions   Lisp also provides facilities to propagate conditions up the call stack when immediate handling is not possible. This is useful in scenarios like deferring error handling to a higher-level context where more contextual information might be available.

```
(defun step-1 ()
  (step-2))

(defun step-2 ()
  (step-3))

(defun step-3 ()
  (signal 'simple-error "Step 3 failed!"))
```

Here, when step-3 signals an error, the condition can propagate back through step-2 to step-1, allowing any function in the stack to catch and handle the error.

The described concepts establish a solid foundation for error management in Lisp programs, ensuring applications can gracefully handle unexpected conditions while maintaining robustness and stability.

9.4   Condition System in Lisp

The condition system in Lisp provides a powerful mechanism for managing errors and exceptional conditions. Unlike conventional programming languages that use a straightforward try-catch model, the Lisp condition system offers more flexibility and control, allowing programs to handle errors in more sophisticated and customizable ways.

Conditions: The Basics

In Lisp, conditions are objects that represent exceptional situations or error states. They belong to classes that can be specialized to represent specific types of errors. Conditions are signaled using the signal function, which begins the process of error handling.

```
(signal 'simple-error :format-control "An error occurred" :
    format-arguments nil)
```

This example signals a simple-error condition with a specific error message. The signal function takes the condition type and additional keyword arguments that provide details about the error.

Handlers and Restarts

Two core components of the condition system are handlers and restarts. Handlers specify actions to take when specific conditions are signaled, while restarts provide possible recovery options to resume normal operation after an error.

handler-bind establishes dynamic associations between condition types and handling functions. When a condition of the specified type is signaled, the corresponding handler is invoked.

```
(handler-bind
```

```
((simple-error (lambda (condition)
                  (format t "Handled ~A~%" condition)))))
 (signal 'simple-error :format-control "This is a test error" :
     format-arguments nil))
```

In this example, when a simple-error is signaled, the anonymous function prints a message indicating that the error has been handled. The handler can perform various actions, such as logging the error, notifying the user, or attempting automatic recovery.

Restarts, defined using restart-case, provide mechanisms to recover from errors. Restarts are akin to checkpoints where execution can resume following an error.

```
(restart-case
    (signal 'simple-error :format-control "Restarts example" :
        format-arguments nil)
    (continue () (format t "Continuing after error"))
    (abort () (format t "Aborting operation")))
```

This code segment signals a simple-error and provides two restarts: continue and abort. Each restart specifies an action to take if it is selected.

Advanced Condition Handling

Lisp's condition system allows for advanced error handling strategies. For more specific control, use handler-case, similar to handler-bind but allows for a more structured way to catch and handle conditions directly.

```
(handler-case
    (error "An error occurred")
    (simple-error (e) (format t "Caught ~A~%" e))
    (error (e) (format t "General catch for any error: ~A~%" e)))
```

In this snippet, handler-case catches simple-error separately from other errors, demonstrating its capability for precise condition handling.

Custom conditions can be defined to suit specific needs by creating new condition types using define-condition.

```
(define-condition my-custom-error (error)
    ((details :initarg :details :reader error-details))
    (:documentation "A custom error type with additional details"))
```

```
(handler-case
    (signal 'my-custom-error :details "Custom error encountered")
  (my-custom-error (e)
    (format t "Caught custom error: ~A~%" (error-details e))))
```

Here, a custom condition my-custom-error is defined, including an additional slot details for extra error information. When this error is signaled within a handler-case, the handler can access and process the additional details.

Best Practices for Using the Condition System

When using Lisp's condition system, some best practices help in maximizing effectiveness:

- Define specific condition types for different error scenarios to allow precise handling.

- Use handler-bind for dynamically scoped error handlers that can adapt based on the program's execution context.

- Provide multiple restarts for critical sections of code, empowering users or other parts of the program to choose the most appropriate recovery action.

- Leverage custom conditions to encapsulate and convey detailed information about errors, making debugging and error reporting more informative.

- Document condition types and handlers thoroughly to maintain clarity and ease of maintenance.

Lisp's condition system, with its robust mechanisms and flexible error-handling capabilities, provides developers with the tools needed to write resilient and maintainable code. Its integration ensures that programs can gracefully handle exceptional situations, improving reliability and enhancing debugging processes.

9.5 Using Handler-Bind and Restart

Error handling in Lisp is considerably advanced, providing robust mechanisms to manage runtime issues gracefully. Two core constructs in this domain are handler-bind and restart. These forms allow developers to define complex interactions for error handling and recovery, offering both flexibility and control.

handler-bind is a macro that allows associating specific handlers with particular types of conditions. When an error matching the condition type occurs, the corresponding handler is invoked.

The basic syntax for handler-bind is as follows:

```
(handler-bind ((condition-type condition-handler))
  body)
```

To illustrate, consider the following code, which handles division by zero errors:

```
(handler-bind ((division-by-zero
               (lambda (c)
                 (format t "Handled division by zero.")
                 (invoke-restart 'use-zero))))
  (restart-case
    (/ 10 0)
    (use-zero () 0)))
```

In this example, handler-bind associates the division-by-zero condition with a specific handler function. When the division by zero occurs, the handler outputs a message and invokes the use-zero restart to substitute the division result with zero.

restart-case is another pivotal construct that defines potential recovery strategies for conditions encountered during program execution. The setup includes a primary expression that may trigger a condition and one or more restarts that offer recovery strategies.

The following example elaborates on using restart-case to manage file opening errors:

```
(defun open-file-safe (filename)
  (restart-case
      (with-open-file (stream filename)
        (process-file stream))
```

```
(use-default-file ()
  (open-file-safe "default.txt"))
(skip-file ()
  nil)))
```

This function attempts to open a specified file and processes it. If the file is not available, two restarts are provided: use-default-file and skip-file. The use-default-file restart reattempts processing with a default file, while skip-file skips the operation altogether.

Combining handler-bind and restart-case enables a nuanced approach to error handling, as demonstrated below:

```
(defun process-user-input (input)
  (handler-bind ((parse-error
                  (lambda (c)
                    (format t "Parsing error: ~a" (slot-value c '
                      message))
                    (invoke-restart 'retry))))
    (restart-case
        (parse-input input)
      (retry ()
        (let ((new-input (get-new-input)))
          (process-user-input new-input)))
      (terminate ()
        (format t "Terminating process")))))
```

Here, the function process-user-input parses user input. If a parse error occurs, handler-bind directs control to a handler that displays an error message and invokes a retry restart, prompting the user for new input. Another restart, terminate, allows graceful termination if continued attempts are not viable.

Custom conditions can be created to extend the versatility of error handling. This involves defining new condition types, such as:

```
(define-condition my-error (error)
  ((message :initarg :message :reader error-message)))

(defun demonstrate-custom-condition ()
  (handler-bind ((my-error
                  (lambda (c)
                    (format t "Caught a custom error: ~a"
                      (error-message c))
```

```
                    (invoke-restart 'recover))))
(restart-case
    (signal 'my-error :message "An issue occurred!")
    (recover ()
      (format t "Recovery is in progress..."))))))
```

In this example, my-error is a custom condition type with an associated message slot. The function demonstrate-custom-condition binds a handler to my-error, printing the message and invoking a recover restart to manage the situation.

Using handler-bind and restart effectively enhances the robustness of error handling in Lisp programs. These constructs empower developers to encapsulate fault-tolerant behavior, ensuring logical responses to runtime anomalies. This integration fosters resilience and aids in maintaining uninterrupted program flow, even during unforeseen conditions.

Understanding these mechanisms is crucial for advancing toward expert-level Lisp programming, where error management and recovery are indispensable.

9.6 Creating Custom Conditions

Custom conditions in Lisp provide a powerful mechanism to signal and handle application-specific errors in a flexible and modular manner. By defining new condition types, programmers can tailor error handling to context-specific needs, enhancing robustness and maintainability.

A condition in Lisp can be any instance of a condition class, which inherits from the base class condition. New condition types can be created by defining a new class that inherits from condition or one of its subclasses such as error or warning.

To create a custom condition, you use the defclass macro. This allows you to define a class with slots for any additional information relevant to the condition. Conditions are typically signaled using signal, error, or warn, depending on whether the condition is considered non-fatal, fatal, or a simple warning.

Example of Defining a Custom Condition   Consider a scenario where we need to define a custom condition for a missing configuration file. We need to create a class for this custom condition that includes information about the missing file.

```
(defclass missing-config-file (error)
  ((filename :initarg :filename
             :accessor missing-config-file-filename
             :initform nil
             :type string
             :documentation "The name of the missing configuration
                file."))
  (:documentation "Condition raised when a required configuration
     file is missing."))
```

In the above code, we define a new class missing-config-file that inherits from error. It has a single slot filename, which stores the name of the missing file. The :initarg keyword specifies the keyword argument to use when creating an instance of the condition, and the :accessor keyword defines a function to retrieve the value of the slot.

Signaling a Custom Condition   Once the custom condition is defined, it can be signaled using the error function.

```
(defun load-config (filename)
  "Load the configuration from the specified FILENAME."
  (unless (probe-file filename)
    (error 'missing-config-file :filename filename))
  (with-open-file (stream filename)
    ;; Code to read configuration data
    ))
```

In this example, the load-config function attempts to load a configuration file. If the file does not exist, it signals an missing-config-file condition, passing the filename as an argument.

Handling a Custom Condition   To handle the custom condition, we use the condition system with constructs like handler-bind or handler-case.

```
(handler-case
    (load-config "config.lisp")
  (missing-config-file (e)
    (format t "Config file ~A is missing.~%" (
```

```
        missing-config-file-filename e))))
```

In this code, handler-case is used to handle the missing-config-file condition if it is signaled during the execution of load-config. The handler prints an error message including the name of the missing file.

Using Restart to Recover from Conditions Lisp supports the use of restarts as a mechanism to recover from conditions. By providing restarts, programs can offer ways to resolve the condition and continue execution.

```
(defun load-config (filename)
  "Load the configuration from the specified FILENAME."
  (restart-case
      (unless (probe-file filename)
        (error 'missing-config-file :filename filename))
    (use-default-configuration ()
      :report "Use the default configuration."
      (format t "Using default configuration.~%")) ;; Code to use
          default configuration
    (try-another-file ()
      :report "Try another configuration file."
      (let ((new-filename (prompt-for-filename)))
        (load-config new-filename)))))
```

In this revised version of load-config, a restart-case is used to define two restarts: use-default-configuration and try-another-file. If the configuration file is missing, the error is signaled, but the user is given the option to either use a default configuration or try loading a different file.

Conclusion By defining custom conditions and leveraging Lisp's condition system, developers can create sophisticated error handling mechanisms tailored to their specific needs. This permits a high degree of granularity in error reporting and resolution while maintaining the clarity and maintainability of the codebase. Custom conditions, in conjunction with handlers and restarts, provide a robust framework for managing errors in a Lisp application.

9.7   Debugging Basics

Debugging is a critical skill in programming, which entails identifying and resolving bugs or defects in software. This section will introduce fundamental debugging techniques in Lisp, providing a foundation for more advanced practices. Lisp offers a rich environment for debugging, integrating various tools and methods to help developers efficiently troubleshoot and improve their programs.

Begin by examining the role of the trace function, an essential tool in the Lisp debugger's toolkit. The trace function allows you to monitor the calls to a specific function, displaying each call with its arguments and results. This aids in identifying the flow of execution and understanding how data changes throughout the function calls.

To use the trace function, simply call it with the name of the function you want to trace. For instance, consider a function that calculates the factorial of a number:

```
(defun factorial (n)
  (if (<= n 1)
      1
      (* n (factorial (- n 1)))))
```

To trace the factorial function, use the following command:

```
(trace factorial)
```

With tracing enabled, any invocation of factorial will now output details about the call:

```
(factorial 3)
```

The output will be:

```
0: (FACTORIAL 3)
  1: (FACTORIAL 2)
    2: (FACTORIAL 1)
    2: FACTORIAL returned 1
  1: FACTORIAL returned 2
0: FACTORIAL returned 6
```

This output shows a hierarchical view of the function calls, with indentation representing the call depth. Each entry indicates when a call is made, displaying the function name and arguments, followed by the returned value upon completion of that call.

To stop tracing a function, use the untrace command:

```
(untrace factorial)
```

Another valuable debugging technique in Lisp is the break function, which can be inserted into your code to create breakpoints. When execution reaches a break function call, it pauses, allowing you to interact with the Lisp environment and inspect the current state. For example:

```
(defun debug-fact (n)
  (if (<= n 1)
      1
      (progn
        (break "Reached recursive case with n=~A" n)
        (* n (debug-fact (- n 1))))))
```

When calling debug-fact with a value, execution will halt at the break point, enabling examination of the current value of n and other aspects of the environment.

```
(debug-fact 3)
```

This call will emit the following prompt:

Reached recursive case with n=3Break (type 'c' to continue, 'ab' to abort, 'q' to quit):

At this prompt, you can: - Type c to continue execution. - Type ab to abort the current function call. - Type q to quit the program.

Lisp also provides the assert function, which is useful for runtime verification. assert checks a condition and signals an error if the condition is false. This is instrumental in ensuring certain invariants or conditions hold true at specific points in a program. For instance:

```
(defun safe-divide (numerator denominator)
  (assert (/= denominator 0) (denominator)
          "Denominator cannot be zero.")
  (/ numerator denominator))
```

Calling safe-divide with a zero denominator causes an error with a descriptive message:

```
(safe-divide 10 0)
```

Resulting in:

265

Assertion failed: Denominator cannot be zero.
  [Condition of type SIMPLE-ERROR]

These basic debugging techniques form the foundation for more complex error-handling and debugging strategies. Mastery of trace, break, and assert can significantly enhance your capability to identify and resolve issues in Lisp programs. Applying these methods facilitates a deeper understanding of your code's behavior and better assurance of its correctness and robustness.

9.8   Using the Debugger

The debugger in Lisp is a powerful tool for diagnosing and resolving issues within programs. It allows for inspection of the call stack, variables, and execution flow. Mastering the use of the debugger is crucial for effective debugging practices. This section explores the functionalities and utilization of the debugger within a Lisp environment.

When an error occurs, the Lisp system enters the debugger automatically. Consider the following example:

```
(defun example-function (x y)
  (/ x y))
(example-function 10 0)
```

Executing this code results in a division by zero error, which triggers the debugger. The immediate response from the Lisp system provides a prompt with information about the error and the current state of the program. This is exemplary output:

Error: Division by zero.
    [Condition of type DIVISION-BY-ZERO]

Restart options:
0: Return to Top Level (an "abort" restart)
1: Retry evaluation of the form (example-function 10 0).
2: Return a value (specify value).
3: Retry once again.

The debugger provides several tools and commands for inspecting and managing this error state.

To inspect the call stack, the backtrace command can be used. This command displays the sequence of function calls that led to the current error condition. Consider the following usage within the debugger:

```
(backtrace)
```

The output elucidates the stack frames:

```
0: (EXAMPLE-FUNCTION 10 0)
1: (EVAL (EXAMPLE-FUNCTION 10 0))
...
N: TOP-LEVEL
```

This backtrace enables the user to trace the sequence of function calls that culminated in the error.

Another valuable command is frame-variable, which inspects the variables within a selected stack frame. For example, to examine the values of x and y in the function example-function, one can use the following:

```
(frame-variable 0 'x)
(frame-variable 0 'y)
```

Where 0 is the index of the stack frame corresponding to example-function. The output indicates the values of these variables at the point of the error.

```
X = 10
Y = 0
```

Modifying variable values is also feasible within the debugger. This can be done by setting new values to the variables in a specific frame. Employ the setf command to achieve this:

```
(setf (frame-variable 0 'y) 1)
```

The above command modifies the value of y within the zeroth stack frame to 1. After altering the state, one can resume program execution using suitable restart options provided by the debugger.

Custom debugging utilities can also be established through handler-bind and restart. These constructs allow for the arrangement of handlers and restarts that are visible within the context of the debugger, providing control over error handling and recovery.

For example:

```
(handler-bind ((division-by-zero
                (lambda (condition)
                  (invoke-restart 'use-value 1))))
  (example-function 10 0))
```

In this code, a custom handler for the division-by-zero condition is defined, initiating the use-value restart with a value of 1. Within the debugger, these defined handlers and restarts can be integrated seamlessly, facilitating advanced debugging mechanisms.

Finally, conditional breakpoints can be set within the code to halt execution upon certain conditions. For example:

```
(trap '(example-function)
    (lambda () (when (= y 0) (break "Y is zero!"))))
```

This code sets a trap on example-function, invoking a break when y equals 0. Upon encountering the breakpoint, the debugger activates, pausing execution and enabling inspection and modification of the program state.

These tools and techniques form the core aspects of utilizing the Lisp debugger effectively, aiding in immersive and interactive debugging to address and mitigate program errors.

9.9   Breakpoints and Step-through Debugging

Breakpoints and step-through debugging are essential techniques in Lisp for pausing program execution and examining the program state. These techniques facilitate identifying and resolving errors by allowing developers to inspect variable values, program flow, and logic at specific points in their code.

Breakpoints can be set in Lisp using various methods depending on the development environment and tools being used. A breakpoint is essentially an intentional stopping point set in the source code where program execution will halt. This allows developers to inspect the state of the program at that specific location.

To set a breakpoint in a typical Lisp environment, such as SLIME (Superior Lisp Interaction Mode for Emacs), you can use the following methods:

```
(break)
```

Inserting (break) in your Lisp code will halt the program when it reaches that point, invoking the debugger and allowing you to inspect the current state.

Another method to set a breakpoint dynamically is by using the :b command in the SLIME REPL:

```
(slime-break "function-name")
```

Breakpoints are particularly useful in combination with step-through debugging, which allows you to execute your program one step at a time. This way, you can closely observe how the program state changes with each executed line or function call.

Step-through debugging in SLIME can be controlled using commands like:

- :next - Execute the next expression.

- :step - Step into the next expression.

- :out - Step out to the caller of the current function.

- :continue - Continue executing until the next breakpoint or error.

Consider the following example function in Lisp:

```
(defun factorial (n)
  (if (<= n 1)
      1
      (* n (factorial (1- n))))))
```

To debug this function, you can insert a breakpoint and start step-through debugging as follows:

```
(defun factorial (n)
  (break "Debugging factorial function")
  (if (<= n 1)
      1
      (* n (factorial (1- n))))))
```

When the factorial function is called, execution will halt at the breakpoint. Then, using the step-through commands, you can execute and inspect each expression:

```
* (factorial 5)

Breakpoint hit at: (FACTORIAL N)
Debugging factorial function

1. Return to Break level.
2. Next (Step to the next expression).
3. Step (Step into the next expression).
4. Out (Step out to the caller of the current function).
5. Continue (Continue executing until the next breakpoint or error).
6. Quit (Quit the debugger).

Debugger> 3
Step-in:
Inspecting: (if (<= n 1) 1 (* n (factorial (1- n))))
Current frame location: 0

Debugger> 2
Next:
Inspecting: (<= n 1)
Current frame location: 0

Debugger> 2
Next:
Inspecting: (* n (factorial (1- n)))
Current frame location: 0

Debugger> 2
Next:
Inspecting: (factorial (1- n))
Current frame location: 0

...
```

Using these step-through commands allows you to trace through the execution of the recursive calls made by the factorial function. You can inspect the value of n at each step and understand how the factorial of a number is being calculated recursively.

Inspecting variable values is also crucial in step-through debugging. Using the inspect command, you can view and modify values during the debug session:

```
(inspect n)
```

Changes to variable values can be performed interactively:

```
* (inspect n)

Debugging value of n:
1. Inspect the object.
2. Modify the object's slots.
3. Display the description.
4. Continue.
5. Quit debugger.

Debugger> 2
Enter new value: 10

New value set: 10
```

Breakpoint and step-through debugging techniques offer detailed insights into the program's execution process, making it easier to locate and correct logical errors. By dynamically setting breakpoints, stepping through code, and inspecting or modifying variables, developers gain a powerful toolkit for effective troubleshooting and refining of Lisp programs.

9.10 Inspecting and Modifying Program State

Understanding how to inspect and modify the state of a program is fundamental to effective debugging in Lisp. This section provides a comprehensive exploration of techniques for examining program variables, stack frames, and other elements of the program state during execution. By gaining proficiency in these methods, developers will be capable of diagnosing and correcting errors with greater precision.

Inspecting Variables: One of the primary tasks in debugging is to inspect the values of variables at various points in the execution of a program. Lisp provides several tools for this purpose. The Common Lisp *debug-io* stream is commonly used to print variable values and other debug information.

```
(defun compute-factorial (n)
  (if (zerop n)
      1
      (* n (compute-factorial (1- n)))))
```

To inspect the variable n at each recursive call, we can insert a format statement.

```
(defun compute-factorial (n)
```

271

```
(format t "n: ~d~%" n) ; Print the value of n
(if (zerop n)
    1
    (* n (compute-factorial (1- n))))))
```

Running this modified function will output the value of n at each step.

```
CL-USER> (compute-factorial 5)
n: 5
n: 4
n: 3
n: 2
n: 1
n: 0
120
```

This output helps trace how the variable changes and provides insights if an unexpected value is found.

Using the Debugger to Inspect State: Lisp environments typically include a built-in debugger that allows you to inspect the state of a program interactively. When an error occurs, the debugger is activated, and you can examine variable values, control the flow of execution, and more.

Consider the following example with an intentional division by zero error:

```
(defun divide-by (x y)
  (/ x y))
```

If you call this function with y as zero, an error will occur, invoking the debugger.

```
CL-USER> (divide-by 10 0)
Error: Division by zero.
```

In the debugger, you can inspect the values of x and y to understand the cause of the error. Most Lisp debuggers provide commands to print variable values, such as :p or :inspect.

```
CL-USER> :p x
10
CL-USER> :p y
0
```

Modifying Program State: There are times when modifying the state of a program during debugging is necessary to test solutions or understand error behavior. Many Lisp debuggers allow changing variable values. Using the same example, suppose you want to change y to a non-zero value to continue the execution.

272

```
CL-USER> :set y 2
CL-USER> :continue
5
```

This shows how you can dynamically alter variable values to modify the program's behavior and check for potential fixes.

Inspecting Stack Frames: In debugging, inspecting stack frames helps understand the call sequence leading to an error. Each stack frame represents an active function call, along with its local variables and arguments.

Consider a slightly more complex example:

```
(defun foo (a)
  (bar a 2))

(defun bar (x y)
  (baz x y))

(defun baz (m n)
  (/ m n))
```

Calling (foo 10) will invoke baz via bar, and if baz hits an error, the debugger allows inspection of the stack frames.

```
CL-USER> (foo 10)
Error: Division by zero.
CL-USER> :backtrace
0: (DIVIDE-BY 10 0)
1: (BAZ 10 0)
2: (BAR 10 2)
3: (FOO 10)
4: toplevel
```

Using the backtrace, you can navigate up the stack, check the state of each frame, and identify the root cause. Commands like :up and :down help move between frames.

Using Special Variables: Special variables in Lisp, also known as dynamic variables, play a crucial role in debugging as their values are accessible across different scopes during runtime. Special variables are declared using defparameter or defvar.

```
(defvar *my-special-variable* 42)
```

During debugging, they can be accessed and modified regardless of the current scope, aiding in inspecting and adjusting program state on-the-fly.

```
(defun modify-special-variable (value)
  (setq *my-special-variable* value))
```

This function modifies the special variable, and any changes remain effective globally.

```
CL-USER> (modify-special-variable 100)
CL-USER> *my-special-variable*
100
```

The ability to inspect and modify special variables significantly simplifies the process of debugging scoping issues and global state.

By mastering these techniques, Lisp programmers can develop a profound understanding of their program's execution flow, isolate anomalies effectively, and implement corrective measures efficientl.

9.11 Popular Debugging Tools

Effective debugging demands the right tools that can streamline the process of identifying and resolving issues. In Lisp programming, several debugging tools stand out for their utility and power. This section delves into these tools, explaining their features and usage comprehensively.

- SLIME (Superior Lisp Interaction Mode for Emacs): SLIME is a productive environment for interactive programming for Lisp. It is built on top of Emacs and offers an advanced development environment with features such as a REPL (Read-Eval-Print Loop), integrated debugger, inspectors, and a sophisticated editor. Installation can be performed using Emacs package managers such as MELPA. The primary interface to SLIME integrates seamlessly with Common Lisp through its backend, SWANK, providing a host of debugging functionalities.

```
; Install SLIME via MELPA
(require 'package)
(add-to-list 'package-archives '("melpa" . "https://melpa.org/packages
    /"))
(package-initialize)
(package-refresh-contents)
(package-install 'slime)
```

```
; Load SLIME when opening a Lisp file
(require 'slime-autoloads)
(setq inferior-lisp-program "/path/to/your/lisp/implementation")
(slime-setup)
```

SLIME's debugging capabilities include the following:

- When an error occurs, SLIME presents a detailed backtrace.

- It allows restarting the program from specific restart points.

- The environment supports stepping through code, inspecting variables, and modifying their values on the fly.

- Integration with Emacs enables customizable key bindings to streamline navigation.

- Slynk and Sly: Slynk is a server, similar to the Swank server used by SLIME, but it is aligned with Sly, which is a friendly fork of SLIME offering additional features and performance improvements. Slynk and Sly offer an enriched REPL experience, proper integration with the Common Lisp type system, and efficient debugging features.

```
; Install Sly via MELPA
(require 'package)
(add-to-list 'package-archives '("melpa" . "https://melpa.org/packages
    /"))
(package-initialize)
(package-refresh-contents)
(package-install 'sly)
; Load Sly when opening a Lisp file
(require 'sly-autoloads)
(setq inferior-lisp-program "/path/to/your/lisp/implementation")
(sly-setup)
```

- LDB (Lisp Debugger): LDB is the native debugger for a variety of Lisp implementations, including SBCL (Steel Bank Common Lisp) and others. LDB presents an interface for inspecting backtraces, stepping through code, and managing breakpoints. When an error occurs, LDB is invoked, providing options to examine the program state and apply fixes directly.

Here's how to enable LDB in an SBCL environment:

```
; Invoking the debugger in SBCL
(defun buggy-function (x)
  (if (zerop x)
      (debug) ; Triggers the debugger
      (/ 10 x)))

(buggy-function 0)
; This will drop you into the LDB, showing a backtrace and options.
```

In the LDB, you can navigate through stack frames, inspect variable values, and execute arbitrary Lisp expressions within the context of the program.

- DGB (Common Lisp Debugger): Clozure CL's (CCL) debugger, named DGB, offers visualization of call stacks, control over execution flow, and integration with CCL's IDE. It supports breakpoint management and has powerful inspection capabilities.

To use DGB in Clozure CL:

```
; Set a breakpoint
(set-breakpoint #'my-function)
; Run your program
(my-top-level-function)
; When the breakpoint is hit, DGB will be invoked, illustrating the
    current call stack and environment.
```

- Quicklisp: While not a debugger per se, Quicklisp simplifies the management of Lisp libraries and dependencies. It supports the installation and loading of various debugging utilities and extensions for different debuggers.

```
; Load Quicklisp
(ql:quickload "package-name")
; Example: Loading a specialized debugging tool
(ql:quickload "slynk")
```

Utilizing Quicklisp ensures that you have swift access to the best libraries and tools available, streamlining the setup and enabling a more productive debugging experience.

Collectively, these tools empower Lisp developers to address issues expediently and accurately. Whether it's through integrated environments like SLIME and Sly or the command-line proficiency of LDB and DGB, leveraging the right tools is paramount to mastering error handling and debugging in Lisp.

9.12 Best Practices for Error Handling and Debugging

Developing robust Lisp applications requires diligent error handling and effective debugging strategies. This section outlines best practices to help you achieve these goals. These guidelines are designed to enhance the stability and maintainability of your code while streamlining the debugging process.

1. Anticipate Errors:

Anticipating potential errors is the first step toward robust error handling. Identify parts of your program where errors are likely to occur and proactively check conditions that could lead to unexpected behaviors. Integrate assert statements to validate assumptions made in your code.

```
(assert (vectorp my-vector) (my-vector) "Expected a vector.")
```

This ensures that if my-vector is not a vector, the program raises an error immediately, making the source of the issue easier to identify.

2. Use Meaningful Condition Types:

Create specific condition types rather than relying on generic errors. This allows for more precise error handling and easier debugging.

```
(define-condition invalid-parameter (error)
  ((parameter :initarg :parameter :reader invalid-parameter-parameter
     )))
```

By defining custom condition types, you enhance the granularity of your error handling, making it easier to distinguish between different error scenarios.

3. Leverage the Condition System with Handler-Bind and Restart:

Utilize handler-bind and restart to manage errors without disrupting pro-

277

gram flow. Proper use of these constructs allows programs to recover from errors dynamically.

```
(handler-bind ((invalid-parameter
                (lambda (condition)
                  (invoke-restart 'use-default-value))))
  (progn
    (signal 'invalid-parameter :parameter 'foo)
    (handler-case
        (do-something)
      (error (e)
        (format t "Caught an error: ~a" e)))))
```

handler-bind assigns a handler for specific conditions, while invoke-restart attempts a recovery action defined elsewhere in the codebase.

4. Structured Logging:

Implement structured logging to capture detailed information about the program's operation and any encountered errors. Log entries should include timestamps, error types, and relevant data.

```
(defun log-error (message &rest args)
  (format *error-output* "~%[ERROR] ~a: " (get-universal-time))
  (apply #'format *error-output* message args))

(handler-case
    (do-something-critical)
  (error (e)
    (log-error "Caught an error: ~a" e)))
```

Structured logging allows you to save contextual information, making it easier to trace back the cause of an error.

5. Use the Debugger Thoughtfully:

Engage the debugger prudently to understand the program state at the time of error occurrence. This entails setting breakpoints, stepping through code, and examining local variables.

6. Continuous Testing:

Incorporate unit tests and continuous integration to catch errors early in the development cycle. Regular testing prevents bugs from accumulating and becoming harder to diagnose and fix.

```
(deftest test-array-sum
```

```
(check-equal (array-sum #(1 2 3 4 5)) 15))
```

Incorporating tests as part of your development routine ensures your code remains robust over time.

7. DRY Principle:

Adhere to the Don't Repeat Yourself (DRY) principle to minimize errors caused by redundancy. Reuse code by defining functions and macros, which centralize and simplify maintenance.

```
(defun safe-divide (numerator denominator)
  (if (zerop denominator)
      (error "Denominator must not be zero")
      (/ numerator denominator)))
```

Encapsulating potential error-prone operations within reusable functions promotes consistency and reduces the probability of errors.

8. Educate and Document:

Thoroughly document your code and error handling mechanisms. Comprehensive documentation aids in understanding the software architecture and facilitates debugging by making code intentions clear.

```
(defun calculate-interest
    "Calculate interest based on principal and rate.
    :param principal The initial amount of money.
    :param rate The interest rate as a decimal.
    :raises invalid-parameter if either parameter is non-numeric."
    (declare (double-float principal rate))
    ...)
```

By documenting each function's purpose, parameters, and conditions, you create a clear reference that simplifies future debugging tasks.

These strategies, when applied consistently, contribute to the creation of resilient, maintainable Lisp applications capable of graceful error handling and efficient debugging. They empower developers to diagnose and rectify issues promptly, maintaining smooth and reliable software operation.

Chapter 10

Interfacing with External Libraries

This chapter addresses the methods for interfacing Lisp with external libraries. It begins with an introduction to the Foreign Function Interface (FFI), covering the basics of calling C and C++ functions from Lisp. The chapter discusses the use of shared libraries, interfacing with Java through JNA, and handling callbacks. Techniques for managing data exchange and error handling in FFI are explored, along with practical examples of working with popular external libraries. Performance considerations and best practices are provided to ensure efficient and effective integration of external functionalities into Lisp programs.

10.1 Introduction to Interfacing with External Libraries

Interfacing with external libraries is a capability that significantly extends the functionality of Lisp programs. By leveraging external libraries, Lisp can utilize functionalities that are either infeasible or inefficient to implement directly within the language. This capability is facilitated by the Foreign Function Interface (FFI), which provides a standardized mechanism for calling functions written in other programming languages, such as C or C++.

The primary purpose of interfacing with external libraries is to enhance Lisp programs by using established and optimized external functionalities. This is particularly useful when dealing with system calls, graphic rendering, and mathematical computations, where mature libraries already exist.

FFI (Foreign Function Interface) is the fundamental concept that underlies the interfacing process. It acts as a bridge between Lisp and other programming languages, allowing Lisp programs to call functions and pass data to and from external libraries. Using FFI is crucial when there is a need to optimize performance, integrate with hardware, or reuse legacy code.

- Calling external functions: The FFI allows Lisp programs to invoke functions defined in external libraries, written in languages like C, C++, or Java. This involves specifying the function's signature and handling the data types for arguments and return values appropriately.

- Data exchange: One of the key aspects of interfacing with external libraries is the correct management of data exchange. Data has to be converted between Lisp representations and the data formats expected by the external functions.

- Error handling: Ensuring robust error handling mechanisms is critical when dealing with external functions. This includes managing exceptions and ensuring that the external function calls do not introduce vulnerabilities or instability in the Lisp application.

- Callbacks: Some external libraries may demand callback functionality, where the library calls back into the Lisp program. Handling such interactions requires the Lisp program to provide compatible callback mechanisms.

- Performance considerations: FFI introduces overhead due to context switching between Lisp and other languages. Thus, it is important to minimize these context switches and judiciously use external function calls to ensure performance-efficient integration.

The Lisp programming environment typically provides built-in facilities to aid interfacing with external libraries. For instance, Common Lisp offers the cl-foreign library, and various Scheme implementations provide their respective FFI libraries. These libraries facilitate the declaration of

282

foreign functions, marshalling and unmarshalling of data, and managing memory allocation and deallocation, which are integral to interfacing with external libraries.

Defining Foreign Functions: To interface with an external function, the FFI requires the function's signature to be defined in Lisp. This usually includes the return type, the function name, and the types of its parameters. Here is an example of how to define a foreign function in Lisp using the Common Lisp cl-foreign library:

```
(define-foreign-function add
  ((x :int) (y :int)) :int
  "add")
```

In the example above, the define-foreign-function macro specifies that a function named add with parameters x and y, both of type :int, will return an int. The string "add" indicates the actual name of the function in the external library.

Handling Data Types: One of the complexities in interfacing with external libraries is the handling of data types. Different programming languages have different representations for various data types. When calling an external function, it is essential to convert Lisp data into the appropriate format expected by the external function and vice versa.

- Primitive types: Primitive data types such as integers, floats, and characters are generally straightforward to convert between Lisp and C.

- Complex types: More complex data types like structs, arrays, and strings may require custom conversion routines to ensure that the data is marshalled correctly between Lisp and the external library.

Invoking External Functions: Once the foreign function is declared, it can be invoked just like any other Lisp function. The FFI library ensures that the appropriate conversions and checks are performed, facilitating seamless integration.

```
(let ((result (add 10 20)))
  (format t "The sum is: ~d" result))
```

In this example, the add function is invoked with the arguments 10 and 20. The result is stored in the variable result, and then printed using the format function.

Understanding the intricacies of interfacing with external libraries not only enhances the capabilities of Lisp programs but also requires a comprehensive understanding of both Lisp and the external library's language. Proper error handling, efficient data conversion, and careful function invocation are essential elements in achieving robust and efficient integration.

10.2 FFI (Foreign Function Interface) Basics

The Foreign Function Interface (FFI) is essential for extending Lisp programs with functionality written in other programming languages, particularly C and C++. FFI enables seamless inclusion of external code, allowing Lisp programs to utilize libraries and functions outside their native environment. This section elucidates fundamental aspects of FFI, emphasizing practical techniques for calling external functions from Lisp.

def-foreign-library registers a foreign library with Common Lisp. The following example illustrates how to load a C library named libmath:

```
(def-foreign-library libmath
  (:unix (:or "libmath.so" "libm.so"))
  (:darwin "libmath.dylib")
  (:windows "libmath.dll"))
```

def-foreign-function binds a C function to a Lisp symbol, facilitating direct calls to the external function. Consider a function sqrt from the libmath library:

```
(def-foreign-function (sqrt libmath)
  ((number :double) :double))
```

This directive allows the Lisp system to call the C sqrt function, passing a double value and receiving a double result.

Here is an example to compute the square root of 9.0:

```
(print (sqrt 9.0))
```

The output, as expected, would be:

3.0

FFI requires careful handling of data types to ensure correct interoperability between Lisp and external libraries. Common data types include:

- :int - Maps to C int

- :double - Maps to C double

- :float - Maps to C float

- :char - Maps to C char

- :pointer - Maps to C void*

Functions that return pointers require special care. To illustrate, consider a function malloc:

```
(def-foreign-function (malloc "malloc" :library "libc")
  ((size :size_t) :pointer))
```

free must be used to deallocate the memory:

```
(def-foreign-function (free "free" :library "libc")
  ((ptr :pointer) :void))
```

To allocate and release memory:

```
(let ((memory (malloc 100)))
  (unwind-protect
      (progn
        ;; Use the memory
        )
      (free memory)))
```

Error handling in FFI is crucial. Functions returning error codes often need to have their error handling encapsulated. Consider the following example with a hypothetical open function:

```
(def-foreign-function (open "open" :library "libc")
  ((pathname :string)
   (flags :int) :int))

(defun safe-open (pathname flags)
  (let ((fd (open pathname flags)))
    (if (= fd -1)
        (error "Failed to open: ~A" pathname)
        fd)))
```

285

Data exchange between Lisp and external functions may involve structures. When defining and using structures, the def-c-struct macro creates mappings between Lisp and C structures. Consider the following C structure:

```
struct point {
  double x;
  double y;
};
```

Declare the corresponding Lisp structure:

```
(def-c-struct point
  (x :double)
  (y :double))
```

This mapping allows Lisp programs to manipulate C structures directly:

```
(let ((p (make-point :x 10.0 :y 20.0)))
  (setf (point-x p) 15.0)
  (print (point-x p))) ;; Prints 15.0
```

Managing calls to functions involving these structures:

```
(def-foreign-function (compute-distance "compute_distance" :library "
    libgeom")
  ((p1 :pointer)
   (p2 :pointer) :double))
```

```
(let ((p1 (make-point :x 1.0 :y 2.0))
      (p2 (make-point :x 4.0 :y 6.0)))
  (print (compute-distance p1 p2)))
```

This FFI foundation provides a robust toolkit for integrating external libraries, elevating the capabilities of Lisp programs.

10.3   Calling C Functions from Lisp

Interfacing Lisp with C functions plays a pivotal role in enhancing the functionality and performance of Lisp programs. By leveraging the Foreign Function Interface (FFI), Lisp programs can call C functions directly, enabling access to a vast array of libraries and system-level functions that are crucial for certain applications.

To call C functions from Lisp, several steps must be meticulously followed. This section outlines the essential steps and provides a detailed explanation of the process using practical examples.

1. Define the C functions

Before calling a C function from Lisp, the function must be properly defined in a C source file. Consider the following simple example:

```c
#include <stdio.h>

int add(int a, int b) {
    return a + b;
}

void print_message(const char *message) {
    printf("%s\n", message);
}
```

In this example, two C functions are defined:

- add: Adds two integers and returns the result.

- print_message: Prints a given message to the console.

2. Compile the C source file

The next step involves compiling the C source file into a shared library object ('.so' on Linux, '.dll' on Windows, '.dylib' on macOS). This process is typically conducted using a C compiler like GCC for Linux.

```
gcc -o libexample.so -shared -fPIC example.c
```

The -shared flag signifies the creation of a shared library, and the -fPIC flag ensures position-independent code, necessary for shared libraries.

3. Load the shared library in Lisp

To call the C functions from Lisp, the shared library must first be loaded. This is achieved using the ffi:load-foreign-library function from the relevant FFI library, such as CFFI (Common Foreign Function Interface). Below is an example of how to load the shared library in Lisp:

```
(ql:quickload :cffi)
(cffi:load-foreign-library "/path/to/libexample.so")
```

This ensures that the shared library containing the C functions is available for use within the Lisp environment.

4. Define the foreign function interfaces in Lisp

Using CFFI, we define the interfaces for the C functions. This allows Lisp to understand the function signatures and call them correctly. The following example demonstrates how to define the foreign function interfaces:

```
(cffi:define-foreign-library example
  (:unix (:default "libexample.so"))
  (:windows (:default "example.dll"))
  (:darwin (:default "libexample.dylib")))

(cffi:use-foreign-library example)

(cffi:defcfun ("add" add) :int
  (a :int)
  (b :int))

(cffi:defcfun ("print_message" print-message) :void
  (message :string))
```

In this example:

- define-foreign-library specifies the shared library for different operating systems.

- use-foreign-library loads the corresponding library.

- defcfun defines the foreign function interfaces: add and print-message.

The defcfun macro maps the C function names to their corresponding Lisp function names, specifying the return and argument types.

5. Call the C functions from Lisp

Once the foreign function interfaces are defined, the C functions can be called from within Lisp as if they were native Lisp functions:

```
(let ((result (add 3 5)))
  (format t "Addition result: ~d~%" result))

(print-message "Hello from C!")
```

Program execution output is as follows:

```
Addition result: 8
Hello from C!
```

The example demonstrates calling the add function to compute the sum of two integers and the print-message function to display a message via standard output.

Careful adherence to the function signatures and data types ensures that the correct values are passed between Lisp and C, preventing runtime errors and undefined behavior.

6. Handling complex data types

While the examples above involve simple data types (integers and strings), interfacing with more complex data types like structures requires additional steps. Consider the following C structure and function:

```c
typedef struct {
    int x;
    int y;
} point;

int calculate_distance(point p1, point p2) {
    return abs(p2.x - p1.x) + abs(p2.y - p1.y);
}
```

The corresponding Lisp interface definition involves a combination of defcstruct and defcfun macros to correctly map the structure and function:

```lisp
(cffi:defcstruct point
  (x :int)
  (y :int))

(cffi:defcfun ("calculate_distance" calculate-distance) :int
  (p1 (cffi:struct point))
  (p2 (cffi:struct point)))
```

Calling the calculate-distance function is straightforward once the structure is correctly mapped:

```lisp
(let* ((p1 (cffi:make-struct 'point :x 0 :y 0))
       (p2 (cffi:make-struct 'point :x 3 :y 4))
       (distance (calculate-distance p1 p2)))
  (format t "The Manhattan distance is: ~d~%" distance))
```

The structure point is instantiated using the make-struct function, and its fields are populated accordingly.

These steps demonstrate the fundamental process of calling C functions from Lisp. Meticulous definition and handling of function signatures, data types, and appropriate library loading techniques ensure successful integration of external C functionalities into Lisp programs.

10.4   Interfacing with C++

Interfacing with C++ from Lisp requires a more complex approach than interfacing with C due to C++'s support for features like classes, overloading, and namespaces. The Foreign Function Interface (FFI) must be used in conjunction with additional tools or libraries that facilitate the interaction with C++. One commonly used technique is the use of C++'s 'extern "C"' feature to create a C-style API for C++ code, making it accessible from Lisp.

To start, consider a C++ class that we wish to interface with from our Lisp program. Below is an example of a simple C++ class:

```cpp
class MyClass {
public:
    MyClass(int value) : value(value) {}
    void setValue(int value) {
        this->value = value;
    }
    int getValue() const {
        return value;
    }
private:
    int value;
};
```

We can create a C-style interface to this class by writing wrapper functions. These functions will be defined within an 'extern "C"' block, ensuring that they use the C naming convention, which avoids name mangling.

```cpp
extern "C" {
    MyClass* MyClass_new(int value) {
```

```
        return new MyClass(value);
    }
    void MyClass_setValue(MyClass* obj, int value) {
        obj->setValue(value);
    }
    int MyClass_getValue(MyClass* obj) {
        return obj->getValue();
    }
    void MyClass_delete(MyClass* obj) {
        delete obj;
    }
}
```

These wrapper functions allow the Lisp program to create, manipulate, and destroy instances of 'MyClass'. Next, we will write the Lisp FFI definitions needed to call these functions. We assume that the compiled shared library is named 'libmylib.so'.

```
(ffi:define-ffi-lib mylib
  (:unix "libmylib.so"))

(ffi:foreign-func MyClass_new (:pointer (int)) :lib mylib :name "
    MyClass_new")
(ffi:foreign-func MyClass_setValue (void (pointer int)) :lib mylib :
    name "MyClass_setValue")
(ffi:foreign-func MyClass_getValue (int (pointer)) :lib mylib :name "
    MyClass_getValue")
(ffi:foreign-func MyClass_delete (void (pointer)) :lib mylib :name "
    MyClass_delete")

(defun create-myclass (value)
  (MyClass_new value))

(defun set-myclass-value (obj value)
  (MyClass_setValue obj value))

(defun get-myclass-value (obj)
  (MyClass_getValue obj))

(defun delete-myclass (obj)
  (MyClass_delete obj))
```

With these definitions in place, we can now create a Lisp function to demonstrate the usage of the interfaced C++ class:

```
(defun demo-myclass ()
  (let ((obj (create-myclass 10)))
    (format t "Initial value: ~a~%" (get-myclass-value obj))
    (set-myclass-value obj 20)
    (format t "Updated value: ~a~%" (get-myclass-value obj))
    (delete-myclass obj)))
```

Upon executing (demo-myclass), the expected output will be:

```
Initial value: 10
Updated value: 20
```

When dealing with more complex C++ features like templates, exceptions, or advanced type hierarchies, additional tools may be required. SWIG (Simplified Wrapper and Interface Generator) is one such tool that can automate much of the process.

A simple SWIG interface file for the above example might look like this:

```
%module mymodule

%{
#include "MyClass.h"
%}

class MyClass {
public:
    MyClass(int value);
    void setValue(int value);
    int getValue() const;
};
```

This automatically generates the corresponding Lisp FFI code, greatly simplifying the process. To use SWIG, the following command could be issued:

```
swig -cffi -module mymodule MyClass.i
```

The result is a set of generated files that can be directly included in the Lisp project. By leveraging tools like SWIG, the complexity of interfacing with C++ is significantly reduced, allowing Lisp programs to tap into the extensive functionality offered by C++ libraries without excessive manual effort. Proper handling of memory management, consistent exception handling, and adherence to naming conventions are crucial for maintaining robust and maintainable interlanguage operability.

Additional best practices include thorough testing of the FFI interface, careful management of resource lifetimes, and encapsulation of FFI calls in higher-level Lisp abstractions to simplify their usage and reduce the risk of errors.

10.5 Using Shared Libraries

Shared libraries, also commonly referred to as dynamic-link libraries (DLLs) on Windows and shared objects (SOs) on Unix-like systems, are a crucial concept when interfacing Lisp programs with external codebases. The use of shared libraries allows Lisp programs to leverage precompiled routines and functions created in languages such as C or C++, thus promoting reusability, reducing memory overhead, and enabling modular parallel development.

Loading Shared Libraries

To utilize shared libraries in Lisp, the first step is to load the shared library into the Lisp environment. This can be done using the cffi:load-foreign-library function provided by the Common Foreign Function Interface (CFFI) library. The following example illustrates how to load a shared library named libexample.so.

```
(cffi:load-foreign-library "example")
```

The function cffi:load-foreign-library looks for the shared library libexample.so in standard system paths. If the library resides in a nonstandard location, the path must be explicitly specified:

```
(cffi:load-foreign-library "/path/to/libexample.so")
```

Defining Foreign Functions

Once the shared library is loaded, the next step is to define the functions within the library that your Lisp program will call. The cffi:defcfun macro is employed for this purpose. Below is an example where a function named add_integers, residing in the shared library, is defined in Lisp:

```
(cffi:defcfun ("add_integers" c-add-integers) :int
  (a :int)
  (b :int))
```

This declaration exposes the add_integers function from the shared library as the Lisp function c-add-integers. The function takes two integer arguments and returns an integer.

Calling Foreign Functions

With the functions defined, they can now be called within the Lisp code as regular functions. Here's an example usage of the c-add-integers function:

```
(let ((result (c-add-integers 3 5)))
  (format t "The result is ~d~%" result))
```

Upon execution, the above code will output the sum of 3 and 5:

The result is 8

Handling Data Types

Data type compatibility between Lisp and the external library is a critical aspect of interfacing. It is vital to ensure that the types specified in the cffi:defcfun declaration match the types expected by the foreign functions. Commonly used C types such as int, float, and double have corresponding CFFI types :int, :float, and :double respectively. More complex types such as structures and pointers can be handled using :struct and :pointer definitions.

Here is an example where a function process_data takes a pointer to an integer array and its size:

```
(cffi:defcfun ("process_data" c-process-data) :void
  (data (:pointer :int))
  (size :int))
```

Memory Management Considerations

Since shared libraries may perform memory allocation internally, it is essential to manage memory properly to avoid leaks. Lisp provides mechanisms to allocate and free memory using the cffi:foreign-alloc and cffi:foreign-free functions. For instance, you can allocate memory for an integer array before passing it to the process_data function:

```
(let* ((size 10)
       (data (cffi:foreign-alloc :int :count size)))
  (unwind-protect
      (progn
        ;; Initialize the array
```

```
          (dotimes (i size)
            (setf (cffi:mem-aref data :int i) i))
          ;; Pass the array to the C function
          (c-process-data data size))
    ;; Ensure memory is freed
    (cffi:foreign-free data)))
```

Error Handling

Interfacing with shared libraries may introduce errors, such as invalid memory access or type mismatches. Proper error handling ensures that such errors are gracefully handled. CFFI provides the cffi:foreign-funcall and cffi:foreign-funcall-unsafe functions. cffi:foreign-funcall includes additional safety checks, while cffi:foreign-funcall-unsafe is more performant but requires that the programmer ensures type correctness and memory validity.

```
(cffi:foreign-funcall ("process_data" :void) data :pointer :int size :int)
```

In most cases, using cffi:defcfun is sufficient and preferred due to its clarity and ease of use. However, cffi:foreign-funcall can be useful in scenarios requiring dynamic function invocation or additional error handling control.

By understanding the process of loading shared libraries, defining and calling foreign functions, handling data types, managing memory, and dealing with potential errors, you can leverage powerful external code in your Lisp applications. Integrating shared libraries effectively allows for a significant extension of Lisp's capabilities, enabling access to an extensive range of preexisting software functionalities.

10.6   Interfacing with Java through JNA

Interfacing Lisp with Java can significantly broaden the scope of applications, enabling developers to leverage Java's rich ecosystem. The Java Native Access (JNA) library provides a straightforward mechanism to access native shared libraries without writing any custom JNI (Java Native Interface) code. In this section, we will delve into the configuration, usage, and best practices for interfacing Lisp with Java through JNA.

JNA allows Java programs to call functions in dynamic libraries written in other languages, such as C or C++, and vice versa. The following steps outline the process to interface Lisp with Java using the JNA library.

Setup and Configuration

1. Ensure JNA is included in your Java classpath. Typically, this is done by downloading the JNA library and adding it to the project's dependencies.

2. Load the JNA library in your Java code. Below is a sample Java class that uses JNA to access a native library:

```
import com.sun.jna.Library;
import com.sun.jna.Native;
import com.sun.jna.Platform;

public interface CLibrary extends Library {
    CLibrary INSTANCE = (CLibrary)
        Native.loadLibrary((Platform.isWindows() ? "msvcrt" : "c"),
                            CLibrary.class);
    void printf(String format, Object... args);
}

public class JNAExample {
    public static void main(String[] args) {
        CLibrary.INSTANCE.printf("Hello, World\n");
    }
}
```

In the example above, JNA is used to call the printf function from the standard C library. The Printf method is mapped from the native library method.

Bridging Java and Lisp

To interface Lisp with this Java setup, we will use a Lisp library capable of invoking Java methods via JNA. One such library is the abcl (Armed Bear Common Lisp), a Common Lisp implementation that runs on the Java Virtual Machine (JVM).

1. Load the abcl library into your Lisp environment:

```
(require 'abcl)
```

2. Create a JNA Java instance in Lisp:

```
(defpackage :com.example.jna
  (:use :common-lisp)
  (:import-from "com.sun.jna" :library :native)
  (:import-from "com.example.jna" :clibrary))

(in-package :com.example.jna)
```

3. Define a function in Lisp that communicates with the Java code:

```
(defun call-java-printf ()
  (jcall (jfield "com.example.jna.CLibrary" "INSTANCE")
         "printf"
         "Hello from Lisp\n"))
```

In this function, jcall is used to invoke the Java method printf on the instance of CLibrary.

Handling Callbacks

Callbacks are critical in scenarios where Java needs to invoke Lisp functions. JNA supports callbacks, allowing you to define a Java interface for the callback and implement it in Lisp.

1. Define a Java callback interface:

```
public interface CallbackInterface extends com.sun.jna.Callback {
    void callbackMethod(int number);
}
```

2. Implement this interface in Java and set up a method to receive the callback:

```
public class CallbackExample {
    private CallbackInterface callback;

    public void setCallback(CallbackInterface callback) {
        this.callback = callback;
    }

    public void triggerCallback(int number) {
        if(callback != null) {
            callback.callbackMethod(number);
        }
    }
}
```

297

```
}
```

3. In Lisp, create an instance of the interface and use it for the callback:

```
(defclass callback-impl ()
  ((java-instance :initform (jnew "com.example.jna.CallbackExample"
    ))))

(defmethod callback-impl (obj number)
  (format t "Callback received with number: ~a" number))

(let ((callback (jnew "com.sun.jna.CallbackInterface" 'callback-impl)))
  (jcall (jfield "com.example.jna.CallbackExample" "INSTANCE") "
    setCallback" callback))
```

In this snippet, an instance of the callback interface implemented in Lisp is created, and the callback method `callback-method` responds to trigger events from Java.

Best Practices

1. Ensure synchronization when accessing shared resources across Java and Lisp to avoid race conditions. 2. Handle exceptions gracefully on both sides to maintain stable inter-operation. 3. Use consistent data encoding and decoding mechanisms to prevent data corruption. 4. Optimize the JNI layer to reduce overhead and improve performance.

Efficient interfacing between Java and Lisp through JNA requires careful handling of data types and consistent method invocation patterns. Following these guidelines ensures a robust and performant integration of Java functionalities within Lisp applications.

10.7   Handling   Callbacks   from   External Libraries

Handling callbacks is an essential aspect of interfacing with external libraries, especially when dealing with asynchronous operations or event-driven programming. This section will cover the fundamentals of setting up and managing callbacks when working with external libraries in Lisp.

Callbacks serve as a mechanism that allows external libraries to execute Lisp functions. This backward interaction between the external library functions and Lisp is achieved by passing a function pointer or similar reference from Lisp to the external library, which can then call the provided function when certain events occur or conditions are met.

To handle callbacks effectively, we need to understand the following key aspects:

- Defining and registering the Lisp callback function.

- Creating a bridge between the external library and Lisp.

- Ensuring proper data exchange between Lisp and the external library during callbacks.

- Managing the lifecycle of the callback to avoid memory leaks and dangling pointers.

Defining and Registering the Lisp Callback Function

First, we define the Lisp callback function. Assume we are interfacing with a C library that will call our Lisp function when a certain event happens. The callback function needs to adhere to the signature expected by the C library. For instance, consider a C library function that expects a callback function with the following signature:

```
void callback_function(int event_code, const char *message);
```

In Lisp, we can define a corresponding function as follows:

```
(defun lisp-callback (event-code message)
  (format t "Event code: ~A, Message: ~A~%" event-code (ffi:
     foreign-string-to-lisp message)))
```

Here, ffi:foreign-string-to-lisp is a utility that converts a foreign string (pointer to char) to a Lisp string. The lisp-callback function takes two arguments: event-code (an integer) and message (a C string), and prints them in a readable format.

Creating a Bridge Between the External Library and Lisp

To register the callback function with the external library, we need to provide the library with a function pointer to our lisp-callback. This process typically involves using the Foreign Function Interface (FFI) to create a function pointer and pass it to the external library.

Using the CFFI (Common Foreign Function Interface) library in Lisp, we can achieve this as follows:

```
(cffi:defcallback callback-function :void
  (event-code :int)
  (message :string))

(defparameter *callback*
  (cffi:callback-pointer #'lisp-callback))

(cffi:defcfun ("register_callback" register-callback) :void
  (callback :pointer))
```

In this example:

- defcallback defines the callback-function, specifying the return type (:void) and parameter types (:int for event-code and :string for message).

- callback-pointer creates a pointer to the lisp-callback function.

- defcfun declares a foreign function named register-callback that takes a function pointer (:pointer) and returns void (:void).

Next, we register the Lisp callback with the external library:

```
(register-callback *callback*)
```

Ensuring Proper Data Exchange Between Lisp and the External Library during Callbacks

During the callback invocation, it is essential to handle data exchange correctly, converting data types as necessary. This often involves converting C strings to Lisp strings and vice versa, and ensuring numeric types match the expected formats.

In the lisp-callback example, ffi:foreign-string-to-lisp converts the C string message to a Lisp string. Conversely, if the callback required sending data back to the C library, appropriate conversion functions would be utilized.

Managing the Lifecycle of the Callback

To manage the lifecycle of the callback and avoid memory leaks or dangling pointers, it is crucial to maintain references correctly and clean up

300

resources when they are no longer needed.

Ensure that the Lisp callback function and the function pointer remain valid for the duration of their use by the external library. If the callback registration is dynamic, unregister or re-register the callback appropriately when no longer needed or when the Lisp environment is being reset.

```
(defun unregister-callback ()
  "Unregister the callback to prevent further calls."
  (register-callback cffi:null-pointer))
```

By setting the registered callback to cffi:null-pointer, the external library will no longer have a valid function to call, effectively unregistering the existing callback.

Correct management of these elements ensures that callbacks from external libraries integrate seamlessly with Lisp, providing robust and efficient interaction.

The considerations and steps detailed above lay out a systematic approach to handling callbacks from external libraries, ensuring that Lisp programs can react to and interact with asynchronous events generated externally.

10.8 Managing Data Exchange

Efficient data exchange is a crucial aspect of interfacing Lisp with external libraries. Ensuring that data types are properly converted and managed between Lisp and other languages such as C, C++, or Java is essential for maintaining both the stability and performance of your applications. This section will delve into the mechanisms and best practices for managing data exchange, including type mapping, memory management, and marshaling techniques.

Type Mapping: When exchanging data between Lisp and another language, careful consideration must be given to type mapping. This ensures that the data is correctly interpreted by both languages, preventing data corruption or application crashes. The following table outlines common type mappings between Lisp and C:

301

Lisp Type	C Type
integer	int
float	float
double-float	double
char	char
string	char*
pointer	void*

Memory Management: One of the significant challenges in managing data exchange is ensuring proper memory management, particularly concerning allocation and deallocation of memory. When an external library allocates memory, the responsibility to deallocate it often falls to the Lisp program, or vice versa. Using the Common Foreign Function Interface (CFFI), below is an example of managing memory when passing a string from Lisp to a C function that expects a char* type.

```
;; Define the C function in Lisp
(cffi:defcfun ("c_function_name" c-function-name) :void
  (string :string))

;; Allocate a managed pointer for the string
(let ((managed-str (cffi:foreign-string-alloc "Lisp calling C!")))
  ;; Call the C function with the managed string
  (c-function-name managed-str)
  ;; Deallocate the memory after use
  (cffi:foreign-string-free managed-str))
```

This example demonstrates how to use cffi:foreign-string-alloc to allocate memory and cffi:foreign-string-free to deallocate memory, ensuring no memory leaks occur.

Marshaling Techniques: Marshaling refers to transforming the memory representation of an object to enable data exchange. In Lisp, CFFI offers various marshaling functions to convert between Lisp data structures and foreign data structures.

Consider an example where a C function expects a structure containing an integer and a float. First, define the corresponding structure in C:

```
typedef struct {
  int num;
  float value;
} DataStruct;
```

Next, define the same structure in Lisp and use CFFI to marshal the data:

```
(cffi:defcstruct data-struct
  (num :int)
  (value :float))

;; Define the C function in Lisp
(cffi:defcfun ("process_data" process-data) :void
  (data :pointer))

;; Create an instance of data-struct and initialize it
(let* ((data (cffi:make-foreign-instance 'data-struct))
       (num 42)
       (value 3.14))
  ;; Set the fields of the structure
  (setf (cffi:foreign-slot-value data 'data-struct 'num) num)
  (setf (cffi:foreign-slot-value data 'data-struct 'value) value)
  ;; Call the C function with the pointer to the structure
  (process-data data))
```

Complex Data Structures: For more complex data structures such as arrays and linked lists, similar principles apply, but additional care must be taken to correctly manage nested structures and arrays. CFFI provides functions like cffi:make-foreign-array and utility macros to aid in managing such data types.

Below is an example demonstrating how to pass an array of integers to a C function:

```
;; Define the C function in Lisp
(cffi:defcfun ("sum_array" sum-array) :int
  (arr :pointer)
  (length :int))

;; Create a foreign array and initialize it
(let* ((length 5)
       (arr (cffi:make-foreign-object :int :count length)))
  ;; Initialize the array with values
  (dotimes (i length)
    (setf (cffi:mem-aref arr :int i) i))
  ;; Call the C function and retrieve the sum
  (let ((sum (sum-array arr length)))
```

```
(format t "The sum is: ~a~%" sum)))
```

In this example, cffi:make-foreign-object is used to create an array, and cffi:mem-aref initializes the array with values. The C function sum-array computes and returns the sum of array elements.

Proper management of data exchange between Lisp and external libraries ensures the reliability and robustness of interfaces created, allowing Lisp programs to leverage powerful external functionalities seamlessly.

10.9   Error Handling in FFI

Effective error handling is critical when interfacing with external libraries via the Foreign Function Interface (FFI). Errors can arise from numerous sources, including miscommunication between Lisp and the foreign function, mismanagement of memory, or improper use of the foreign library. This section provides an in-depth discourse on techniques for identifying, managing, and resolving errors in FFI.

When calling foreign functions, it is imperative to detect and handle errors promptly to maintain the integrity and robustness of the Lisp program. The catch and throw mechanism built into Lisp can be supplemented with custom error handling strategies designed to address the specifics of FFI interactions.

1. Detecting Errors in Foreign Functions

Foreign functions typically signal errors through return values or by setting global error variables. For instance, C functions often return NULL or -1 to indicate failure and may set the errno variable to provide specific error codes.

To integrate this in Lisp, you must invoke the foreign function within an error-checking context. The following example demonstrates checking the return value of a foreign function that returns a pointer:

```
(defun call-foreign-function ()
  (let ((result (ffi-call "foreign_function")))
    (if (null result)
        (error "Foreign function call failed: ~A" (ffi-get-last-error))
        result)))
```

In this example, ffi-call invokes the foreign function, returning a result that is checked for a NULL value, indicating an error. If an error is detected, the error function raises a Lisp error with a descriptive message.

2. Mapping Foreign Errors to Lisp Conditions

To facilitate more structured error handling, map foreign errors to Lisp conditions. Conditions in Lisp allow you to define custom error types that can be caught and handled separately using handler-case or handler-bind.

First, define the condition class:

```
(define-condition foreign-function-error (error)
  ((code :initarg :code :reader foreign-function-error-code)
   (message :initarg :message :reader foreign-function-error-message)))
```

Next, incorporate this condition into the foreign function call:

```
(defun call-foreign-function ()
  (let ((result (ffi-call "foreign_function")))
    (if (null result)
        (signal 'foreign-function-error
                :code (ffi-get-last-error-code)
                :message "Foreign function call failed.")
        result)))
```

To handle the error in the calling code, use handler-case:

```
(handler-case
    (call-foreign-function)
  (foreign-function-error (e)
    (format t "Error code: ~A, message: ~A"
            (foreign-function-error-code e)
            (foreign-function-error-message e))))
```

3. Managing Memory and Resource Cleanup

Errors can lead to resources being left in an inconsistent state. Proper cleanup and memory management are essential, especially when interfacing with low-level foreign functions. Use the unwind-protect construct to ensure that resources are released even if an error occurs:

```
(defun call-foreign-function-with-cleanup ()
  (let ((resource (allocate-resource)))
    (unwind-protect
```

305

```
(let ((result (ffi-call "foreign_function" resource)))
   (if (null result)
       (signal 'foreign-function-error
               :code (ffi-get-last-error-code)
               :message "Foreign function call failed.")
       result))
 (release-resource resource))))
```

unwind-protect guarantees that release-resource is called irrespective of whether the foreign function completes successfully or signals an error.

4. Propagating and Logging Errors

In complex systems, it is often necessary to propagate errors up the call stack and log them for diagnosis. You can use a combination of condition objects and logging functions to achieve this.

Define a logging function:

```
(defun log-foreign-error (condition)
  (with-open-file (log-stream "error.log" :direction :output :if-exists :
      append)
    (format log-stream "~A - Error code: ~A, message: ~A~%"
            (get-universal-time)
            (foreign-function-error-code condition)
            (foreign-function-error-message condition))))
```

Augment the error handling code to log errors:

```
(handler-case
    (call-foreign-function)
  (foreign-function-error (e)
    (log-foreign-error e)
    (format t "Error code: ~A, message: ~A"
            (foreign-function-error-code e)
            (foreign-function-error-message e))))
```

In the above example, if call-foreign-function signals a foreign-function-error, the error details are appended to an error log file, aiding post-mortem analysis and debugging efforts.

Effective error handling in FFI not only involves detecting and reporting errors but also includes proper resource management and comprehensive logging. By carefully mapping foreign errors to Lisp conditions and ensuring deterministic cleanup of resources, you can build resilient and maintainable Lisp applications interfacing with external libraries.

10.10 Working with Popular External Libraries

Integrating external libraries with Lisp can provide a wealth of function-alities that are not natively available within the Lisp ecosystem. This section explores how to work with several popular external libraries, emphasizing practical usage, data exchange, and performance opti-mization.

SQLite: A Lightweight SQL Database Library

SQLite is a widely used SQL database engine that is both lightweight and easy to integrate with Lisp. The following example demonstrates how to interface SQLite with Common Lisp using the Foreign Function Interface (FFI):

```
(defpackage :lisp-sqlite
  (:use :cl :cffi))

(in-package :lisp-sqlite)

(cffi:define-foreign-library libsqlite3
  (:darwin "libsqlite3.dylib")
  (:unix "libsqlite3.so")
  (:windows "sqlite3.dll"))

(cffi:use-foreign-library libsqlite3)

(cffi:defcfun ("sqlite3_open" sqlite-open) :int
  (filename :string)
  (db :pointer))

(cffi:defcfun ("sqlite3_close" sqlite-close) :int
  (db :pointer))

(defun open-database (path)
  (let ((db (cffi:foreign-alloc :pointer)))
    (when (zerop (sqlite-open path db))
      db)))
```

```
(defun close-database (db)
  (sqlite-close db))
```

The code above defines the interface to the essential functions of SQLite. The open-database and close-database functions manage connection operations with the SQLite database.

OpenSSL: Secure Communications

OpenSSL provides robust cryptographic functionalities. To use OpenSSL in Lisp, you can define the necessary bindings and function calls as shown:

```
(defpackage :lisp-openssl
  (:use :cl :cffi))

(in-package :lisp-openssl)

(cffi:define-foreign-library libssl
  (:darwin "libssl.dylib")
  (:unix "libssl.so")
  (:windows "libssl.dll"))

(cffi:use-foreign-library libssl)

(cffi:defcfun ("SSL_library_init" ssl-library-init) :void)
(cffi:defcfun ("SSL_CTX_new" ssl-ctx-new) :pointer
  (method :pointer))

(defun initialize-ssl ()
  (ssl-library-init))

(defun create-ssl-context ()
  (let ((method (cffi:foreign-symbol-pointer "TLSv1_2_method" :
      pointer libssl)))
    (ssl-ctx-new method)))
```

The initialize-ssl function initializes the SSL library, while create-ssl-context attempts to create a new SSL context using the TLS method.

Zlib: Compression and Decompression Library

Zlib provides essential compression and decompression functionalities. Here is how you can interface with Zlib:

```lisp
(defpackage :lisp-zlib
  (:use :cl :cffi))

(in-package :lisp-zlib)

(cffi:define-foreign-library libz
  (:darwin "libz.dylib")
  (:unix "libz.so")
  (:windows "zlib.dll"))

(cffi:use-foreign-library libz)

(cffi:defcfun ("compress" zlib-compress) :int
  (dest :pointer)
  (dest-len :pointer)
  (source :pointer)
  (source-len :int))

(cffi:defcfun ("uncompress" zlib-uncompress) :int
  (dest :pointer)
  (dest-len :pointer)
  (source :pointer)
  (source-len :int))

(defun compress-buffer (source)
  (let* ((source-len (length source))
         (dest (cffi:foreign-alloc :uchar (* source-len 2)))
         (dest-len (cffi:foreign-alloc :uint (length dest))))
    (setf (cffi:mem-aref dest-len :uint) (* source-len 2))
    (when (zerop (zlib-compress dest dest-len (cffi:foreign-alloc :uchar
                  source source-len) source-len))
      (let ((compressed (cffi:foreign-string-to-lisp dest)))
        (cffi:foreign-free dest)
        (cffi:foreign-free dest-len)
        compressed))))
```

The compress-buffer function compresses a given buffer using Zlib's compress function. This example highlights dynamic memory allocation and conversion between Lisp and C data structures.

Correctly interfacing with these libraries hinges on precise memory management and an understanding of both Lisp and the underlying libraries' native interfaces. Properly managing the data exchange between Lisp's garbage-collected environment and the manually managed memory of external libraries is where meticulous attention to detail is crucial. Understanding and implementing these interfaces can significantly expand Lisp's capabilities, leveraging powerful external libraries effectively.

10.11   Performance Considerations

When interfacing Lisp with external libraries, performance optimization must be a primary focus to ensure seamless multi-language integration. Several factors influence the performance of Foreign Function Interface (FFI) calls, and understanding these elements can lead to more efficient and effective implementations. This section discusses various performance considerations, ranging from data conversion overhead to the cost associated with context switching between Lisp and the external library.

One significant source of performance overhead in FFI is the data type conversion between Lisp and the external language (e.g., C, C++). FFI requires the translation of data structures from Lisp's native representation to the format expected by the foreign library. This conversion process can involve copying data, alignment adjustments, and other transformations that introduce latency.

For example, consider a scenario where a Lisp program repeatedly calls a C function that expects an array of integers. Each function call might involve converting Lisp lists or vectors to C arrays. The resulting overhead can be significant, especially if the array is large or the function is called frequently.

```
(defun call-c-function (lisp-array)
  (let ((c-array (convert-to-c-array lisp-array)))
    (c-function-call c-array)))
```

In the above code, convert-to-c-array would be any function responsible for handling the conversion process. Profiling these conversions is essential to identify bottlenecks.

To mitigate such costs, a strategic approach involves minimizing the number of conversions. One way to achieve this is to batch multiple data items into a single call whenever possible. Instead of calling the

C function for each element, interact with a batch of elements at once:

```
(defun call-c-function-batch (lisp-arrays)
  (let ((c-arrays (map 'vector 'convert-to-c-array lisp-arrays)))
    (dolist (c-array c-arrays)
      (c-function-call c-array))))
```

Additionally, lightweight data structures such as simple arrays and primitive types (e.g., integers, floating-point numbers) should be preferred when frequent FFI calls are necessary. Complex data structures increase overhead due to more intricate conversion and memory allocation requirements.

Another critical aspect to consider is the overhead associated with context switching between Lisp and the external library. Each FFI call incurs a context switch, which involves saving and restoring the state of the Lisp environment and the foreign library's environment. This is particularly pertinent in a high-frequency call pattern.

One optimization technique is to reduce the frequency of FFI calls by integrating more logic and processing within the foreign library itself. By offloading entire units of work rather than piecemeal operations, fewer context switches are required, leading to performance gains. For example, if performing mathematical computations, instead of calling an external library function per operation, it is more efficient to pass an array of operations to be computed in a single call:

```
(defun perform-complex-computation (data)
  (c-complex-computation data))
```

Profiling tools specifically designed for multi-language environments can provide insights into the performance characteristics of FFI calls. These tools can measure the time spent in data conversion, context switching, and execution within the foreign library. With profiling data, developers can make informed decisions on optimizing their FFI interactions.

Memory management is another aspect affecting performance, particularly in languages with garbage collection, like Lisp. Allocating memory for FFI, especially when dealing with large datasets or lengthy operations, must be approached cautiously. Developers should be aware of memory allocation patterns and potential leaks in the foreign library, as well as the interaction between Lisp's garbage collector and the foreign library's memory management routines.

Leverage static memory allocation within the foreign library whenever feasible, as dynamic memory allocation can introduce additional latency. In situations requiring dynamic memory, ensure that appropriate cleanup routines are implemented to avoid memory leaks.

Finally, consider the potential for parallel processing. Modern processors often come with multiple cores, allowing for concurrent execution of parallelizable tasks. Since FFI calls inherently introduce a boundary between Lisp and the foreign library, designing the system to perform parallel execution can leverage these multiple cores for improved performance. However, developers must handle concurrency control mechanisms effectively to avoid race conditions and ensure thread safety.

Adopting the abovementioned strategies contributes significantly to enhancing the overall performance of integrating Lisp with external libraries. Robust profiling and diligent optimization practices ensure that the benefits of using external libraries outweigh the performance overhead introduced by FFI.

10.12 Best Practices for Interfacing with External Libraries

When interfacing Lisp programs with external libraries, it is essential to adhere to best practices to ensure maintainability, performance, and robust error handling. This section details these best practices, emphasizing clear and meticulous programming techniques.

1. Clear API Design

Design the foreign function interface (FFI) layer with clarity and simplicity. Clearly separate the FFI layer from your core Lisp code. Use descriptive and consistent naming conventions for functions, variables, and data types to enhance readability and maintainability.

2. Consistent Data Type Matching

Ensure that the data types in Lisp match those expected by the external library functions. Misalignment can lead to critical errors. Use precise declarations when defining data types in Lisp. For example, when dealing with integers, ensure the bit-widths (e.g., 32-bit, 64-bit) are consistent:

```
(ffi:def-foreign-type int32_t :integer 32)
```

```
(ffi:def-foreign-type int64_t :integer 64)
```

3. Safe Memory Management

Handle memory allocations and deallocations diligently to avoid memory leaks or corruption. When the external library allocates memory, make sure to release it appropriately in Lisp and vice versa:

```
(let ((ptr (ffi:malloc 1024)))
  (unwind-protect
      (use-memory ptr)
    (ffi:free ptr)))
```

Using unwind-protect ensures that ptr is freed even if an error occurs during the use of the memory.

4. Error Handling Mechanisms

Implement comprehensive error checking and handling when interfacing with external libraries. Check return codes or outputs from foreign functions and handle them appropriately:

```
(let ((result (ffi:call-foreign-function "some_function")))
  (if (zerop result)
      (process-success)
    (process-error result)))
```

Integrate consistent error logging and recovery mechanisms to make diagnosing issues easier.

5. Optimize Performance

Avoid unnecessary conversions or data transfers between Lisp and the external library. Minimize crossing the FFI boundary by batching operations when possible. Use efficient data structures that align well with both Lisp and the external library.

6. Utilizing Shared Libraries Effectively

Load shared libraries dynamically only when necessary and release them correctly to conserve resources. Example of loading and using a shared library:

```
(defvar *my-library* (ffi:load-shared-library "libexample.so"))

(defun call-example-function ()
  (ffi:call-foreign-function "example_function" *my-library*))
```

7. Maintain Compatibility

Ensure your interface is compatible with different versions of the external library. Use conditional compilation or runtime checks to adapt to changes or enhancements in the library's API:

```
(when (ffi:external-library-version *my-library*)
  (cond
    ((>= version 2.0) (use-new-api))
    (t (use-legacy-api))))
```

8. Documentation and Comments

Document the interfacing code comprehensively. Include details about the external library version it was developed with, specific data type mappings, memory management strategies, and examples of function usage. This ensures that future developers (or even your future self) can understand and maintain the code:

```
;; Interface to example library - version 1.2
;; Function: example_function
;; Parameters: none
;; Returns: integer result code
(defun call-example-function ()
  (ffi:call-foreign-function "example_function" *my-library*))
```

9. Testing and Validation

Implement rigorous testing, including unit tests and integration tests that cover various scenarios and edge cases. Mock external dependencies where possible to isolate and test the Lisp component of your code:

```
(def-test test-example-function
  (assert (equal (mock-ffi-call-example-function) expected-result)))
```

10. Security Considerations

Be mindful of security implications when interfacing with external libraries. Validate inputs and sanitize outputs to prevent security vulnerabilities such as buffer overflows or injection attacks. Implement proper access controls and isolation mechanisms to mitigate potential risks.